In pursuit of science and technology in Sub-Saharan Africa

This volume examines the progress of Sub-Saharan African countries in advancing science and technology in the context of the Structural Adjustment Programmes they have undertaken.

John Enos looks at the pursuit of science and technology both before and after structural adjustment programmes have been attempted in Ghana, Kenya, Tanzania and Uganda. He looks at the efficiency with which the research and development has been carried out, the transferability of scientific and technical resources from one activity to another and the directions in which advances are channelled. The institutions that receive resources are identified as well as the rates at which those resources are allocated. Finally, John Enos looks at who makes the decisions governing the resources devoted to furthering science and technology and with what objectives.

The findings in this important study will be of interest to students and academics in economic development and to professional economists and administrators directing economic development agencies, as well as to officials in economic planning and finance ministries in developing countries.

J. L. Enos is a Fellow of Magdalen College, Oxford.

UNU/INTECH Studies in New Technology and Development

Series editors: Charles Cooper and Swasti Mitter

The books in this series reflect the research initiatives at the United Nations University Institute for New Technologies (UNU/INTECH) based in Maastricht, the Netherlands. This institute is primarily a research centre within the UN system, and evaluates the social, political and economic environment in which new technologies are adopted and adapted in the developing world. The books in the series explore the role that technology policies can play in bridging the economic gap between nations, as well as between groups within nations. The authors and contributors are leading scholars in the field of technology and development; their work focuses on:

- the social and economic implications of new technologies;
- processes of diffusion of such technologies to the developing world;
- the impact of such technologies on income, employment and environment;
- the political dynamics of technology transfer.

The series is a pioneering attempt at placing technology policies at the heart of national and international strategies for development. This is likely to prove crucial in the globalized market, for the competitiveness and sustainable growth of poorer nations.

1 Women Encounter Technology
Perspectives of the Third World
Edited by Swasti Mitter and Sheila Rowbotham

2 In Pursuit of Science and Technology in Sub-Saharan Africa
The impact of Structural Adjustment Programmes
J.L. Enos

3 Politics of Technology in Latin America
Edited bu Maria Inês Bastos and Charles M. Cooper

4 Exporting Africa
Technology, Trade and Industrialization in Sub-Saharan Africa
Edited by Samuel M. Wangwe

In pursuit of science and technology in Sub-Saharan Africa

The impact of structural adjustment programmes

J. L. Enos

London and New York

Published in association with the UNU Press

First published 1995
by Routledge
11 New Fetter Lane, London EC4P 4EE

Simultaneously published in the USA and Canada
by Routledge
29 West 35th Street, New York, NY 10001

© 1995 UNU/INTECH

Typeset in Times by LaserScript, Mitcham, Surrey
Printed and bound in Great Britain by
Mackays of Chatham PLC, Chatham, Kent

British Library Cataloguing in Publication Data
A catalogue record for this book is available from the British Library

Library of Congress Cataloguing in Publication Data

Enos, John L. (John Lawrence), 1924–
In pursuit of science and technology in sub-Saharan Africa: the impact of
structural adjustment programmes / J.L. Enos.
    p. cm. – (UNU/INTECH studies in new technologies and development)
    Includes bibliographical references and index.
    1. Structural adjustment (Economic policy) – Africa, Sub-Saharan – Case
studies. 2. Technology and state – Africa, Sub-Saharan – Case studies.
3. Science and state – Africa, Sub-Saharan – Case studies. I. Title. II. Series.
HC800.E56   1995
338.967– dc20   95-58
                                                                  CIP

ISBN 0–415–12689–4
ISSN 1359–7922

Contents

Figures

Tables

Preface

There have been many studies of the effects of the Structural Adjustment Programmes on the countries in Sub-Saharan Africa, but, almost without exception, they have concentrated on the macro-economics: effects on government revenues and expenditures, imports, exports and the balance of payments; and output, income and growth. The effects of Structural Adjustment Programmes on smaller units of the countries' economies – sectors – and on smaller units still – have been very few. Yet it is the smaller units in the economies – the organizations and individuals – which bear the costs of adjustment and which derive the benefits. The macro-economic changes are just the statistical summaries of the micro-economic adjustments.

It is, therefore, appropriate that there should now be micro-economic studies of the effects of Structural Adjustment Programmes; and it seems, to us at least, particularly appropriate that one of these studies should address, albeit at one remove, the future that the programmes are designed to ameliorate. That future will be influenced greatly by the technical progress that the Sub-Saharan African countries are able to achieve. And that progress will be greatly influenced by their relative success in advancing their science and technology.

That their advance starts from a pitifully low platform is one of the facts that emerges from our study: countries whose current spending on advancing science and technology, so defined as to include not only formal R&D, but also informal R&D, and technical education and training, should not surpass a few US dollars per capita, are securing little advance. Countries whose current incomes and expenditures are so low are little equipped to shift substantial resources into achieving more rapid advance of science and technology.

It was within such a depressing context that the Institute for New Technologies (UNU/INTECH), one of the research institutes of the United Nations University, decided to investigate the current situation and future prospects for pursuing science and technology in Sub-Saharan Africa. The idea came from UNU/INTECH's Director, Professor Charles Cooper, and the task was assigned to us. In order to be able, within the time and research funds available, to penetrate sufficiently deeply into the subject, we decided to concentrate on four anglophone countries' experiences: one country selected from West Africa – Ghana – and three from East Africa – Kenya, Tanzania and Uganda. What follows are their stories, augmented with occasional incidents from their Sub-Saharan neighbours.

The first of our accomplishments, and it is no minor one, is a statistical one. We have been able to compile time series of the four countries' expenditures on advancing science and technology, covering a span of at least several years, up to the present, which include periods before and after Structural Adjustment Programmes took effect. These time series measure aggregate expenditures on advancing science and technology, and are further broken down into those expenditures on formal R&D and technical education and training; and into expenditures by sector (public vs private; agriculture vs industry vs services; and domestically financed vs financed from abroad).

Armed with these various measures of the extent of pursuit of science and technology we embarked upon their analysis, in addressing those questions that seemed to us to be most important. Theory suggested that we examine the efficiency with which R&D is carried out, the transferability of scientific and technical resources from one activity to another and, most significantly, the directions in which advances are channelled. Present concern suggested that we examine the rates at which resources are allocated to the various activities, what institutions are engaged in providing those resources, and who make the choices that decide the outcomes. Our findings appear in the various chapters of the text, and our policy recommendations, based upon these findings, appear in its last chapter.

Performing a task such as this was well beyond the capability of a single individual. Besides the advice and criticism of Professor Cooper we sought those invaluable aids to inquiry from Professor Sam Wangwe at UNU/INTECH, and from all their able and solicitous colleagues. In carrying out the field work we profited in Kenya from the assistance of Mohammed Mwamadzingo, now of the Institute of Development Studies at the University of Sussex; in Tanzania from introductions to leaders of research institutes and of the University of Dar es Salaam by Dr S. Nyantahe; and in Uganda from Mr Alan Whitworth and his colleagues at the Ministry of Finance and Economic Planning. In Ghana, M. Gebril Mersha single-handedly gathered the data, doing a splendid job. The staff of the UNDP offices in the capital cities were most helpful in enabling us to make the best use of our limited time and in bringing to our attention their detailed compilations of statistics on foreign donations in Kenya and Tanzania. Finally, our thanks must deservedly go to the directors of the research institutes and advisory bodies in the four countries and to their associates; to the Vice-Chancellors and their faculties in the universities and to the directors and their staff in the technical colleges; to the administrators in the government ministries; and to businessmen and consultants in the private sector. That all these men and women should have gone to so much trouble to give us guidance and support has made our study more enjoyable. They all enabled us to eliminate many errors; any that do remain, in spite of their efforts, are our responsibility alone.

J.L. Enos
Magdalen College, Oxford
February, 1994

Part I
Introduction

1 Scope and method

INTRODUCTION

Until the middle of the twentieth century the history of Africa was not one of a continent acting, but of one acted upon. It was only with the attaining of national sovereignty that the constituent countries of the continent began to achieve some independence of action. Yet independence is not easily won, it is not effortlessly retained; even now, Africans are frequently required to reserve certain areas of decision-making to foreigners, or to relinquish other areas over which they have previously gained control.

Such an area is that of economic policy-making. Typically, the newly sovereign African country is able to choose its own economic policies, and apply them to the best of its ability. Nevertheless, the environment within which the policies have been applied has not been conducive to success: dissent from within and shocks from without have put African economies under great stress. Moreover, the high expectations of the liberated populace have raised the standards which that policy must attain if it is to be successful.

It is not surprising, therefore, that many African countries have been unable to meet the aspirations of their people. It is also not surprising that, in their disappointment, they have had to turn to those with wealth for help.

When help is sought by one or two, the response can take into account the particular characteristics of both grantor and recipient: each programme of assistance is specific to the occasion. When, however, many countries appear on the international scene seeking help, the wealthy – wealthy countries, wealthy institutions – naturally establish rules and procedures governing their response. They systematize or regularize the provision of assistance. Moreover, if the number of appeals places pressure on the administrative capacity of the wealthy to respond, they tend to create new agencies which specialize in the allocation and management of assistance:

the IMF and the World Bank are today the two primary agencies. Finally, if the number of appeals is rising sharply, the grantors, in fear of still further commitments and in their superiority, begin to impose conditions upon the help they provide.

The help they do provide can be, and usually is, substantial. Grants, loans and other financial support, and technical assistance from the primary agencies, from the wealthy countries that support them, and from commercial and philanthropic organizations are great attractions for developing countries. But along with financial help come the conditions – multifacetted, nearly uniform and primarily economic in nature, imposed upon the poor African countries by the agencies of the wealthy countries, designed both to raise the productive capacity of the recipients and to achieve other, possibly associated, ideological and political goals. Together, the provision of funds and the imposition of conditions are commonly called Structural Adjustment Programmes.

OBJECTIVES OF THE STUDY

If the enunciated objective of Structural Adjustment Programmes is to help make the recipients more productive, the enunciated objective of this study can be posed as the question: do Structural Adjustment Programmes help to make a few of the institutions of the recipients more productive? Not all the institutions, for the study is not of sufficient scope to address such a monumental question, but only those institutions which attempt to advance the recipient country's science and technology.

Why focus on the advance of science and technology? The answer is clear, if not entirely lacking in controversy: the productivity of a country's population depends more than anything else in the long run on that country's ability to achieve technical progress. In the short run, to be sure, improvements may be secured through increases in the efficiency with which existing scarce resources are applied, through reallocations of the scarce resources to different sectors of the economy and different types of organizations, and through increased availability of imports financed by foreign loans; but these are once-and-for-all advances. After the short-run improvements have been secured, subsequent progress depends greatly upon the country's developing and absorbing new techniques, upon its making and exploiting advances in science and technology. In the long run it is advances in science and technology that are crucial for economic success.

Hence our concern with science and technology, and with the effects of Structural Adjustment Programmes on their advance. But just as we shall be able to study only a sample of those institutions that are assigned the task of advancing science and technology, so we can only consider a few countries. Since the majority of developing countries have adopted, or are adopting, Structural Adjustment Programmes, there is a large universe to select from. A lack of readily available material on the achievements of institutions engaged in furthering science and technology has prevented us from carrying out the sort of statistical analysis on the macro-economic effects of Structural Adjustment Programmes attempted by several authors (World Bank, 1988a and 1990; Harrigan and Mosley, 1991; Faini *et al.* 1991; and Stewart, 1991). We therefore limit ourselves to a few countries, choosing Ghana in West Africa, and Kenya, Tanzania and Uganda in East Africa. Like most countries in Sub-Saharan Africa these four are quite poor, with few reserves to cushion themselves from external shocks and internal dislocations. The majority of their populations is engaged in agriculture; their manufacturing is erected on a fragile base; their governments' revenues are scanty and expenditures over-committed; and a large fraction of their overseas earnings are consumed in servicing foreign debt. Adjustment to the IMF/World Bank's satisfaction would be expected to be very difficult, and to take a very long time, years or even decades, rather than months. Like other grave economic matters – capital investment, education, health, the birthrate – the phenomena on which we are focusing are not altered on short notice. Nor can our observations, extending over at most a decade, provide other than a guess at what will be the lasting effects of Structural Adjustment Programmes on the pursuit of science and technology.

Definition of terms

Science and technology are imprecise terms; yet if we are to measure the effects of Structural Adjustment Programmes upon them, and their effects, in turn, upon the economies under adjustment, we must consider the terms' meaning.

Figure 1.1 may be of some use in setting limits to the terms 'science and technology'. The figure displays the chief scientific and technological institutions within a country, comprised of those which provide scientific and technical education; those independent institutions which carry out R&D; and producers (firms, government ministries, para-statals, plantations, etc.), a few of which conduct R&D, as commonly defined, and many of which also assimilate and improve upon the techniques they employ. The main flows between these institutions – flows of individuals and flows of information (or knowledge and know-how, which tend, in Sub-Saharan Africa to flow with individuals) – are indicated by the arrows. Like others who write about science and technology (e.g. Forje, 1989: 18) we shall consider all the institutions and their links, human and intellectual, i.e. all the stocks and flows in Figure 1.1, to constitute science and technology. We shall also include, to the extent possible, the mores encountered, i.e. those attitudes, inducements, rules and procedures that set the environment within which science and technology are advanced.

To draw a figure, and to say that our subject is all it contains, is not to make the task any easier nor the measures any more precise. Everyone who studies science and technology recognizes that the terms are not only imprecise but also incomprehensible. Relevant outputs from scientific and technical education and R&D institutions are unquantifiable; those from the educational establishments, to whose graduates numbers can be attached, do not reveal their standards of attainment nor their future potential. Where numbers can be ascribed to the scientific and technical education, and R&D institutions they are of the nature of inputs – so many scientists employed within and R&D laboratory or so many engineers and

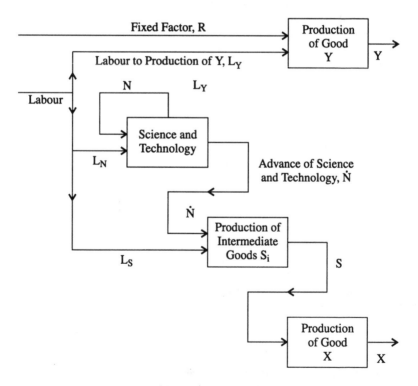

Figure 1.1 Flow diagram of the model of structural adjustment

technicians working on improving a company's manufacturing process. These data give no indication of whether or not the individuals are working together harmoniously, whether or not the results of their efforts will be applied expeditiously. Data of this last sort, qualitative material on the effectiveness of institutions' expenditures on science and technology, emerge only after thorough investigation.

SAMPLING PROCEDURE

We have already mentioned that our sample of countries numbers four, from among the larger number comprising Sub-Saharan Africa. For these four countries we shall try to obtain as much data as possible on the overall commitment to science and technology. To place these aggregative measures in some perspective we shall relate them to other more familiar macro-economic data.

Completeness of measure is beyond our means for the institutions indicated in Figure 1.1: we did not have the resources to investigate more than a few R&D organizations nor more than a few firms which, in addition to producing their goods and services, improve upon their techniques. Our sample is thus quite small. The reader should not be too disappointed, however, for the universe of institutions is not so much larger. In Forje's 'Directory' of major research establishments in Africa (Forje, 1989: 267–81) 14 are listed for Ghana, of which we investigated five plus two more not listed; 16 for Kenya, of which we covered two, plus two more not listed; seven for Tanzania, of which we covered three, plus two more not listed; and seven also for Uganda, of which we covered one (with multiple establishments), plus one more not listed.

In total, for the four countries, 44 R&D establishments are listed; we covered 11, plus seven others, in depth. Adding the seven extra establishments to the 44 in Forje's 'Directory' brings the total of 51, and our sample to 18, which is one-third of the universe. Such a small sample does not warrant a sophisticated statistical analysis, so we shall use the quantitative material derived from the case studies as illustrative, attributing to it little more credence than the qualitative material simultaneously gathered. But to write of sophisticated analysis is to broach the topic of methodology to which we come next.

APPROACH TO THE STUDY

There is thought to be an ideal way to approach a study similar to this one. In brief, one draws upon an established body of theory, which yields, as logical deductions, hypotheses. Some hypotheses may be obvious, some surprising, but all should be relevant to the issues arising in the study. One then collects data with which to confront the hypotheses. Provided that hypotheses have not been falsified by the data, their implications can be drawn; if they fail to pass the tests, the hypotheses must be rejected, the theory reformulated, and data gathering and testing renewed. These five stages – formulating theory, deriving hypotheses, collecting data, testing hypotheses against data, revising, and determining implications – may have to be undertaken again and again, before one can be satisfied with the outcome.

In the social sciences the ideal is never attained. Theories are never sufficiently precise: often, two or more incompatible bodies of theory purport to cover the same issues. Even if there is only one generally accepted body of theory, it may not yield enough interesting hypotheses. When the issues to be studied are complex, as they usually are, the theory may be equally complex, so complex as to make it impossible to deduce hypotheses logically, i.e. to determine the general behaviour of the system the theory encapsulates.

Succeeding difficulties that arise in attaining the ideal are a lack of conformity between the elements of the theory (variables, parameters) and the units of observation. The data may not provide the exact measures of the hypothetical terms or, alternatively, the hypotheses may not contain variables which rank large in the data. Even if the hypothetical terms and the categories of data match perfectly, data are seldom available in sufficient number and precision to permit the application of discriminating tests. Finally, the time and resources devoted to carrying out a study are usually so limited as to prevent more than one circuit, or perhaps one-and-a-half circuits of the five-stage scheme.

How close does this study of the effects of Structural Adjustment Programmes on the pursuit of science and technology come to the ideal? We shall attempt to answer this methodological question in terms of the five-stage scheme already mentioned. First, as regards the theory, there is none that perfectly suits our purpose. The phenomena we are dealing with – Structural Adjustment, as defined by the IMF and World Bank, and the pursuit of science and technology – are respectively, macro-economic and micro-economic (and macro-political). Theory that contains both macro- and micro-economic variables is rare. In the formulation of macro-economic theory, the behaviour of individual economic agents is usually neglected or, if it is included, is embedded in a highly simplified system (usually specified to be perfectly competitive) from which a representative agent is detached. In the formulation of micro-economic theory, phenomena external to the agents or to some collection of agents, say an industry, are not accommodated explicitly. In conventional micro-economic theory, for example, structural adjustment would be an exogenous factor, i.e. a set of elements not represented in the theory itself. In between the realms of macro-and micro-economic theory there are a few formulations upon which we can draw, although even in these few there are some unwelcome assumptions.

But we will address these matters more fully in the next chapter, which will be devoted to theory, where we will also observe how numerous and provocative are the hypotheses that can be deduced. Moving on to the third of the five stages of the typical study we can ask now to what extent are the data we can collect likely to be similar in their definitions to the variables in the theory?

At the level of the economy, data, and their counterparts in theories, are often closely connected, if not entirely congruent. Aggregate statistics like GNP, investment, exports and imports, government revenue and expenditures, etc. provide reasonable estimates of the same variables appearing in theory. Prices, e.g. wage and profit rates, interest rates, exchange rates, can diverge, in practice and in theory, both as regards their definitions and their coverage. A few of the theoretical terms used to set standards or support judgements, such as welfare and utility, do not have statistical counterparts.

If there are some difficulties at the overall level in matching theoretical variables with their empirical counterparts, these are as nothing compared to the difficulties in matching at a micro-economic level. These variables which rate so large in micro-economic theory – outputs, inputs, prices, costs, profits – are almost impossible to measure at the level of the producer. What is the output of an R&D laboratory? What is the likelihood that one can discover the costs of manufacture of a small, privately owned company? What are any firm's profits? And those assumptions which underlie the theory – e.g. profit-maximizing entrepreneurs directing institutions staffed with knowledgeable, rational and dedicated workers carrying out orders with supreme efficiency; costless and instantaneous shifting of resources from one activity to another in response solely to market signals etc. – can they be brought within the scope of an enquiry? Can data of any kind measure the mobility of resources to inducements that may never have been offered before? Yet, as we shall see almost all theory, the micro-aspects of the IMF/World Bank theory of Structural Adjustment for example, depends for its solution on just these sorts of assumptions. If all economic agents are presumed to exhibit these attributes, the assumptions may be acceptable, in the interest of obtaining solutions to the theory. But if some agents, say those operating in the private sector, are presumed to exhibit them, and other agents, say public sector operators, are presumed not to exhibit them, data should be available to reflect this distinction. Yet it is extremely unlikely that data sufficiently precise and reliable to satisfy all critics, will be available. There may be enough indications for us to make up our minds, and enough of these may be communicable to enable others to come to similar conclusions, but there will never be enough to confirm or reject the assumptions, and consequently to confirm or reject the hypotheses derived from that part of the body of theory that is supported by the assumptions.

Summarizing, our data will in all likelihood not conform closely to the variables in the theory, and if perchance they did, they will not be of sufficient number and precision to be wholly persuasive. Moreover, considering the fourth stage of investigation, the stern testing of hypotheses against evidence, this must be imperfectly performed. With few countries, few institutions, and a short time span, we are not able to provide enough observations to warrant any econometric analysis. Our statistical measures will be simple, as befits the data, and our conclusions tentative, as necessitated by the wide departure from the ideal.

OUTLINE OF THE BOOK

As mentioned above, the next chapter will be devoted to theory, which provides the guide to our inquiry. Several theories will be considered, one of which generates hypotheses relevant to the issues we are studying. This most useful theory, presented as a model, will be covered in as much detail as necessary to instruct the reader; the others in much less detail.

In Part II, consisting of four chapters, one each on Ghana, Kenya, Tanzania and Uganda, we will present our data. The same format will be followed for each country: beginning with a brief recording of recent economic events and statistical aggregates; continuing with a report on individual institutions in the fields of agriculture, industry, appropriate technology and education; ascending to a compilation of resources devoted to advancing science and technology; and finally drawing a few implications for the country's future progress.

Part III contains the analysis. The data from the four countries will be assembled, together with other relevant information. To the extent possible the effects of Structural Adjustment Programmes on the pursuit of science and technology will be determined, first at the level of the entire economy (Chapter 7), next at the level of the sector of economic activity – agriculture and industry, exports and imports and non-traded goods, public and private activities (Chapter 8), and finally at the level of the individual institutions where scientific and technological tasks are performed (Chapter 9).

Part IV contains the conclusions, divided into two chapters, the first (Chapter 10) devoted to summarizing the results of the analysis in the preceding three chapters; and the second deriving implications for the future, both under the current regime of Structural Adjustment and under alternative, possibly more attractive regimes.

We now move on to the exposition of the theory, which not only suggests questions but also provides a framework which can support different programmes of Structural Adjustment, for there is little to be gained by trying to evaluate current programmes in the absence of alternatives.

2 Choice and application of economic theory

INTRODUCTION

Economic theory can be put to many uses. The conventional use is the clarification of thought: specifically the explicit recognition of certain phenomena, their precise definition, the determination of their relations one to another, the elimination of logical inconsistencies, and the deduction of principles, often too subtle to be grasped intuitively. These principles, or hypotheses, can then be confronted with evidence and, if they are in conformity with the evidence, can be given some credence.

There are other, less methodologically pure, uses for economic theory. Theory can be used to buttress policy which was formulated previously in time or chosen for different, non-economic reasons. In economics, theory describes an Ideal, an environment organized in a simple fashion, containing elements identical in nature and following identical rules of behaviour. If the focus of the theorist is on the individual economic agents, and if the theory is powerful, it will generate interesting hypotheses about their performance and, perhaps, on the performance of all other agents of their type. If the focus is on the entire economy, the theory will generate interesting hypotheses on the performance of all the agents together. Whether the theoretical environment is small, containing just one agent, or vast, containing an infinite number, it describes completely and perfectly an economy: the economy is Ideal in the sense that its performance is predictable under the conditions specified. If the policy already chosen properly meets the conditions, then the performance of the system under the chosen policy can be predicted. If, in addition, the performance is an improvement upon the performance of the system in the absence of the policy, support for the policy is gained. The theory tends to justify the policy.

Theory is also used to contradict other theories. If an hypothesis, or set of hypotheses, is unattractive, an alternative theory may be formulated which yields, as its logical deductions, more attractive hypotheses. If one does not like one Ideal, one can create a better Ideal. Ideals are, after all, only imaginary representations of reality, and one's own imagining may produce a representation superior to that of one's predecessors. It has been said that much of the struggle of life is to persuade others of the correctness of one's own view of reality; the creation of theory is part of the process of persuasion.

Attractive or not, a theory can be made obsolete by a change in the environment that it purports to describe. If the changes are very slow to occur, or if the theory is particularly powerful and in conformity with contemporary ideological views, the theory may have a lease on life; in such cases the existing theory may coexist with a more recent one devised to take account of the changed circumstances. When the world contains actors operating under the old set of conditions and actors operating under the new, both theories can prosper. Methodologically, one should formulate a meta-theory, comprised of both sorts of actors, but this means of resolving dispute is usually unavailable: the meta-theory is either too complex to solve or can only be solved for specific, not general, conditions. One only has to imagine the difficulties of formulating a micro-economic theory governing an industry comprised of firms run by entrepreneurs with different motivations, or a macro-economic theory describing an economy controlled by a government with inconsistent policies, to understand how formidable a task it is to develop meta-theories.

Nonetheless, even though it cannot in principle be said to be superior, the new theory formulated to take account of changed circumstances can be useful in suggesting directions in which research should move. This is theory in the role of guide to inquiry. ('Guide' is a modest word; often theory is used to justify undertaking inquiry.) The deduction from the newly-established theory is that such-and-such a phenomenon is important in the governance of a system; consequently that phenomenon should be studied. Its investigation is made respectable, is even made imperative, by the strategic position that the phenomenon holds in the theory.

Theories as examples of scientific method, as buttresses for policy, as contradictions to other theories, as guides to inquiry: these all represent practical uses. One final use must be mentioned, namely theories as aesthetic objects. Theories, like paintings or music, can be beautiful. 'Elegant' is the word used to describe a theory that is spare, balanced, well-defined and pregnant with hypotheses; and the formulation of such a theory can be a joy. It can give pleasure to the observer too, and may be assigned an importance because of the pleasure it confers. Like a sculpture carved by a member of a tribe that has disappeared from the face of the earth, a long-familiar theory may have an appeal that causes it to be cherished; in a museum of theories it may bear a proud place.

Having argued that theory can serve several functions, we would be remiss if we claimed that the only purpose to which *we* will put theory is the first, i.e. as an application of scientific method. We shall also display theory as the representation of an Ideal, as a justification for policy, and as a guide to our own inquiry, although not in that order. The first use, rather, will be as a justification for our focusing on the pursuit of science and technology.

CONSEQUENCES, IN THEORY, OF ADVANCING SCIENCE AND TECHNOLOGY

The first use to which we shall put theory, as well as some statistical evidence, is in addressing two issues faced by all developing countries: is it worth while allocating to the pursuit of science and technology some of those so very scarce resources such as scientists, engineers and managers, capital, and time? The second issue follows upon the answer to the first: if it *is* worth while allocating scarce resources to the pursuit of science and technology, at what stages in a country's development should allocations be made? It is these issues that we shall use theory to explore.

Since the 1950s, much theory has been devoted to trying to capture, in the abstract, the effects that advancing science and technology may have upon a country's economy. The attempts were inspired by Solow's study (Solow, 1957), which indicated that only a minor portion of the economic growth of the USA could be explained by increases in the amounts of labour and capital applied to the production of the country's goods and services. The major portion was explained by a factor exogenous to the system described in the model, labelled by Solow 'technical change'. Technical change the factor surely includes, but not exclusively, for what the factor represents is everything other than labour and capital; it explains what labour and capital do not explain.

As might be expected, such a provocative statement as Solow's stimulated inquiries into just what 'technical change' signified. The response of Denison was, from our point of view, the most significant (e.g. Denison, 1967). What Denison did was to decompose the residual, left after the contribution of the growth of labour and capital had been subtracted, into several distinct elements plus, inescapably, a residual of the original residual.

Since Denison's decompositions covered the growth of the US and Western European economies they are of less interest to us than a similar decomposition of the elements explaining the growth of the economy of the

Republic of Korea, carried out by Kim and Park (quoted in Westphal, 1986). In this rapidly developing country, between the years 1963 and 1982, increases in the supplies of labour and capital accounted for 55 per cent of the growth. The remainder, 45 per cent, is Solow's 'technical change'. How does this remainder break down? Kim and Park found that roughly 10 per cent could be assigned to increases in the amount of education gained by the workforce; 40 per cent to the attainment of economies of scale; nearly 20 per cent to an improved allocation of labour; and 30 per cent to unassigned causes, of which one involved was the greater utilization rate of capital equipment. The extent to which these different sorts of productivity increase can be attributed to the advance of science and technology in Korea is, of course, subject to argument; but, given the elastic definition of science and technology that we adopted in Chapter 1, we would be inclined to assign almost all.

Questionable an assignment as this may be, it does at least give some support to the proposition that advances in science and technology contribute to economic growth, and to our focus upon science and technology in countries eager to reproduce Korea's process of rapid economic growth from a low platform.

THE TIMING, IN THEORY, OF ADVANCING SCIENCE AND TECHNOLOGY

Presuming that it is desirable for developing countries to pursue science and technology, the next issue that arises is when they should do so. Here, again theory has something to say. The economic theory that we shall draw upon is the so-called optimal growth theory, 'growth' in that it attempts to describe, in the abstract, the growth of an economy over the long run; and 'optimal' in that it attempts, for the economy so described, to determine how scarce resources should be allocated through time so as best to achieve the economy's overall objective. The objective is often specified as maximizing the discounted stream of consumption per capita, over some long, perhaps infinite, horizon; in less technical language as obtaining as high a standard of living as possible throughout the future.

Since the optimal programme is somewhat surprising and, at first at least, extremely austere, it might be useful to describe the theory of optimal economic growth, under advancing science and technology, in some detail. The first piece of theory that we shall draw upon is that formulated by Phelps (1966).

Phelps' objectives in formulating his theory were twofold. First, he wanted to represent, in the abstract, the mechanism by which advances in science and technology led to increases in the productivity which scarce resources achieved in production. He called the activity which generated increases in productivity 'research': research is one of the two sectors comprising his economy. In the mathematical model describing the economy, laid out in detail in the article, research is undertaken by only one of the two factors of production: labour, allocated to the research sector, yields technical progress, or, as we would call them, advances in science and technology.

These advances have profound effects on the performance of the economy. In the research sector already identified, advances in science and technology make subsequent research easier to undertake. Advances achieved today enable labour engaged in research to be more productive tomorrow; in other words, undertaking research now creates a momentum which leads to more effective research in the future. The other effect of research is to make the remaining portion of the labour force, engaged in the (second) sector of the economy which produces its physical output, more productive also. The advances in science and technology are assumed to disseminate throughout the productive sector immediately and costlessly, so that all the labour there employed becomes more efficient as a result.

Having represented the pursuit of science and technology in this manner, Phelps then asks how should an economy allocate its labour supply between the research sector and the productive sector so as to maintain, throughout all time, maximum consumption per capita, for the growing population. Phelps is not concerned with how that economy reaches this optimum state, merely with the properties of this optimum. This optimum he calls the 'golden age', since it can, without changes in the system or its parameters, exist in this happy state forever. It is the dynamic equivalent of static equilibrium: and can be thought of as a momentary equilibrium for all moments of time. Mathematicians call this a 'steady state'.

What is the allocation of labour among the two sectors in the steady state? In that steady state characterizing the 'golden age' (there may be other steady states which fail to maximize consumption per capita) it happens that the portion of the labour force devoted to research is exactly half the total. This coincidental result comes about from the mathematics, in particular the functional forms chosen to express the outputs of the research and productive sectors, but may not be as unrealistic as seems. If, instead of science and technology (our collective term for technical progress; or 'research', the term used by Phelps) one thinks of 'information', the term used by information scientists, one can recognize their claim that approximately half of all labour in the developed countries is devoted to generating, processing and applying information. They say that the Japanese, US or Western European economies are 'information economies'; Phelps would say that they are 'research economies', and we that they are scientific and technological economies. And Phelps' prescription for an under-developed economy is that it be, somehow, an 'information economy'.

Phelps also illustrates the benefit that accrues to the research economy in its 'golden age': with the labour force growing at a constant rate (as elements do in a steady state) and without any research being conducted, i.e. with all the labour force allocated to production, the economy grows at a slower, although constant, rate. In other words, the economy grows at the same rate as the labour force, or in this abstract economy, as the population. Consumption, per capita, is static. The economy is growing, to be sure, but no faster than its population. However, with research undertaken so exten-sively as to occupy half the labour force, the rate of growth of the economy, and of consumption too, is twice the rate of growth of the population. In other words, the economy is growing twice as fast as the population; and consumption at the same rate. How superior an outcome this is!

There are two qualifications that we may wish to impose upon Phelps' model: that it has a narrow view of what resources are utilized in under-taking research and that it does not address the issue of how the economy attains the 'golden age'. The first of these qualifications does not really hold, neither in theory nor, perhaps unfortunately, in practice in the part of the world that we are investigating. In his development of the theory, Phelps does consider how his results would differ if capital, a second factor of production already necessary for production in his model, is also neces-sary for 'research'. He thus considers an augmented model in which both inputs, labour and capital, are needed in both sectors. When capital, as well as labour, is a necessary ingredient for the conduct of 'research', a 'golden age' is still attainable in principle. The results indicate that it is even more golden – 24 carat as against say 16 carat in the case of 'research' requiring labour alone – in that the steady state rate of growth of the economy can exceed twice the rate of growth of the labour force. The reason would seem to be that the scarcest input in this economy is labour; and if something can be substituted for labour, then the labour constraint on growth can be relaxed. The something that can substitute for labour is capital.

The qualification that Phelps took too narrow a view of the inputs necessary for research may not hold in Sub-Saharan Africa, because labour seems to be almost the sole input to research. We are anticipating the results of our inquiries into the conduct of R&D there, but one of our findings is that almost all the expenditures of the institutes are devoted to wages and salaries. What Phelps would designate as capital – such things as laboratory equipment, supplies, scientific books and journals, etc; the wherewithal of research – are severely lacking in practice. Advances in science and technology are secured almost solely by the unassisted labour of scientists and technologists.

The second qualification to Phelps' analysis is that it neglects what in a practical sense would be the *development* of the economy. How does the economy reach perfection? What happens before the 'golden age'? For an answer to this question we must move to a different sort of growth model, one which considers the path to be followed from *any* initial situation, to that of the 'golden age'. In mathematical terms, this means considering the transition from a non-steady state to that particular steady state characterized as the 'golden age'. Posing the task as a question: what is the optimal path to be followed by an economy, given that it commences from a non-optimal position? And what allocations, through time, will ensure that the economy adheres to this path?

To answer these related questions we shall move on to the work of Uzawa and Enos. Uzawa's was much the more original and grand contribution (Uzawa, 1965). He, like Phelps, assumes that, of the two inputs the economy utilizes, only labour is needed to advance science and technology. The sector in which science and technology are advanced is called, by Uzawa, 'education'. When allocated to the educational sector, labour achieves an output which raises the productivity of all the (remaining) labour assigned to the productive sector. As in Phelps' case, the productivity of labour in the productive sector is raised, through 'education', universally and immediately. The cost thereof is in the output of the productive sector forgone through the alternative allocation of otherwise productive labour to 'education'.

In Uzawa's model there are two sequences of decisions which the economy must make at every instant of time, if it is to achieve its objective. The objective is rather more complicated than in Phelps' model; in Uzawa's it is to maximize the discounted sum of consumption per capita over an infinite horizon. In the 'golden age', the issue of discounting does not arise, since every instant is the same, and the future identical to the present. In the interval, perhaps infinite in time, before the 'golden age' is attained, however, a little more consumption today, and its necessary concomitant, a little less in the future, must be weighed against a little less today and a little more in the future. Discounting future units of goods consumed against present consumption makes some sense as a weighting process. The two decisions the economy must make are in what portions to allocate its scarce labour supply among the two sectors, 'education' and production, and in what portions to allocate the current output of goods among the two competing uses, as consumption and as investment. Although education in Uzawa's model needs only labour, production needs both labour and capital; and the capital stock available for production is enlarged only by investment.

What are the two optimal allocations through time, for an economy that is initially short of 'education'? Remember that being short of 'education' means having a low productivity of labour in production, and consequently producing little output with the labour and capital initially available. In our terms, it means having initially a low level of science and technology, less, probably far less, than would be accessible in the 'golden age'.

Taking first the output of the productive sector, which is either consumed or invested, it is optimal initially, and for some extended length of time, to allocate the entire amount to investment. In other words, the capacity of the productive sector to produce goods should be built up as quickly as possible. Current consumption should be halted; only the ability to produce for future consumption should be considered. Only after an appropriate stock of capital has been accumulated should some of current output be made available for consumption.

In Uzawa's artificial world, consumers (= labour) are compensated for not consuming today by consuming more in the future; but in reality such abstinence is not practicable. Economists immediately recognized the extreme nature of the optimal programme, the absurdly high value of the optimal savings rate. A more realistic savings/investment rate, one which might be politically and socially feasible, is to maintain consumption per capita constant and allocate all the remaining output to investment; i.e. to invest the economy's surplus. But, whatever allowance is made for maintaining current consumption, the optimal policy continues unrepentant – start by investing everything that one can, for as long as is necessary, or, in more emotive terms, sacrifice today's pleasures for tomorrow's good.

Of more concern to us is the second sequence of decisions, derived as the optimal policy for the allocation of labour between production and 'education'. The choice is not easy, nor simple. If labour is allocated to the productive sector, investment can flourish; if it is allocated to the educational sector, the productivity of labour in the productive sector can flourish. Unlike the decision to consume or to save/invest, this seems not so much to involve a trade-off between present and future: the trade-off is between utilizing one means to the end – applying more labour to production – and the other means to the same end – applying more labour to 'education', thereby raising the productivity of the fewer remaining workers in the productive sector.

What is the optimal programme for the assignment of labour? In Uzawa's model it is not so clear as in Phelps': given Uzawa's assumptions of labour being perfectly mobile and supplied in a perfectly competitive market, its allocation will depend upon its relative contribution, at the margin, in the two sectors. Its contributions will be measured by its shadow prices, which are established according to the discounted future value of the consumption their output permits, be it via the investment goods it produces in the goods sector, or via the increase in labour productivity through the advance in science and technology in the educational sector. There is no magic result, as in Phelps' case; but just as the optimal policy for the allocation of goods involves maximizing, initially, their assignment to investment, so the optimal policy for labour involves assigning initially more than the steady state amount to the educational sector.

The optimal allocation of labour in a model reflecting the advance of science and technology can be seen somewhat more clearly in another growth model, this one attributable to Enos (Enos, 1991). In this model, there are the customary two sectors: one, in which goods are produced; and the other, in which 'training' takes place. The difference between Enos' model, on the one hand, and Phelps' and Uzawa's on the other, lies in what are identified as the scarce inputs: in the latter's models the scarce inputs are labour and capital; in the former unskilled labour and skilled labour. Both types of labour are assumed to be necessary for the production of goods, and both for the training of unskilled labour so that it acquires skills. Progress occurs through the increasing prevalence in the economy of the more productive skilled labour.

What is the optimal policy in Enos' model, given that the objective of the economy is, as in the other models, to maximize the discounted sum of future consumption per head? Not surprisingly, given the previous results, for the economy initially short of skilled labour the optimal policy is to initially allocate all labour to the 'training' sector, provided there is not too great a difference in the degrees to which the two types of labour can be substituted one for the other in the two sectors. If the degree of substitutability in the 'training' sector is low, and that in the production sector high, almost all the skilled labour will be assigned to training, until the proportion of skilled to unskilled labour has become sufficiently high. Again, this is an austere outcome, for with the assignment of most of the skilled labour to training unskilled labour, little physical output is produced, and little consumption takes place. Moreover, another issue arises, one that also arises in the case of Uzawa's and Phelps' models but is left implicit there: the issue of absorption. Along the optimal path, incomes are maintained as both skilled and unskilled labour earn wages in both sectors, but there are few goods to purchase with these earnings. Total income of the economy is undiminished, but the total volume of goods available falls: under the optimal programme it falls to a very low level. The immediate effect of reallocating large amounts of labour to 'training', therefore, would be to put the economy under great stress, as existing incomes chase fewer goods.

The implications of Enos' model for our study are twofold. The first is that the best policy for the developing country would be to assign as much labour as feasible to raising the skill level of the population, or in our words, to advancing science and technology. The second is that the degree of substitutability of the relatively more scarce input for the relatively less scarce is of importance. This phenomenon – substitutability – will appear again in the next model we draw upon, the model that comes closest to including Structural Adjustment.

Before we go on to consider theory devoted to explaining Structural Adjustment we may find it useful to recapitulate the theory, and the few statistical results already described. The various theories have three elements in common: first they are all rigorously developed, using mathematical language to secure consistency and exactness. Secondly, they are all sufficiently powerful to yield interesting, and usually testable, hypotheses. These two elements are the characteristics of all theory in economics; it is the third that divides our theories from the very much larger universe of all economic theories, namely that our sample focuses on the long run. Short term phenomena are missing, and consequently there are also missing those fluctuations in economic activity that occur from month to month or from year to year, and those policies that governments and other economic agents adopt in response. Our theories are concerned with trends, with what can happen over the longer horizon when economic fluctuations are irrelevant.

Given that the theories take the long view, they yield a set of mutually consistent ideas about economic development. Most germane to our study is the idea that the advance of science and technology, to use our term, contributes greatly to the growth of an economy. The demonstrations were initially made by Solow and Denison. The next ideas, that we have attributed to Phelps, are that advances in science and technology can be modelled as a separate activity, utilizing the resources that are scarce in the economy, and therefore useful elsewhere (for example in production), but organized in its own fashion and following its own rules and procedures. When organized separately, the evolution of the sector that generates advances in science and technology can be related to that of the rest of the economy, and their joint progress observed. In the steady state, described by Phelps, the growth of the economy and the advance of science and technology move in step, at a rate greater than that at which physical resources, specifically the labour force, multiply. Equally consequently, a substantial portion of the labour force is always allocated to further and further advancing the scientific and technological level of the society.

To determine how the economy best reaches the steady state, that state where the economy is organized so as to achieve throughout all time the highest level of material satisfaction, we drew upon two optimal growth theories, those of Uzawa and Enos. Like Phelps, they formulated models of long-run economic growth in which the sector generating advances in science and technology was identified separately, but unlike Phelps they addressed the issue of how the economy attained the 'golden age' of steady, maximal growth. Their simple but self-denying conclusion was that the best course of action for the economy to follow was to allocate all the resources that it could spare foremost to building up its scientific and technological potential. Using their language, the optimal policy was first to allocate all the available resources to investing in capital and 'education' (Uzawa) or 'skills' (Enos). Until capacity to advance science and technology had been created in sufficient amount to permit its rapid advance, little attention should be given to increasing physical output. Only afterwards should producing goods lay claim upon the economy's scarce resources.

So, in summary, advancing science and technology is vital; its advance can be considered separately from the growth of the productive economy; the economy in its highest state has a flourishing ambience of science and technology, in which are usefully employed a substantial fraction of the working population; and finally, to reach this highest state from one less abundantly endowed, with the least sacrifice and in the quickest time, the entire surplus of the economy should, immediately and for an extended interval, be channelled to accelerating scientific and technological progress.

These are the implications of the theory that we have chosen to describe, and these are the theses that underlie our analysis. But we have not yet exhausted our search among economic theories, for we need additional guidance in conducting our inquiry among developing countries with very low levels of science and technology and under great stress. In the language of the theorists, we need guidance for an inquiry into economies formulating their optimal policies with distressing parameter values and under dreadful initial conditions.

THEORIES OF STRUCTURAL ADJUSTMENT

The nature of theories is that they are abstract, for otherwise they would not reveal the general properties of the systems they describe. Yet, it can certainly be argued that the theories hitherto described are too abstract, for they fail to include two other crucial issues, the allocation of scarce resources *within* the productive sector and the destination of its outputs. These two issues are interrelated, and so can best be considered – logically and coherently – in the context of an expanded mathematical model of economic growth. The model will necessarily be one that expands upon our earlier models but, also necessarily because of its increased complexity, one that is not so clear in its policy implications, i.e. one that does not yield, as a logical deduction, an optimal policy. For the model that we will describe, the optimal policy cannot be derived, only guessed at.

Of all the theories available, this model appears to be the most relevant to our research and the most suggestive for policy, not only domestic (that is within a developing country) but also foreign (that is within the international agencies and the overseas donors). If our prescriptions are to be international, our theory must be international too, so it is within the international elements of the theory that we will commence our description. The theory is recent, having been formulated only recently by Ka-yiu Michael Fung and Jota Ishikawa (Fung and Ishikawa, 1992). In their paper the authors start by assuming that the prices which govern in the developing economy are those established in the world at large. The developing country under examination can trade at those prices, but must also accept them for its own internal transactions. It is, in the language of trade theorists, an open economy. The country is also assumed to have such a meagre effect in the world's demand for and supply of the tradeable commodities that it alone has no effect on their prices. It is a small open economy.

For us, the tradeable commodities must be defined with great care. In Fung and Ishikawa's model they are two in number and labelled X and Y: both X and Y are final goods, which can either be traded abroad, generating foreign exchange, or consumed at home, yielding satisfaction (see Figure 1.1). Taking the world market price of good X as unity, the world sets a price of P^* on good Y. Since the goods within the developing country are valued at world market prices, their domestic prices are also 1 (unity) and P^*. These prices are assumed to remain constant throughout all time.

Since the relative prices of the two goods are exogenous and fixed, something else must distinguish the two. The distinguishing characteristics are the resources that they need for their production and the impact upon them of advances in science and technology. Briefly, good Y is produced under constant returns to scale, using labour and a second factor unique to itself, labelled R. For the moment, we will say no more about R, beyond that it is necessary in the production of good Y, is in fixed supply, and, consequently, yields to its possessors an income, or rent, hence the letter R.

Good X, the other traded good, is produced under increasing returns (to be explained later) using a single factor, intermediate goods. Intermediate goods, S, are an exception to the category of goods consisting of X and Y: they are assumed not to be tradeable. In other words, goods X and Y can enter into international trade but goods S, the intermediate goods, cannot. They have a price in the domestic economy alone, and that price is determined solely in the domestic economy.

We cannot bring out the important distinction between goods X and Y without going further into the origin of the intermediate goods S. This can most clearly be done by counting up the sectors in Fung and Ishikawa's model. So far we have identified three, those responsible for the production of goods X, Y and S. But there is a fourth and final sector, called by the authors the R&D sector, but by us the sector that generates advances in science and technology.

In the sector that generates advances in science and technology, there is only one factor, labour. In this assumption, Fung and Ishikawa's model is similar to Phelps' simpler model, and to those of Uzawa and Enos; but not to Phelps' more complicated model. Working with the accumulated science and technology, labour engaged in this sector is able to advance it, the rate of advance being proportional to the number of workers allocated, and to its existing level. Thus the higher is the current level of science and technology, the faster it will advance; and the more workers that are employed in advancing it, the faster it will advance. The two elements (the state of science and technology and the number of scientists, technologists and allied workers) reinforce each other. Each alone is capable of promoting science and technology, but together they have a greater capability. This greater capability is acknowledged in the expression 'increasing returns to scale'.

Increasing returns to scale are the characteristic of production of tradeable good X, but accrue not directly but indirectly through the production of the intermediate good S. Recall that S, and S alone, is necessary for the production of good X; yet labour and the accumulated amount of science and technology is necessary for the advance of science and technology, which is incorporated in good S. The way in which Fung and Ishikawa account for the effect of advances in science and technology in S is now relatively common in economic theorizing and owes its formulation to Romer and Lucas (Romer 1989 and 1990; Lucas, 1988). The properties of the specific function chosen are discussed in Grossman and Helpman, 1989. Essentially, Fung and Ishikawa assume that the further has science and technology advanced, the greater is the number of different intermediate goods available to producers of X; and the greater the number of intermediate goods available, the lower are their prices. Thus, the further advanced is science and technology, the cheaper is the production of X. This section of the model itself is more complicated, involving many producers of differentiated intermediate goods in a monopolistically competitive industry.

In résumé, the two tradeable goods, Y and X, are produced under different conditions: Y is produced employing a technology that is static, whereas X is produced under an advancing technology. The more labour that is allocated to securing advances, the faster are those advances; also, the further has the technology advanced already, the faster are those advances. To concentrate today on advancing science and technology is to lower the costs of producing X today; moreover, to have concentrated on advancing science and technology in the past is to have lowered the cost of producing X today. Concentrating on advancing science and technology provides two dividends, one immediate and the other from past accumulations.

Perhaps it is now obvious why it is so important for us to define our goods X and Y carefully. Depending upon what real commodities we assign to the category X and what other commodities to category Y, we will be determining deductions from the model and influencing the recommendations for policy. One's intuition can be relied upon already; it suggests that whatever commodities receive the attention of grantors of money for R&D will have greater prospects for the future than those which receive no attention. But there is a danger of circular reasoning: since, according to the model, the commodity towards whose production R&D is directed will have its costs of production lowered, so it will be worth while directing R&D towards that commodity. That commodity automatically falls in category X. The allocation is self-fulfilling. But there may well be another commodity whose cost of production would fall even further if the same amount of R&D were devoted to advancing its technology. Yet, if that potentially more attractive commodity does not receive the attention of the potentially less attractive commodity, it would fall in category Y.

So, we must assign commodities to categories X and Y not on the basis of whether or not they currently have R&D directed towards them but on the basis of whether or not they have great potential, potential that could become manifest were R&D to be directed towards them. It is potential to respond to R&D that determines in which category actual commodities belong. This is not a theoretical issue but a practical one; this is not an issue that we can dispose of now, but one that will occupy us throughout our study.

Even before our theory has been fully formulated it has already illuminated one issue that we must address – the issue of the direction of R&D. In our language, the issue is in which areas and on behalf of which commodities are advances in science and technology to be sought? It is not enough for us to identify those areas in which advances in science and technology are currently being sought; we must ask if these are the *best* areas. Are there better areas to be exploited? Why are these areas not being opened? Why is R&D not being undertaken there?

Other collateral questions immediately come to mind: on what basis and through what mode of analysis is the potential of individual commodities determined? Who makes the choice? With what objective in mind? These are all questions that we must ask, questions that are of consequence not only for the narrow purpose of ensuring as good a fit between our model and reality in Sub-Saharan Africa but also for the much graver purpose of ensuring that those resources necessary to advance science and technology there, so scarce as they be, be put to their best use.

Having interrupted our description of Fung and Ishikawa's model to identify our first set of questions, we shall now proceed to determine its solution and its policy implications. Although we are avoiding mathematics in this chapter, we will find it useful to appeal to five further diagrams, in the hope that they will make the analysis clearer. The first is Figure 2.1 which purports to illustrate the state of the economy before and after substantial resources are allocated to advancing science and technology. The output of good Y (the good whose potential is low, i.e. whose response to future R&D would be less beneficial from the point of view of the developing economy) is measured on the vertical axis; that of good X (the good with potential) on the horizontal. The curve, concave to the origin, joining the two axes, is the locus of the maximum amounts of the two goods, X and Y in combination, that can be produced currently, assuming that all the resources in the economy are fully employed, that they can be allocated to the production of X and Y in any proportion, and that they can be shifted costlessly from the production of less of one good to the production of more of the other. In other words, any combination of goods X and Y indicated by the coordinates of a point on the concave curve labelled $(X,Y)^c$, the 'c' for current, is assumed to be feasible.

How, in theory, will the developing country allocate its scarce resources? Assuming that internal prices of the two commodities match world market prices, and assuming also that the objective of the country is to maximize the total value of output (equal, in macro-economic terms, to maximizing GDP), it should allocate them so as to produce the amounts Y^c and X^c, as indicated by the intersections on the vertical and horizontal axes respectively. Graphically, coordinates of the amounts Y^c and X^c are located where the concave production possibility curve and the dashed relative price line (P^* is the slope of the dashed line) are tangent.

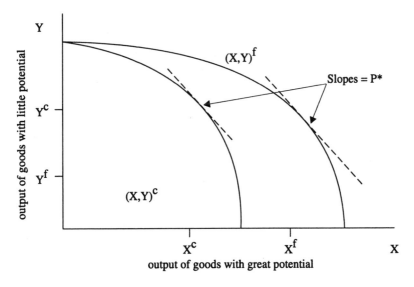

Figure 2.1 Production of goods X and Y by the economy, before and after advances in science and technology

This exercise established the equilibrium for the economy before there is any shift of resources into advancing science and technology. In the absence of the allocation of resources to advancing science and technology, this equilibrium will persist through time: the economy described by the model will be static; i.e. it will not grow in per capita terms. For ease of display, it is also assumed that population is static; relaxing this assumption does not change the results in per capita terms.

An economy that grows is presumably better than one that does not. In Figure 2.1 we also depict the optimal allocation of resources some time in the distant future, based on the assumptions that the relative prices of X and Y do not change, that the scarce resources have been devoted to advancing science and technology in the production of the good X, where the potential lies, and that the country's objective is still that of maximizing GDP. The optimal allocation is determined in exactly that same manner as for the 'current' case; the only change graphically is that the production possibility curve has moved outwards to the right. The new curve, $(X,Y)^f$ where the superscript 'f' indicates future, illustrates the greater productivity of the country's resources when assigned to the production of good X, but a constant productivity through time when assigned to the production of good Y.

In the future, the country will maximize its GDP by producing Y^f of good Y and X^f of good X. Total GDP will be higher in the future than the present, by the amount by which $(1)(X^f) + (P^*)(Y^f)$ exceeds $(1)(X^c) + (P^*)(Y^c)$. The production of good Y will have fallen, and that of good X will have risen more than proportionately. Resources will have been shifted from the production of Y to that of X, although in lesser proportion than the shift in output, because of the growth of productivity of the country's resources in the production of the good X towards which it was worth directing R&D expenditures.

Although Figure 2.1 displays the before and after, it does not give any indication of the process by which growth was obtained. This is the function of Figures 2.2–2.3. There, the initiation of R&D is depicted; the changes have come about as a result of the reallocation of scarce resources away from the production of good Y. Logically, given the properties of the model, its output will fall from Y^c to a new level Y^1. The resources reallocated will have two competing uses, to increase the immediate output of X, and to advance science and technology so as to increase the productivity of these resources that are devoted to producing X. How should the newly available resources, withdrawn from the production of good Y, be split between the two competing uses? The optimal growth theories already laid out in the preceding section of this chapter (those attributable to Phelps, Uzawa and Enos) deduce that the bulk of the newly available resources should be allocated to advancing science and technology.

So, previous theory suggests that it is optimal to shift most of the newly available resources into R&D; but the models that yield this theorem are simpler than Fung and Ishikawa's, lacking both the sector which does not benefit from advances in science and technology and the expression which provides increasing returns through the accumulation of scientific and technological knowledge. Therefore previous theory is silent about whether the output of good X will rise or fall. Fung and Ishikawa recognize that there are the two possibilities. These are reflected in Figures 2.2 and 2.3 by the alternative production possibility curves $(XY)^{1a}$ and $(XY)^{1b}$; the implication of the former is that shifting the resources previously utilized in the production of good Y to advancing science and technology will lead to less X being produced too; the implication of the latter that shifting the resources will lead to producing more X. To Fung and Ishikawa, as to ourselves, which of the two alternatives will be forthcoming is not obvious, but they have been able to specify, quite ingeniously, the conditions that will determine the answer. The determining condition is expressed by two parameters (para = determined outside; meter = the model) which they label δ and β, plus one initial condition and one control variable. The initial

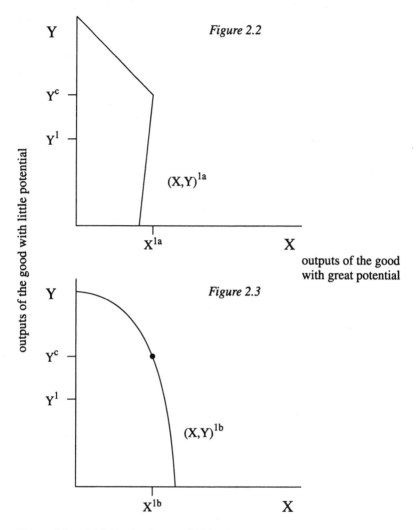

Figures 2.2 and 2.3 Production possibilities for the economy with different elasticities of substitution for intermediate goods

condition, which we label N^c, reflects the level of science and technology at the time the shift occurs; the control variable is labelled L_N (as in figure 1.1), and measures the amount of labour allocated to advancing science and technology.

The first of the two parameters, δ, is easy to interpret: it represents the efficiency with which the labour employed in the research sector advances science and technology. The 'production function' for advances in science and technology contains the efficiency parameter, δ, together with the other two factors determining the advance, namely the level of science and technology already reached and the number of workers assigned to the sector.

The other parameter, β, is difficult to interpret, although no less important in determining the outcome. It is contained in the 'production function' for the output of the good, X, whose potential is being realized through advances in science and technology. This equation states that the output of good X is directly dependent upon the number of intermediate goods available, which themselves are dependent upon the current state of the arts. The production function exhibits constant returns to scale at any instant; the parameter β represents the elasticity of substitution between the various intermediate goods. Since β is a constant, the production function can be recognized as one with a constant elasticity of substitution (abbreviated, commonly, as a CES function).

What does the elasticity of substitution signify? Its significance can perhaps be understood most easily if we consider the two polar cases, those of no substitutability and of perfect substitutability. Imagine the case of no substitutability; in this case there is no possibility of substituting in production one intermediate good for another (say, one lathe for another lathe). Intermediate goods must be combined in fixed proportions, and a lack of one sort, necessary for the production of X, cannot be compensated for by a surplus of another sort. The case of perfect substitutability is the antithesis of no substitutability: all lathes are perfectly substitutable; and none will be in surplus. In the case of perfect substitutability, the parameter β takes on the value of zero; in the case of perfect substitutability, the value of infinity. A realistic value would be somewhere in between – greater than zero and less than infinity. What value β does take on is an empirical matter, but presumably subject to influence through policy, an issue to which we will return shortly.

Let us now illustrate the effects of various values of the two crucial parameters δ and β on the total output and income of the country. For this purpose we will utilize Figures 2.2–2.3. In these, are displayed the alternative outcomes in cases of relatively low (less than one-half) and relatively high (more than one half) for β, the elasticity of substitution. Note that in the first case, illustrated in Figure 2.2, the production possibility curve $(X,Y)^{1a}$ bends back upon itself at lower outputs of good Y than the previous equilibrium output $(X,Y)^c$ (refer to Figure 2.1, for the deter-

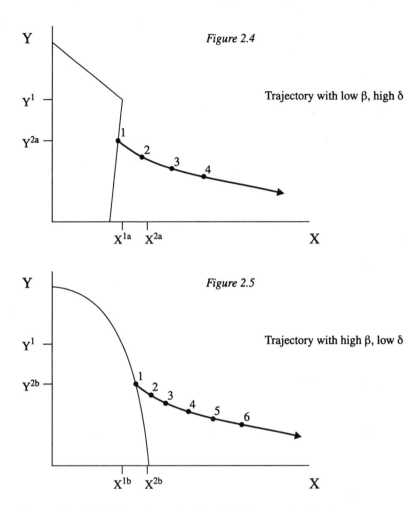

Figures 2.4 and 2.5 Alternative trajectories with different values for the parameters measuring the elasticity of substitution (β) and the efficiency of inputs (δ)

mination of the pre-research equilibrium). The reason that the production possibility curve bends backwards is that the productivity of intermediate goods is low because of their scarcity and lack of substitutability. Points lower down on the production possibility curve $(X,Y)^{1a}$ indicate greater allocation of labour to advancing science and technology, and, consequently, a lesser allocation to production of good X. This reflects the trade-off between lower production today, with more resources assigned to R&D, and higher production in the future, as a result of the advances in science and technology which today's research workers achieve.

But, if the value of β exceeds one-half, it is possible to allocate some resources to advancing science and technology *and* produce more of good X simultaneously (although, of course at the expense of producing less of good Y). This more favourable outcome is illustrated in Figure 2.3, in which the production possibility curve does not bend back upon itself for outputs of Y less than X^c, Y^c.

We have therefore seen the difference between lower and higher values of the parameter β, the difference being that, with lower values of β committing resources to advancing science and technology reduces, in the short run, the output of both final goods. With higher values of β committing resources to advancing science and technology reduces only the output of good Y.

How can we illustrate the effect of changing values of the other crucial parameter, δ, the efficiency with which resources are employed in the research sector? To illustrate varying efficiencies, we have drawn Figures 2.4 and 2.5. These two consider a longer period than the previous figure, and depict outcomes in a succession of years. These yearly outcomes are shown as points along two trajectories; each trajectory is the locus of yearly outcomes of combinations of goods X and Y produced by the economy, with different values for the two parameters δ and β. Taking the upper trajectory, the outcome for the year before resources are committed to advancing science and technology is the familiar X^c, Y^c. Given a low value for the elasticity of substitution β, the outcome for the next year will be represented by the point X^{1a}, Y^1. Assuming that the resources employed in advancing science and technology are very productive (i.e. assigning a high value to the efficiency parameter δ) progress along the trajectory (i.e. progress from point $(X,Y)^{1a}$ to point $(X,Y)^{2a}$, to point $(X,Y)^{3a}$ and so on) will be rapid.

The alternative trajectory represents opposite values for the crucial parameters δ and β. As in Figure 2.3, it is assumed that the value of β is high, and so the first year's outcome is indicated by the point $(X,Y)^{1b}$. But this trajectory is drawn on the assumption that the value of the second parameter, δ, is low, i.e. that resources committed to advancing science and technology are employed less effectively. As a consequence, yearly progress along the trajectory is slower, successive outcomes (points $(X,Y)^{2b}$, $(X,Y)^{3b}$, and so on) being more closely spaced that equivalent points $(X,Y)^{1a}$, $(X,Y)^{2a}$, $(X,Y)^{3a}$.

The best combination for the developing country is high values for both parameters. In such a desirable case, the initial commitment of resources to advancing science and technology would not involve any immediate sacrifice of good X, although there would be a sacrifice of good Y through the reallocation of resources out of the good with no potential to respond to advances in science and technology. Subsequently, progress along the economy's trajectory would be rapid, so that the country would in a relatively short period of time reach, and subsequently surpass, the situation illustrated in Figure 2.1 as the production possibility curve $(X,Y)^f$.

Summarizing the deductions we have made from Fung and Ishikawa's model, we can now recognize the significance of the two parameters β and δ, the elasticity of substitution of intermediate goods in the production of good X and the efficiency with which resources are employed in research, respectively. Added to the other two important variables, L_N and N^c, the number of workers committed to advancing science and technology and the initial level reached by the country, we can see how, within the context of the model, the country's productive future is determined.

Since these four elements, the parameters β and δ and the variables L_N and N^c determine the course of the future in principle, we, who are using economic principles as our guide, should focus upon the actual phenomena they represent. We should attempt to find out the extent to which intermediate goods can be substituted for each other, the extent to which resources allocated to advancing science and technology are employed effectively, the extent to which substantial numbers of workers are actually committed to advancing science and technology, and the level of science and technology already achieved. Moreover, to fulfil the objective of our study, we wish to discover how these phenomena are being affected by Structural Adjustment Programmes, and whether or not their values are being improved. Do the Structural Adjustment Programmes lead to an increase in the value of β, so important in the initial years? Do they lead to an increase in the value of δ, so important along the country's trajectory? Do they lead to an increase in the resources committed to advancing R&D, so important throughout? Do they lead to the country's ability to exploit, to the fullest extent, its current stock of scientific and technological knowledge? These are the questions that our theory suggests are of such importance as to demand answers.

GUIDANCE FOR OUR STUDY

The theories presented in this chapter have been of some use. They, together with some statistical analysis, have provided justification for concentrating our inquiry on advancing science and technology in the developing countries. They have suggested that the optimal policy for these developing countries is to commit, immediately and in substantial volume, additional resources to promoting the advance of science and technology. They have alerted us to the importance of certain phenomena, upon which we should focus our attention. Finally, they will provide us, in Parts III and IV of this study, with a means of separating the effects of Structural Adjustment Programmes from all the other events that impinge upon the developing countries in our sample; i.e. they will enable us to construct counterfactual cases, so as to guess at what would have transpired in the absence of the Structural Adjustment Programmes.

Before moving on to the country studies, let us restate the list of phenomena to which theory has alerted us. First, when defining the terms of out theory we saw that a clear distinction had to be made between those goods which the developing country could, through advances in science and technology, produce increasingly profitability, and those, other, goods which it could not. We called these goods with a 'potential' and goods without, respectively, and admitted that it will be important in principle for our study, and in practice for the developing country and for those who advise it correctly to identify the goods. This is a real issue: in which direction should science and technology be advanced? Which developments should be encouraged? Given that there are never enough resources to pursue all lines of research, which developments should not?

Having distinguished in principle between goods with potential and goods without, we then learned that theory suggests we focus particularly upon four phenomena as having a profound influence upon the future. These are the country's ability to substitute 'intermediate' goods one for another in the production of the good in which the country has potential, the efficiency with which R&D is carried out, the number of individuals committed to advancing science and technology, and the extent to which the already existing body of science and technology is drawn upon. Theory implies that these are vital matters in their own right, and that the effects upon them of the adoption of Structural Adjustment Programmes will be of great importance for the country's progress. Some empirical evidence concerning these phenomena, and others of interest, will be reported in the next four chapters, one each on Ghana, Kenya, Tanzania and Uganda.

Part II

The pursuit of science and technology

3 Ghana

INTRODUCTION

Ghana gained its independence in 1957, and was therefore one of the first countries in Africa to do so. In some ways, the Ghanaian economy has changed substantially since that date; industry and services have increased their role, and agriculture has been reduced. Income in total, and also per capita, rose for a few years, fluctuated around the highest value attained for the next few years, and then fell, until very recently. The country's population has grown very rapidly, from a figure of approximately 7 million inhabitants at the time of independence to over 16 million today. Government's role in the economy has increased.

But among these changes, certain things have remained constant. Ghanaians have sought employment abroad, sometimes in neighbouring countries, at other times in Nigeria, and still other times beyond West Africa, their numbers varying as economic conditions at home fluctuated and as emigrating Ghanaians received different welcomes. Ghana's primary exports, from which almost all of its foreign exchange is derived, have not changed in nature; throughout its history as an independent country Ghana has depended to a substantial extent upon exports of cocoa, timber and gold and, to a lesser extent, of diamonds and bauxite. Through time both the physical quantities of these exports and the price which each unit of them receives in world markets, have declined. Other constants are an increasingly urbanized population, many of whose members are unemployed or only partly employed; pressure on government constantly to increase its level of employment, both internally and within the parastatal companies; an insufficiency of public overhead capital in all branches – transport, communications, energy and education – and, not unexpectedly, political instability.

It is within the economy whose main characteristics are summarized above that we undertook a study of the performance and prospects for those organizations advancing science and technology. In outline, the description of the study will commence with a very brief history of the Ghanaian economy since independence, relying upon the accounts of others and upon the published statistics of the Ghanaian government. Our attention will be drawn to several phenomena: the overall level of economic activity, and that fraction of total output which is allocated to investment, the revenues and expenditures of the Ghanaian government; the country's exports and imports; and the borrowing and repayments it has made abroad. Within the light of these economic events, the Structural Adjustment Programmes undertaken by the Ghanaian government, on its own account and in response to the requirements of the IMF and World Bank, will be summarized. Fortunately, in the case of Ghana we have some indication as to what these conditions were, so that we will be able to list them, focusing on those which are likely to have had an impact on the advance of science and technology.

Once we have described the Structural Adjustment Programmes, and the economy on which they have been imposed, we shall move on to organizations contributing to the advance of science and technology. Three of these, one each in the fields of agriculture, industry and appropriate technology, were the subjects of detailed inquiry; of the remainder, we have merely collected a few statistics. The three organizations which we covered in detail will be described in sequence, with particular attention paid to their scope, their requests for resources, and the amounts which they were finally allocated.

With estimates of the expenditures of other R&D organizations, both in the public and the private sectors, we can derive aggregates for all research institutions within Ghana.

Science and technology were defined in Chapter 1 as including not only the activities of R&D institutions but also the activities of public and private firms of a more applied nature, and expenses of educating and training the technical workforce. These latter activities, ancillary to the carrying out of R&D, will be mentioned, and guesses made as to the amount of resources which they employ. Combining all of our measures of expenditures, in whatever areas of science and technology, we will be able to produce an overall estimate of that portion of the Ghanaian economy which is devoted to their advance. This overall measure of the amount of resources devoted to advancing science and technology, and a few alternative measures provided by others engaged in the same inquiry, will provide the basis for our evaluation in Chapter 7 of Ghana's contribution to the advance of science and technology in Sub-Saharan Africa.

RECENT ECONOMIC HISTORY

Of all the countries which we are studying, it is Ghana about which the most has been written by economists. Every few years has seen the emergence of yet another study of the political economy of this enthralling country (e.g. Apter, 1955; Birmingham *et al.*, 1966/7; Foster and Zolberg, 1971; Killick, 1978; Roemer, 1984; Green, 1987; Younger, 1989; and Rothchild, 1991). Chronologically, these authors have run the course from optimism, through disappointment, to disillusion, depression and finally to optimism once again.

Aggregate economic statistics for Ghana move in parallel with these opinions. At the time of independence, the Ghanaian economy was quite well endowed in respect of natural resources, skills and finance. With a productive agriculture, not only feeding the population but also providing substantial volumes of cocoa for export, the Ghanaian economy had a solid base from which to advance. Industrial output value-added was nearly 20 per cent of GDP. Besides, before independence, education had flourished and capital had been accumulated. In 1957 Ghana's was, by African standards, a flourishing economy, each inhabitant, on the average, receiving an income of approximately US$600 in today's prices (see Tables 3.1, 3.2).

The subsequent history has been one of a rapidly rising population combined with a much less rapidly rising output. The first estimate of Ghana's GDP covered the year 1965 and amounted to 4.64 billion Cedis, measured in constant prices of 1975 (see Table 3.1). Distributed among the 8 million Ghanians this yielded an average of 580 Cedis each, or approximately the same number of US dollars (see Table 3.2). Sixteen years later, in 1981, GDP per capita had fallen to 489 Cedis (again in 1975 prices); both agriculture and industry had suffered, the latter more dramatically, its share of the total national output falling from 19 per cent in 1965 to 9 per cent in 1981 (see Table 3.3; note that in 1984 the figures in Table 3.3 shifted from the basis of current prices to the basis of constant prices of 1975).

By the end of 1981, the economy was in chaos. The response was the return to power of Flight Lieutenant Rawlings, heading a government comprised of both military officers and civilians and dedicated to moral and economic uplift. At first, the Ghanaian government attempted to stabilize the economy through its own efforts, mobilizing the population and emphasizing the need for improved performance. But by the end of 1982 the government recognized that assistance from outside would be necessary and, for the first time, approached international financial agencies for assistance. The following year, Ghana embarked upon a programme of

Table 3.1 Ghana, GDP, 1965–1991

	GDP (billions current Cedis)	GDP deflator (1987 = 100)	GDP (billions Cedis at constant 1987 prices)	GDP (billions Cedis at constant 1975 prices)	Official Exchange Rate (annual average conversion factor, Cedis per $US)	GDP (billions current $US, at official exchange rate)
1965	n.a.	n.a.	n.a.	4.64	n.a.	n.a.
1966	n.a.	n.a.	n.a.	n.a.	n.a.	n.a.
1967	n.a.	n.a.	n.a.	n.a.	n.a.	n.a.
1968	n.a.	n.a.	n.a.	n.a.	n.a.	n.a.
1969	2.0	0.3	580	n.a.	n.a.	n.a.
1970	2.3	0.3	640	n.a.	n.a.	n.a.
1971	2.5	0.4	691	n.a.	1.03	2.43
1972	2.8	0.4	670	n.a.	1.33	2.15
1973	3.5	0.5	689	n.a.	1.16	3.01
1974	4.7	0.6	740	n.a.	1.15	4.08
1975	5.3	0.8	641	n.a.	1.15	4.60
1976	6.5	1.1	619	n.a.	1.15	5.65
1977	11.2	1.8	630	n.a.	1.15	9.75
1978	21.0	3.0	692	n.a.	1.76	11.9
1979	28.2	4.1	680	n.a.	2.75	10.5
1980	42.9	6.3	684	n.a.	2.75	15.6
1981	72.6	10.9	664	5.38	2.75	26.4
1982	86.5	13.9	621	n.a.	2.75	31.4
1983	184	31.0	593	n.a.	8.83	20.8
1984	271	41.9	645	5.16	36.0	7.53
1985	343	50.6	678	5.42	54.4	6.31
1986	511	71.7	713	5.70	89.2	5.79
1987	746	100	746	5.98	153.7	4.85
1988	1,051	133.5	787	6.31	202.4	5.20
1989	1,417	171.6	826	6.63	270.0	5.25
1990	1,904	223.8	851	6.84	326.3	5.83
1991	2,359	264.2	893	7.13	367.8	6.42

Sources: 1965: Ghana, Republic of, 1991
1969–1991: World Bank, World Tables 1991, 1993
1990–1991: Ghana, Republic of, 1991

Table 3.2 Ghana, population, GDP per capita, and annual rate of growth of GDP,
1965–1991

	Population (millions)	GDP per capita (Ghanian Cedis at constant 1975 prices)	GDP per capita (current $US)	Annual rate of growth of GDP (per cent per year)
1965	n.a.	580	n.a.	n.a.
1966	n.a.	n.a.	n.a.	n.a.
1967	n.a.	n.a.	n.a.	n.a.
1968	n.a.	n.a.	n.a.	n.a.
1969	8.4	n.a.	230	n.a.
1970	8.6	n.a.	250	9.7
1971	8.9	n.a.	270	5.4
1972	9.1	n.a.	250	−3.0
1973	9.4	n.a.	260	2.9
1974	9.6	n.a.	290	7.3
1975	9.8	n.a.	280	−13.4
1976	10.0	n.a.	280	−3.5
1977	10.2	n.a.	300	1.8
1978	10.3	n.a.	350	9.8
1979	10.5	n.a.	380	−1.7
1980	10.7	n.a.	410	0.6
1981	11.0	489	410	−2.9
1982	11.4	n.a.	380	−6.5
1983	11.7	n.a.	350	−4.5
1984	12.2	n.a.	370	8.8
1985	12.6	430	370	5.1
1986	13.1	n.a.	390	5.1
1987	13.5	n.a.	390	4.6
1988	14.0	n.a.	400	6.2
1989	14.4	n.a.	380	6.1
1990	14.9	n.a.	390	4.1
1991	15.3	469	400	4.7

Sources: 1965–1991: Ghana, Republic of, 1991
1965–1989: World Bank, *World Tables 1991, 1993*

Structural Adjustment, with its first loan from the World Bank (see
Rothchild, 1991).

More than 10 years have passed since then, and six additional loans from
the World Bank have been secured. Looking at the overall changes in the
Ghanaian economy during this period and comparing the present with the

Table 3.3 Ghana, GDP by sector, 1965–1991

	Agricultural product (billions Cedis)	Share of agriculture in GDP (percentage)	Industrial product (billions Cedis)	Share of industry in GDP (percentage)	Manufacturing product (billions Cedis)	Share of manufacturing in GDP (percentage)	Services (billions Cedis)	Share of services in GDP (percentage)
1965	n.a.	41	n.a.	19	n.a.	10	n.a.	41
1966	n.a.	n.a.	n.a.	n.a.	n.a.	n.a.	n.a.	n.a.
1967	n.a.	n.a.	n.a.	n.a.	n.a.	n.a.	n.a.	n.a.
1968	n.a.	n.a.	n.a.	n.a.	n.a.	n.a.	n.a.	n.a.
1969	0.92	46	0.38	19	0.25	13	0.70	35
1970	1.05	47	0.41	18	0.26	12	0.80	35
1971	1.10	44	0.46	18	0.28	11	0.94	38
1972	1.13	43	0.50	19	0.31	12	1.00	38
1973	1.72	49	0.65	19	0.41	12	1.14	32
1974	2.38	51	0.85	18	0.50	11	1.43	31
1975	2.52	48	1.10	21	0.74	14	1.66	31
1976	3.30	51	1.25	19	0.86	13	1.97	30
1977	6.3	56	1.8	16	1.2	11	3.1	28
1978	12.7	61	2.5	12	1.8	9	5.7	27
1979	16.9	60	3.5	12	2.4	8	7.8	28
1980	24.8	58	5.1	12	3.3	8	12.98	31
1981	38.6	51	6.7	9	4.3	6	27.4	40
1982	49.6	57	5.4	6	3.1	3	31.5	38
1983	109.9	60	12.2	7	7.1	4	61.9	34
1984	2.78	54	0.60	12	0.37	7	1.92	37
1985	2.80	52	0.71	13	0.46	8	2.06	39
1986	2.89	49	0.76	13	0.51	9	2.20	38
1987	2.89	47	0.85	14	0.56	9	2.40	39
1988	3.00	46	0.91	14	0.59	9	2.59	40
1989	3.12	46	0.94	14	0.61	9	2.74	40
1990	3.05	43	0.99	14	0.62	9	2.98	43
1991	3.07	42	1.09	15	0.67	9	3.14	43

Sources: 1965: 1984–1991 Ghana, Republic of, 1991. (GDP at market prices, in constant 1975 prices)
1969–1983: World Bank, World Tables 1991. (GDP at factor cost, in current prices)

Table 3.4 Ghana: public, private and total investment as percentages of GDP, 1970–1991

Year	Public	Private	Total
1970	n.a.	n.a.	14.2
1971	n.a.	n.a.	14.1
1972	n.a.	n.a.	7.1
1973	n.a.	n.a.	9.0
1974	n.a.	n.a.	13.0
1975	n.a.	n.a.	12.7
1976	n.a.	n.a.	8.9
1977	n.a.	n.a.	11.1
1978	n.a.	n.a.	5.4
1979	n.a.	n.a.	6.5
1980	n.a	n.a.	5.6
1981	n.a.	n.a.	4.6
1982	n.a.	n.a.	3.4
1983	n.a.	n.a.	3.7
1984	n.a.	n.a.	7.0
1985	n.a.	n.a.	9.6
1986	8.2	1.2	9.6
1987	9.5	1.0	13.3
1988	9.1	2.2	14.0
1989	7.8	5.8	13.6
1990	7.4	8.6	16.0
1991	8.0	8.9	16.9

Source: 1970–1991: World Bank, *World Tables 1991, 1993*

trough of 1981, the Ghanaian economy has shown remarkable recovery. The overall measure of economic output, GDP, has risen from 4.8 to 7.1 billion Cedis, at 1975 prices. The increase in industrial output has been even more rapid, from 0.4 billion Cedis in 1981 to 1.1 billion Cedis 10 years later. The share of industry in total GDP has very nearly been restored to its value at the time of independence; since total GDP is some 50 per cent higher than at the time of independence, total industrial output has increased by approximately the same percentage. Total investment has risen from approximately 5 per cent of GDP in the initial year to nearly 17 per cent at the present (see Table 3.4). During this time, public investment has remained more or less constant at 8 per cent of GDP; the increase has come about entirely through a resurgence in private investment, which rose from a negligible rate in 1981 to nearly 9 per cent of GDP at the present.

If the domestic economy appears to be recovering, Ghana's international economy has not vouchsafed the same improvement. In Table 3.5 we see data on total exports, imports and the balance on current account for Ghana, as well as figures for the exports and imports of its chief commodities. The improvement in the domestic economy has generated some improvement in exports in recent years, but only to the level of the late 1970s, chiefly because of the debilitated state of the cocoa plantations and the low price which gold commands in world markets. It is the value of imports which has increased so rapidly in recent years. The resurgence of industrial output, and the growth of incomes, has increased the need for imports – of raw materials, capital goods and consumer goods – and the reduction of restraints on imports, through the scheme of liberalization, has encouraged the increase. Financed in part by foreign borrowing, the deficit on the current account has been contained until recently, but the figures for the last few years – 1990 and 1991 particularly – suggest that the deficit on the current account has now reached a dangerous level.

As it is, the pressure on Ghana to service previous borrowing from abroad is already beginning to tell. The figures in Tables 3.6, 3.7, and 3.8 display Ghana's growing international indebtedness. The majority of Ghana's debts are to international financial agencies and to governments in the developed countries; the eight loans which Ghana accumulated in the six years 1983–1989 amounted alone to US$626 million (see Table 3.6). In 1989, Ghana was allocating approximately 10 per cent of its total export earnings to servicing official debt; the servicing of unofficial debt claimed another 2 per cent of Ghana's export earnings.

The annual outflow in payments to creditors has now surpassed the annual inflow, from both official and unofficial sources. In 1989 Ghana became, on balance, a supplier of capital to the developed countries and to their financial institutions. If Ghana is to fulfil its obligations to the international financial community, it will have to continue to export more capital than it receives from abroad.

THE PROSPECTS FOR INDUSTRY

Because it has been undergoing Structural Adjustment, at first on its own initiative and subsequently under the direction of the IMF and the World Bank, Ghana's industry has a history of 10 years' restructuring. The evidence that is available up to the present indicates that there have been substantial changes in Ghana's industrial sector, and that these changes have not been wholly to the country's benefit (Lall *et al.*, 1994).

Table 3.5 Ghana: balance of payments, 1970–1991

	Total exports of goods and services (millions current $US)	Total imports of goods and services (millions current $US)	Balance on current account (before official transfers) (millions current $US)	Exports of primary products (millions current $US)	Exports of cocoa (millions current $US)	Imports of manufacturers (millions current $US)	Imports of fuel (millions current $US)	Exports of manufactures (millions current $US)
1970	477	543	−765	423	n.a.	286	23.9	9.3
1971	389	535	−155	326	n.a.	317	26.5	4.1
1972	443	348	92	374	n.a.	185	33.7	4.9
1973	654	540	108	520	n.a.	275	40.1	13.4
1974	747	942	−199	615	n.a.	503	136	11.6
1975	895	922	−3	697	n.a.	518	131	11.2
1976	894	995	−105	722	n.a.	571	129	11.4
1977	1020	1159	−144	906	n.a.	804	180	18.0
1978	997	1102	−109	960	n.a.	708	139	12.1
1979	1165	1121	41	892	n.a.	567	176	12.1
1980	1213	1264	−54	929	n.a.	682	301	9.0
1981	832	1336	−508	733	n.a.	741	390	5.5
1982	714	905	−192	633	n.a.	529	360	3.8
1983	478	724	−248	431	n.a.	308	166	5.0
1984	612	813	180	557	382	389	210	6.5
1985	676	952	−244	622	412	416	224	7.2
1986	819	1056	166	739	503	457	246	8.6
1987	906	1328	−220	812	493	586	316	9.4
1988	959	1393	−262	867	462	619	333	10.8
1989	889	1410	−319	801	408	625	337	9.3
1990	984	1628	−442	853	355	727	391	9.9
1991	1095	1756	−442P	974P	376P	810	436P	11.3

Sources: 1970–1989: World Bank, World Tables 1991, 1993; total imports and exports from balance of payments; individual items from customs figures 1990–1991: Ghana, Republic of, 1991

Notes: P signifies projected.

Table 3.6 Ghana, debt servicing, 1970–1991

	Total debt outstanding (billions current US dollars)	Official debt (billions current US dollars)	Debt to IMF (billions current US dollars)	Debt to World Bank (IBRD/IDA) (billions current US dollars)	Private debt (billions current US dollars)	Total debt as a percentage of GDP	Service of debt, annual total (billions current US dollars)	Service of official debt (billions current US dollars)	Service of private debt (billions current US dollars)	Total debt service as a percentage of GDP	Total debt service as a percentage of total exports	Service of official debt, as a percentage of government current revenue
1970	0.549	n.a.	n.a.	n.a.	n.a.	n.a.	n.a.	n.a.	n.a.	n.a.	n.a.	n.a.
1971	0.531	0.52	n.a.	n.a.	0.01	22	n.a.	n.a.	n.a.	n.a.	n.a.	n.a.
1972	0.583	0.57	n.a.	n.a.	0.01	27	n.a.	n.a.	n.a.	n.a.	n.a.	n.a.
1973	0.736	0.65	n.a.	n.a.	0.08	25	n.a.	n.a.	n.a.	n.a.	n.a.	n.a.
1974	0.717	0.65	n.a.	n.a.	0.07	18	n.a.	n.a.	n.a.	n.a.	n.a.	n.a.
1975	0.729	0.65	n.a.	n.a.	0.08	16	n.a.	n.a.	n.a.	n.a.	n.a.	n.a.
1976	0.717	0.63	n.a.	n.a.	0.09	13	n.a.	n.a.	n.a.	n.a.	n.a.	n.a.
1977	1.058	0.96	n.a.	n.a.	0.10	11	n.a.	n.a.	n.a.	n.a.	n.a.	n.a.
1978	1.269	1.19	n.a.	n.a.	0.08	11	n.a.	n.a.	n.a.	n.a.	n.a.	n.a.
1979	1.273	1.21	n.a.	n.a.	0.06	12	n.a.	n.a.	n.a.	n.a.	n.a.	n.a.
1980	1.314	1.25	n.a.	n.a.	0.06	8	n.a.	n.a.	n.a.	n.a.	n.a.	n.a.
1981	1.430	1.05	0.03	0.24	0.39	38	n.a.	n.a.	n.a.	1.4	6.4	n.a.
1982	1.610	1.06	0.02	0.26	0.55	45	n.a.	n.a.	n.a.	1.8	8.7	n.a.
1983	1.820	1.33	0.28	0.27	0.49	54	0.10	0.09	n.a.	2.9	20.9	0.3
1984	2.050	1.51	0.47	0.31	0.54	56	0.08	0.08	0.01	2.2	13.5	12.7
1985	2.430	1.76	0.65	0.38	0.67	63	0.08	0.08	0.01	2.1	12.2	10.8
1986	3.130	2.09	0.75	0.55	1.04	77	0.09	0.08	0.01	2.2	10.8	10.7
1987	3,262	3.19	n.a.	n.a.	0.07	67	0.11	0.10	0.01	2.4	12.2	14.9
1988	3,048	2.99	n.a.	n.a.	0.06	59	0.11	0.10	0.01	2.1	11.5	13.7
1989	3,296	3.24	n.a.	n.a.	0.06	63	0.11	0.10	0.01	2.1	12.4	13.7
1990	3,761	3.70	n.a.	n.a.	0.06	65	0.10	0.09	0.01	1.7	n.a.	n.a.
1991	4,209	4.14	n.a.	n.a.	0.06	66	n.a.	n.a.	n.a.	n.a.	n.a.	n.a.

Sources: Column 1–6, 10–11: 1981–1990: Strack and Schönherr, 1989
Columns 1, 2, 5, and 6: 1970–1980: 1987–1991: World Bank, World Tables 1991, 1993; private debt recorded as long term debt of private sector;
official debt by subtraction from total debt
Columns 7–9: 1983–1990: Strack and Schönherr, 1989
Column 12: Service of Offical Debt, from column 8: Government Current Revenues from, Table 3.8, column 1, converted to US dollars by the
official exchange rate (Table 3.1, column 5).

Table 3.7 Ghana, total debt and its composition, 1970–1991 (millions of current US dollars outstanding at end of year)

Year	External debt, total	Long term debt, total	Short term debt, total	Private sector debt, total (including non-guaranteed debt)	Public sector debt, total
1970	549	544	5	10	539
1971	544	537	7	10	534
1972	602	585	16	9	593
1973	756	731	26	82	674
1974	738	729	9	74	664
1975	728	722	6	76	652
1976	717	714	3	85	632
1977	1,074	849	224	96	978
1978	1,286	919	367	80	1,206
1979	1,290	1,087	204	60	1,230
1980	1,407	1,276	131	52	1,355
1981	1,546	1,260	286	49	1,497
1982	1,475	1,267	208	55	1,420
1983	1,650	1,557	93	47	1,603
1984	1,941	1,699	242	52	1,889
1985	2,226	2,038	189	59	2,167
1986	2,726	2,539	187	67	2,659
1987	3,262	3,143	119	73	3,189
1988	3,048	2,976	72	65	2,983
1989	3,296	3,098	198	62	3,234
1990	3,761	3,449	312	62	3,699
1991	4,209	3,826	384	59	4,150

Source: 1970–1989: World Bank, World Tables 1991, 1993. Debt of non-financial public enterprises; amounting to approximately 20% of the total external debt in early years and decreasing to 10% in the later years, is excluded from private sector debt. Public sector debt by subtraction of private sector debt from total external debt.

Table 3.8 Ghana, government revenues, expenditures and investment, 1969–1991

Year	Government current revenue (billions current Cedis)	Government current expenditure (billions current Cedis)	Government surplus (+) or deficit (−) (billions current Cedis)	Government capital payments (billions current Cedis)	Government consumption (billions current Cedis)	Government gross investment (billions current Cedis)	Total gross domestic investment (billions current Cedis)	Private investment (billions current Cedis)
1969	n.a.	n.a.	n.a.	n.a.	0.29	n.a.	0.23	n.a.
1970	n.a.	n.a.	n.a.	n.a.	0.29	n.a.	0.32	n.a.
1971	n.a.	n.a.	n.a.	n.a.	0.32	n.a.	0.35	n.a.
1972	0.42	0.44	−0.16	0.14	0.36	n.a.	0.20	n.a.
1973	0.39	0.45	−0.19	0.13	0.38	n.a.	0.32	n.a.
1974	0.58	0.62	−0.20	0.16	0.57	n.a.	0.61	n.a.
1975	0.81	0.91	−0.40	0.30	0.69	n.a.	0.67	n.a.
1976	0.87	1.10	−0.74	0.50	0.80	n.a.	0.58	n.a.
1977	1.17	1.36	−1.06	0.87	1.41	n.a.	1.24	n.a.
1978	1.39	2.54	−1.90	0.75	2.37	n.a.	1.13	n.a.
1979	2.60	3.50	−1.80	0.90	2.90	n.a.	1.85	n.a.
1980	2.95	4.18	−1.81	0.58	4.78	n.a.	2.41	n.a.
1981	3.28	6.33	−4.71	1.66	6.38	n.a.	3.32	n.a.
1982	4.86	8.60	−4.85	1.10	5.60	n.a.	2.92	n.a.
1983	10.2	13.4	−4.93	1.77	15.8	n.a.	6.90	n.a.
1984	22.6	23.3	−4.84	4.16	20.0	n.a.	19.01	n.a.
1985	40.3	38.5	−7.58	9.43	32.0	n.a.	33.0	n.a.
1986	73.6	60.8	0.30	12.5	46.1	41.7	48.0	6.3
1987	111.0	80.7	4.06	26.3	64.1	70.6	77.8	7.2
1988	153.8	110.0	3.91	38.9	89.4	95.2	118.8	23.6
1989	n.a.	n.a.	n.a.	n.a.	116.2	110.5	193.0	82.5
1990	n.a.	n.a.	n.a.	n.a.	164.3	144.7	313.0	168.2
1991	n.a.	n.a.	n.a.	n.a.	188.9	188.9	399.1	210.2

Source: 1969–1988: Columns 1–4: World Bank, World Tables 1991, 1993
1986–1991: Columns 5–8: Ghana, Republic of, 1991

Like the economy as a whole, the industrial sector in Ghana has been the subject of much inquiry (in chronological order, see Birmingham *et al.*, 1966/7; Steel, 1977; Page, 1980; Andrea, 1981; Ewusi, 1986; Meier and Steel, 1989; Steel and Webster, 1990; Mosley, Harrigan and Toye, 1991; Sowa *et al.*, 1991 and Rothchild, 1991). As mentioned already, industrial output as a whole has been growing since the adoption of the Structural Adjustment Programmes in Ghana. Within the industrial sector, it is small and medium scale industry that are increasing in proportion, and large scale industry that is static. The increase in output of the small and medium scale portion has been primarily through increase in the number of firms; entry into Ghanaian industry has been very rapid in recent years, but once established, the firms tend to remain fixed in size and employment. Large scale firms in Ghana have shown little resilience under the Structural Adjustment Programme. The liberalization of imports has permitted increases in foreign products with which they compete, often with disastrous results for the local industries. A headline from a newspaper (the *Weekly Spectator*, number 1233, Saturday, 9 November 1991) is 'factories collapsing . . . over 120 out of business'. The beginning of the article reads as follows:

> Over 120 industries in the country have closed down since 1988 due to their inability to sell goods they produce. The industries affected include those of garment, leather, agricultural, electrical, electronic, metal and pharmaceuticals. Prominent among them are the Match Factory, Crystal Oil Mills, Ever Ready Battery, Ayrton Drug manufacturing, all the machine shops, Ghana Candle and Brush Company. Others are the Glamour garment factory, Ghana Umbrella Factory, Benya distilleries, Baston Terrazo Works, Akropong farm ltd. and African Motors. A spokesman of the Association of Ghana Industries who disclosed these in an interview on Thursday said that unfair trade competition from unchecked imported items into the country has contributed to this situation.

Even allowing for journalistic exaggeration, the majority of large Ghanaian firms competing with foreign producers have not fared well. The few that have prospered are those that have been endowed with exceptionally talented leadership and foreign technology (Lall *et al.*, 1994).

It is a temptation to blame all of the business failures upon the Structural Adjustment Programme in general and upon the liberalization of imports in particular. What those who have studied the changes in Ghanaian industry since the adoption of the Structural Adjustment Programme, and those who are employed within industry, are coming to realize is that the industrial structure of a country cannot be changed overnight. Embodied in the law, in custom, and in the behaviour of Ghanaians, as well as others in Sub-Saharan Africa, are elements which prevent the quick and easy transfer of resources from one line to another, or from one sector to another, or from one type of enterprise to another. Take as an example the legal requirements on payment of redundancy, for those whose employment is terminated, and for retirement, for those whose working life is ended. Laws passed by the Ghanaian parliament in the late 1950s and early 1960s entitle employees who are declared redundant to payments amounting to approximately five years' wages or salary. Payments to those retiring are, upon their retirement, approximately twice as large. To reduce employment, a large firm, which would be expected to conform to legislation, would incur substantial costs, with no immediate return. It is no surprise that large firms when faced with these costs of retrenchment, prefer to operate for some period and then to close down permanently. The choice for them is not between running at a profit and running at a loss, but between incurring a substantial loss in the short period, through redundancy, and incurring a gentler loss over a much longer period, through unchanged operations with the original workforce, followed by exit from the industry.

It may well be asked why, in a study of the pursuit of science and technology, we direct so much attention to industry in Ghana. Part of the answer lies in the fact that many of the scientists and engineers who have been educated in Ghana are probably working in the industrial sector. We have data on the numbers of scientists and engineers in two countries in our sample of four, Ghana and Kenya. Expressing the number of scientists and engineers in each of the two countries on the basis of a million persons, Ghana has 403; Kenya 26 (UNESCO, 1990). Although Kenya's population is slightly larger than Ghana's, even in absolute numbers the number of scientists and engineers in Ghana exceeds that in Kenya, and probably in our other two countries as well, by an order of magnitude. With so many scientists and engineers, somewhere close to 10,000 in total, many must be employed within Ghanaian industry.

Our focusing on Ghanaian industry is also in part because industry affords an indicator of the success with which science and technology in Ghana have progressed in the past. To the extent that advances in science and technology occur in the industrial sector, and to the extent that they are applied within the firms operating there, we would expect Ghanaian industry to be relatively efficient, adaptable, and technically knowledgeable. To the extent that these virtues are not apparent, we would be forced to conclude that advances in industrial science and technology have not percolated down to the workplace. We should then search for reasons, which we might find in a lack of resources devoted to advancing industrial science and technology, in a failure to disseminate those advances that were obtained, in advances that are inappropriate for the Ghanaian industrial regime, in a disinterest in their application by Ghanaian firms, or in any combination of these. To the extent that reason or reasons have been suggested, we shall cite them; to the extent that these forces have been altered, for the better or for the worse, by the adoption of Structural Adjustment Programmes, we shall try to acknowledge them.

THE STRUCTURAL ADJUSTMENT PROGRAMMES

After the Ghanaian government realized that its own efforts at adjustment would be insufficient, it appealed to the IMF and the World Bank, who imposed their first Structural Adjustment Programme in 1983 (negotiations over this and subsequent programmes are described in Martin, 1991). The conditions which were attached to this first and the subsequent seven loans from the World Bank are summarized by Toye (Mosley *et al.*, 1991: 173) as nine major policy themes, governing:

1 the producer price of cocoa;
2 the cocoa marketing costs of the Ghana Cocoa Marketing Board;
3 the removal of subsidies and price controls;
4 the trade and foreign exchange regime;
5 cost recovery and removal of subsidies in health and education;
6 public sector programming;
7 state enterprise divestiture;
8 public sector management; and
9 banking reform.

Like most of the very poor countries which submit to the IMF and World Bank's conditions, Ghana's attempt at compliance has been sincere and success in compliance has been relatively high. The meeting of some of the conditions can be seen in the macro-economic statistics already cited; for example, in 1986 the Ghanaian government ran a budget surplus, the first year on record (see Table 3.8 above). Imports, particularly those of industrial commodities, have been liberalized, with the dire results for that portion of Ghanaian industry in competition with imports noted above. Employment in government and in the para-statal sector is slowly being reduced; for example 5,000 'ghost-workers' (imaginary persons, whose wages were appropriated by real persons) and 5,000 'retirees' (employees who had officially retired and received the appropriate financial emoluments, but were still receiving wages or salaries from the firm) had been taken off the rolls by 1991.

Other conditions have been much more difficult to fulfil (see, e.g. Rothchild, 1991: 9–14). As has happened in many Sub-Saharan African countries, Ghana's deficit and the balance of payments has risen rather than fallen, by extremely large amounts in the last two years (see Table 3.5 above). This is a common experience in the years following import liberalization and a substantial devaluation of the local currency, bringing it more nearly in line with free market rate: the volume of imports is quick to respond to the first of these regulatory changes; the volume of exports slow to respond to the second. Increases in the volume of Ghana's main export earner, cocoa, have been achieved, but the world market price has fallen, more than cancelling the increase in value terms.

Another change that will take a long time to come about, a change that is just as necessary as increasing Ghana's exports, is improving the ability of Ghana's civil service to plan the government's and the para-statal's future, and then to make the decisions and execute and monitor the programmes that will follow. These activities require many civil servants with technical as well as administrative skills; both these skills take time to acquire and perfect; the Ghanaian government and its ancillary institutions cannot be expected to improve their performance overnight. The acquisition of these skills may depend on previous advances in science and technology, and for these the time scale is even longer.

We have described enough of the recent economic history of Ghana to recognize the fragile nature of the economy; the inefficiencies, improprieties, and degradations that have occurred in the years since independence; and the substantial difficulties that lie in the face of adjustment. That these adjustments to the structure of the Ghanaian economy are necessary appears to all observers to be true; that it will take a long time to secure such an adjustment is beginning to be recognized also. But then the long horizon stretches before us, as well, when we consider the future of science and technology in the country. This consideration will begin in the next section, when we report on our inquiries into the activities of Ghana's R&D institutions.

R&D INSTITUTIONS

Considering R&D institutions in Ghana, we shall first describe the three that we examined in some detail; we will then mention the other R&D institutions within Ghana's public and private sectors; finally we will observe the overall structure of Ghana's activities in science and technology, both from a statistical and from an administrative view.

The first research institution that we investigated was the Industrial

Research Institute (IRI). Ghana was fortunate to have acquired several research institutes whose purview had been all of British West Africa. One of these was the Industrial Research Institute, established originally in 1964 as the Institute of Standards and Industrial Research. Now, as then, it has the function of providing solutions to problems encountered by local industry. As of the latest year for which figures are available, 1989/90, IRI had 24 people on their scientific staff, spread over 13 fields. Seven worked in the area of chemistry and chemical engineering; three in ceramics; two each in metallurgy, mechanical engineering, economics and physics; and one each in electrical engineering, agricultural engineering, planning, geology, statistics and library science. The numbers of scientific staff have varied over the last decade with the general state of the economy and with government expenditures; there were 21 in 1980, 16 in 1983, 20 in 1985, and 15 in 1987. Within these numbers, there is considerable turnover, young researchers being attracted to it because of the immediate incentives which it offers (50 per cent of initial salary as an inducement to take employment, and 30 per cent of any fees earned for the institute by consultancy work). IRI also provides sponsorship for young professionals who wish to pursue further studies either locally or abroad.

In addition to the R&D which IRI undertakes on its own behalf, it also provides technical services, on such matters as technology transfer, technical and managerial training etc., to firms, particularly those in metal working, and agricultural equipment industries, and building materials and ceramics.

The best measure of IRI's activities and aspirations can be gathered from figures on its funding (see Table 3.9). There are eight columns in the table, the first three devoted to recurrent funding, the second three to funding for development or capital investment, and the final two to ratios. Of the total recurrent expenditures, the major portion is consumed in wages and salaries. In 1980, the first year of our compilation, wages and salaries represented two-thirds of the total recurrent expenditures; this figure rose somewhat erratically to a fraction of three-quarters in 1990. In a few years – 1983 and 1985 – more was spent on administration than on the wages and salaries of scientific and technical staff; in the other years the proportions were reversed.

The only other item on which a substantial portion of IRI's recurrent expenditures have been allocated is an item labelled 'Overhead', which includes mainly the use of power, water and other utilities, and maintenance: overheads claim almost all of the residual left over after wages and salaries have been paid.

Moving on to capital expenditures, requests by IRI have always been substantial, approximately equalling, and in some years even exceeding,

Table 3.9 Ghana: Industrial Research Institute (IRI) requests for and allocations of funds, 1980–1991

Year	Recurrent items (millions current Cedis)			Development items (millions current Cedis)			Ratios: expenditures as a percentage of requests by IRI	
	Requests by IRI	Approvals by Finance Ministry	Released for expenditure	Requests by IRI	Approvals by Finance Ministry	Released for expenditure	Recurrent	Development
1980	0.09	n.a.	0.80	0	0	0	89	–
1981	2.38	1.38	1.16	0.79	0.32	0	49	0
1982	2.74	n.a.	1.41	1.15	0	0.10	52	9
1983	3.18	n.a.	1.55	1.70	0	0	49	0
1984	4.52	2.06	2.17	5.60	0	0	48	0
1985	7.52	6.17	6.86	5.35	0	0	91	0
1986	17.1	n.a.	16.5	13.2	n.a.	1.2	96	9
1987	33.7	27.0	22.6	16.6	n.a.	n.a.	67	n.a.
1988	60.6	45.7	35.7	46.2	6.0	5.1	59	11
1989	105	88	54	200	116	61	51	31
1990	135	81	63	429	70	27	47	6

Source: Industrial Research Institute

requests for current expenditures. Only in the last three years which our records cover – 1988, 1989 and 1990 – however, were substantial funds made available for capital expenditures. In the first of these years, 1988, a foreign loan – from the African Regional Centre for Technology, which contributed 200 million Cedis – accounted for a major portion of the capital expenditures in that year, and in the following year, 1989, a large loan from the World Bank (amounting to US$120 million) included one billion Cedis for the IRI. The first tranche was approved by the Finance Ministry and released in 1989, permitting a capital expenditure of 61 million Cedis. Another 27 million Cedis were released in 1990, and, presumably, the balance will be made available over subsequent years. Starting in 1989, therefore, IRI has been building up its capital equipment.

Nonetheless, there is still a considerable backlog of capital expenditures requested by IRI and yet to be carried out, as a comparison of the figures in columns 4 and 6 of Table 3.9 indicates. Whereas requests for current expenditures have usually been approved in the proportions of roughly two Cedis approved for each three Cedis requested, the proportions of approvals to requests in the capital budget have been much smaller. From 1980 through 1987, in only one year were any funds approved at all; in two of the last three years, 1988 and 1990, approvals from the Finance Ministry were only about one-sixth of the amounts requested. To be sure, those undertaking R&D do request more funds than they expect to receive, but a lack of substantial approvals, or no approvals at all, does impose considerable stringency upon a research institute.

The data on IRI presented already are of an overall nature; they reveal little of the day to day activities of the institute. At the moment, these are concentrated in four projects – the development of a local biogas process, the adaptation of a Gari processing machine (Gari is a crude sugar), a machine for removing the hulls from groundnuts (peanuts), and a stove adapted to use liquid petroleum gas. In addition, IRI is involved in collaborating research with the Botany Department of the University of Ghana (involving classification of oil bearing plants and seeds), with the Geological Survey Department (involving the collection of samples of local raw materials with a potential use as glazes in ceramics) and with the Food Research Institute and Crops Research Institute (on the processing of cassava). IRI also trains technicians in welding, foundry operation, machining and toolmaking, drawing the apprentices from both private industrial firms and from the armed forces. Finally, IRI offers the service of its scientists and engineers as consultants to private industry, deriving from it annually an income which supplements government funds by a small percentage.

Towards the end of this chapter we shall consider the role of IRI within the overall conduct of R&D in Ghana, but after one final comment we will move on to the next research institute. The comment is that none of the funds which IRI has utilized over the last 10 years has come in the form of a donation from abroad. In order to augment the funds which it provided itself, the Ghanaian government was forced to borrow money from the World Bank: investment in R&D in industry does not come cheaply to Ghana.

The next two research institutes that we studied do receive foreign bounty. The first is the Scientific Instrumentation Centre (SIC). The Centre was established as a joint undertaking of the Ghanaian government and UNDP. Its major objective is to develop facilities and skills in instrumentation and measurement suited to the educational, industrial and technological development of the country. The Centre undertakes calibration, repair and maintenance of scientific, industrial, educational and medical equipment.

The main divisions of the Scientific Instrumentation Centre are four in number: electrical/electronics; fine mechanics; calibration; and glass blowing. The academic background of the staff is in electrical, electronic and mechanical engineering, in physics, and in glass blowing. Table 3.10 reveals requests for funds, approvals and expenditures in the years 1979 through 1991; included within the totals are the donations, in foreign currency, received from UNDP. It was these donations – US$103,000 in 1984 and US$143,000 in 1985 – that permitted the large capital expenditures in 1985 and 1986.

The second research institute which has benefited from foreign donations is the Food Research Institute. The Food Research Institute conducts investigations into food processing, preservation, storage, marketing and distribution. The Institute employs 30 specialists and ancillary staff, most of whom are engaged in R&D. The areas which are covered are solar crop drying, quality evaluation and grading of grains, fisheries and fish technology, meat and fish processing technology and the growing of horticultural crops for export. The FRI also accumulates knowledge on the quality and characteristics of local food crops such as maize, cowpeas, mango, cassava, and fishes. It has also collaborated with the Cocoa Research Institute on standards and specifications for cocoa processing facilities.

The budgets for the Food Research Institute, to the extent that they are available, are reported in Table 3.11. The funds made available for current expenditures ('Recurrent Items'), have averaged approximately 75 per cent of requests; until 1987, requests for capital expenditures were granted only in very small proportion, but in that year, substantial foreign donations

Table 3.10 Ghana: Scientific Instrumentation Centre (SIC) requests for and allocations of funds, 1981–1991

Year	Recurrent items (millions current Cedis)			Development items (millions current Cedis)			Ratios: expenditures as a percentage of requests	
	Requests by SIC	Approvals by Finance Ministry	Released for expenditure	Requests by SIC	Approvals by Finance Ministry	Released for expenditure	Recurrent	Development
1981	0.67	n.a.	0.2	1.61	n.a.	0.0	30	0
1982	0.88	n.a.	0.3	1.72	n.a.	0.7	34	41
1983	1.51	n.a.	1.0	2.02	n.a.	0.4	66	20
1984	1.48	n.a.	1.7	4.50	n.a.	7.4	114	165
1985	3.18	n.a.	4.5	15.0	n.a.	23.0	141	154
1986	8.25	n.a.	10.0	33.7	n.a.	23.5	121	70
1987	13.8	n.a.	15.0	56.8	n.a.	12.9	109	23
1988	32.3	n.a.	11.5	42.0	n.a.	n.a.	36	n.a.
1989	n.a.	n.a.	n.a.	n.a.	n.a.	n.a.	n.a.	n.a.
1990	36.3	25.6	34.8	180	45	n.a.	96	n.a.
1991	n.a.	39.1	n.a.	98	70	n.a.	n.a.	n.a.

Source: Scientific and Instrumentation Centre

began to arrive. The amounts, in thousands of US dollars, have been as follows: 1987, $51.5; 1988, $21.1; 1989, $7.9; 1990, $70.0; and 1991, $13.9: in total, these donations come to US$164,000. Translated into Cedis at the exchange rates governing at the time of the donations, the figures reveal that foreign contributions covered a little over half of the capital expenditures of the Food Research Institute during those five years. For the Food Research Institute, current expenditures appear to have been financed adequately out of government funds; capital expenditures, however, have been more than double what the Ghanaian government could finance on its own account.

The final public research institute that we will consider is the Technology Transfer Centre (TTC). Although established in 1981 under the Ministry of Industries, Science and Technology, the Technology Transfer Centre did not become active until 1988, by which time its legal status had changed to that of a semi-autonomous research institute. Its activation came about as a result of an interest expressed by UNDP, which decided to finance an institution-building project whose purpose was to promote Ghana's capacity for the transfer, utilization and development of foreign technology. Within this general rubric, the Technology Transfer Centre attempts to identify the technological needs of the national economy, to obtain information on the alternative sources of technology to meet these needs, to gain knowledge as to how best to acquire the preferred technologies, to learn how to 'unpack' imported technology, to assist in negotiating the best possible terms and conditions for the acquisition of foreign technology, and finally, to disseminate to potential users information about foreign technologies which would be appropriate for Ghanaian conditions.

With UNDP's assistance, the Centre has built up a staff of permanent employees, and a core of outsiders, who are hired as consultants. The main activity thus far has been the publication of papers, but it is expected that more attention will be devoted to establishing links with Ghanaian industries.

The budgetary information on the Technology Transfer Centre is given in Table 3.12. From the table, it will be seen that capital expenditures have been as substantial as current costs, a common experience in the establishment of a new research institute. In its first four years, UNDP's contribution has been allocated to capital expenditures, and has amounted to a substantial portion of the total. Given the fact that so much of Ghana's industrial investment in the first 20 years of its independence was not appropriate for the factor endowments of the country, being overly capital and skill intensive, and given that much of the capital equipment was acquired, via tied loans, to unduly expensive sources, the investigations of a group such as the Technology Transfer Centre could be extremely beneficial

Table 3.11 Ghana: Food Research Institute (FRI) requests for and allocations of funds, 1981–1991

Year	Recurrent items (millions current Cedis)			Development items (millions current Cedis)			Ratios: expenditures as a percentage of requests	
	Requests by FRI	Approvals by Finance Ministry	Released for expenditure	Requests by FRI	Approvals by Finance Ministry	Released for expenditure	Recurrent	Development
1981	2.7	n.a.	2.2	n.a.	n.a.	n.a.	81	n.a.
1982	5.3	n.a.	3.8	n.a.	n.a.	n.a.	72	n.a.
1983	n.a.	n.a.	n.a.	10.8	n.a.	n.a.	n.a.	n.a.
1984	5.5	n.a.	4.0	4.0	n.a.	n.a.	73	n.a.
1985	6.7	n.a.	n.a.	n.a.	n.a.	n.a.	n.a.	n.a.
1986	n.a.	n.a.	25.6	7.5	7.5	0.19	n.a.	n.a.
1987	n.a.	n.a.	31.4	40.6	7.2	1.9	n.a.	5
1988	n.a.	29.1	50.4	49.4	49.4	4.8	n.a.	10
1989	n.a.	54.4	64.7	62.0	54.1	12.7	n.a.	21
1990	n.a.	69.3	68.5	75.0	57.0	54.7	n.a.	73
1991	n.a.	164.8	81.0	85.0	45.0	8.5	n.a.	10

Source: Food Research Institute

Table 3.12 Ghana: Technology Transfer Centre (TTC) requests for and allocations of funds, 1988–1991

Year	Recurrent items (millions current Cedis)			Development items (millions current Cedis)			Ratios: expenditures as a percentage of requests	
	Requests by TTC	Approvals by Finance Ministry	Released for expenditure	Requests by TTC	Approvals by Finance Ministry	Released for expenditure	Recurrent	Development
1988	4.5	3.7	3.7	0	0	0	82	–
1989	12.0	10.6	10.6	10.0	9.6	9.6	9.6	88
1990	21.6	15.9	15.9	30.0	27.0	13.2	74	44
1991	25.0	19.3	21.5	50.0	40.0	34.3	86	69

Source: Technology Transfer Centre

for Ghana. It is too early to tell, however, whether or not these benefits have begun to accumulate.

At this stage, we should introduce the Council for Scientific and Industrial Research (CSIR), which supervises the three research institutes we have already mentioned, as well as ten other research institutes and the Technology Transfer Centre. CSIR was established shortly after independence, first as the National Research Council and subsequently, in 1968, under its current title. At first, the CSIR was responsible to the Ministry of Finance and Economic Planning, but with the creation of the new Ministry of Industries, Science and Technology in September 1979 the CSIR was transferred to it. The functions, organization, terms of reference and parliamentary authority of the CSIR are all described in the report by Goka *et al.* (1990).

Essentially the CSIR is the overseer of science and technology in Ghana. Its functions include organizing and coordinating scientific, industrial and agricultural research in all its aspects. It also undertakes the collection, publication and dissemination of results of the research and of statistics measuring its performance. For example, the figures on the overall expenditure of monies on advancing science and technology in Ghana, which we will present at the end of this section, were compiled by CSIR. The CSIR itself is primarily an advisory body, and maintains only a small staff: the administration of these individual research institutes is in the hands of their Management Boards, who have the responsibility for determining such matters as the allocation of funds and the determination of research priorities.

Until recently, the CSIR occupied a minor role in Ghana's programmes to advance science and technology, but with the attempts to plan, execute and monitor the national efforts, the CSIR has taken on a larger role. The first attempt to draw up a National Science and Technology Plan was made at the time of the formulation of the National Socio Economic Development Plan of 1981/5. A second attempt is being made currently, not in the context of the formulation of the National Plan but in that of the functioning of Sectoral Technical Committees, which are considering programmes of a scientific and technological nature in greater detail. When a fully fledged programme for the advance of science and technology is developed, the CSIR will presumably be given a strong part in its implementation.

There are other research institutes outside the purview of the CSIR, but still within the realm of government. One of these is the Ghana Atomic Energy Commission, which reports directly to the President of the country and which administers the National Nuclear Research Institute. Employed by the National Nuclear Research Institute (NNRI) are approximately 50 scientists and engineers, 20 technicians and an additional 330 staff in support. The major source of finance for the institute is the International Atomic Energy Authority, which has been providing approximately US$500,000 each year; the government of Ghana also contributes funds for wages and salaries, the major recurrent expense. The focus of the Institute is on the application of those techniques which have been developed in atomic and nuclear establishments in the developed countries to the resolution of agricultural and industrial problems in Ghana. The three main research projects involve training in nuclear instrumentation (primarily the maintenance and repair of advanced electronic equipment) research into nutrition and reproduction of sheep and cattle, so as to improve animal husbandry, and the breeding of sterile insects, particularly tsetse flies, in order to reduce the ravages on herds of ruminants.

With an assured source of funds from abroad, and with the highly sophisticated capital equipment that these funds have procured, working in the Institute offers an opportunity to apply the most modern of scientific techniques. Added to this inducement are incentives upon joining the institute, such as an initial allowance, and the possibility of attending the International Atomic Energy Association's training courses and conferences abroad. As a consequence, the turnover of staff has been extremely low, only four scientists having resigned during the Institute's history. (Two went to analogous institutions; the other two moved into the teaching of electronics.)

There are not many statistics available on the National Nuclear Research Institute's finances. The foreign grant, which has already been mentioned, consists primarily of convertible currencies and was used in part to buy capital equipment, and in part for construction, furnishings and motor vehicles. In 1990, the recurrent expenditures of the Institute were 876 million Cedis, of which 25 per cent went for wages and salaries, 10 per cent for maintenance and repairs, and the balance for other current inputs. In the same year, an almost exactly equal amount, 816 million Cedis, was allocated to capital expenditures; approximately one-third being devoted to construction and the remainder to plant, equipment and vehicles. The estimates for 1992 are divided in approximately the same amounts, somewhat less than half to capital expenditures and somewhat more than half to recurrent expenditures. The main change between 1990 and 1992 is that wages and salaries have increased to consume half the recurrent budget.

Although the National Nuclear Research Institute has been in existence since 1982, and thus spans the last decade, its performance cannot be judged. In this sense, it is similar to the Technology Transfer Centre, the previously mentioned research institute whose purpose it is to try to adapt foreign technology for Ghanaian needs. These are inherently projects whose outputs are impossible to measure, and whose performance can only be evaluated over a very long period.

The next research institute is judged on more pragmatic grounds. It is the Cocoa Research Institute of Ghana (CRIG). The origin of the Cocoa Research Institute of Ghana goes back to June 1938 when the Central Cocoa Research Station was established within the Gold Coast Department of Agriculture. It was located then, as it is now, at Tafo, in one of the cocoa growing regions approximately 50 miles north of Accra. By 1944, the new research station was functioning well enough to be selected as the headquarters for the West African Cocoa Research Institute, covering British colonies in the Gold Coast, Nigeria, Sierre Leone and Gambia. When the West African Regional Association was dissolved, in October 1962, the Station was taken over by the Ghanaian government and given its present name. For the next 15 years, control of the Cocoa Research Institute of Ghana moved back and forth from one organization to another, until July 1979, when it was finally assigned as a division of the Cocoa Marketing Board. Since then it has been under the authority, and received the bulk of its funds from the Cocoa Board, with occasional grants from the Ghanaian government. Only in two recent years have foreign donors provided financial support.

In 1986, the staff of the Cocoa Research Institute of Ghana consisted of 28 scientists, 22 technicians and 50 administrators, as well as a larger number of lesser skilled employees. Five years later, at the end of 1991, the scientific staff had increased to 38, of whom 16 had PhDs and 22 had BScs and MScs. The main purpose of the Cocoa Research Institute of Ghana when it was first established in 1938 was to address the problems threatening the African cocoa industry; the objective is much the same today, although the scope of the institute has been expanded so as to include other indigenous products that yield vegetable oil. The main direction of the research in 1938 was to reducing the depredations of pests and diseases upon the cocoa tree; the direction is much the same today. The main accomplishments of the Institute have been the development of new varieties of cocoa which are resistant to the two main diseases afflicting cocoa, swollen shoot virus and black pod infection. Studies have also led to recommendations on the conditions under which different varieties of cocoa will flourish and the amounts and extent to which fertilizers should be used. The cocoa tree also yields by-products, cocoa pod husks, which can be used for animal feeds, pectin which can be used in the production of alcohol, and fats from cocoa bean waste which can be used in the manufacture of soap. In recent years, attention has been directed also to the rehabilitation of old and abandoned cocoa plantations.

CRIG is divided into six divisions: Agronomy/Soil Science, Etylomology, Plant Breeding, Plant Pathology, Physiology/Biochemistry, and Statistics/Farming Systems. The divisions have approximately equal numbers of the people employed. In addition, CRIG has three research sub-stations, two in the Eastern Region, and one in the Northern Region. In the other four cocoa growing regions of Ghana, CRIG cooperates with the Cocoa Services Division of the Cocoa Board in joint field trials. A small amount of coffee is produced in Ghana and its improvement also falls under the aegis of the Cocoa Research Institute.

Statistics on the Cocoa Research Institute's funding are available since 1975/6, yielding a longer financial history than for any other of the country's research institutes. These statistics are laid out in the familiar fashion in Table 3.13. In the case of the Cocoa Research Institute, the requests are those of its Director; these requests go first to the Cocoa Board, where they are scrutinized. From the Cocoa Board the requests are passed to the Ministry of Finance, which gives final approval. In the final two columns of Table 3.13 we see that there is a much closer correspondence between requests and approvals for the Cocoa Research Institute than for the research institutes under the Council for Scientific and Industrial Research. In part this is because the Cocoa Research Institute receives the bulk of its funds as a levy upon the sales of cocoa by the Cocoa Board; it therefore has a reasonably assured source of income. In part, the government recognises the importance of cocoa to the Ghanaian economy and so supplements the receipts from the Cocoa Board from its own resources. These two resources have provided the Cocoa Research Institute with extraordinary financial stability, which is reflected in its considerable accomplishments. We shall have something to say about the institutional nature of the CRI's support in the final part of this study.

SCIENCE AND TECHNOLOGY AT THE GHANAIAN UNIVERSITIES

In Ghana, the universities appear to contribute as much to advances in science and technology as do the research institutions. In addition to their regular task of training scientists and engineers, the universities conduct R&D and disseminate the results throughout the Ghanaian economy. We therefore felt it correct to devote as much attention to the universities as we did to the R&D institutes.

There are three universities in Ghana; the University of Ghana (Legon), the University of Science and Technology (Kumasi), and the University of Cape Coast (Cape Coast). The first is located in a suburb of Accra, the

Table 3.13 Ghana: Cocoa Research Institute of Ghana (CRIG) requests for funds and actual expenditures 1975/6–1990/1

Year	Recurrent items (millions current Cedis)			Development items (millions current Cedis)			Ratios: expenditures as a percentage of requests	
	Requests by CRIG	Approvals by Finance Ministry	Released for expenditure	Requests by CRIG	Approvals by Finance Ministry	Released for expenditure	Recurrent	Development
1975/1976	4.0	3.2	n.a.	0.7	0.5	n.a.	80	71
1976/1977	3.4	2.7	n.a.	1.0	0.8	n.a.	79	80
1977/1978	9.1	7.2	n.a.	1.3	1.1	n.a.	79	85
1978/1979	11.7	9.4	n.a.	1.9	1.5	n.a.	80	79
1979/1980	12.6	10.1	n.a.	0.7	0.6	n.a.	80	86
1980/1981	21.7	17.3	n.a.	1.4	1.1	n.a.	80	79
1981/1982	28.5	22.8	n.a.	3.5	2.8	n.a.	80	80
1982/1983	37.5	30.0	n.a.	1.8	1.4	n.a.	80	78
1983/1984	73.1	58.5	n.a.	0	0	n.a.	80	–
1984/1985	141	113	n.a.	25.3	20.2	n.a.	80	80
1985/1986	309	281	n.a.	106	96.0	n.a.	91	91
1986/1987	717	651	n.a.	434	395	n.a.	91	91
1987/1988	651	592	n.a.	135	123	n.a.	91	91
1988/1989	1,189	1,081	n.a.	579	526	n.a.	90	91
1989/1990	1,205	1,095	n.a.	99	90	n.a.	91	91
1990/1991	912	829	n.a.	54	49	n.a.	91	91

Source: Cocoa Research Institute of Ghana

capital; the second in an industrial city in the south central part of the country; and the third, as its name suggests, on the coast some four hours' drive west of Accra. Of these three, it is the University of Science and Technology that is host to the largest number of organizations involved in advancing science and technology. The major organizations located at UST are five in number: the Bureau of Integrated Rural Development; Energy Associates Limited; the Solar Energy Laboratory; the Technology Consultancy Centre; and the Animal Science Group. We shall focus on the Technology Consultancy Centre, which is most intimately engaged in disseminating the results of science and technology to Ghanian industry, and on the Animal Science Group, which receives the most foreign assistance.

The Technology Consultancy Centre (TCC) was established in 1972. The purpose of the Centre was, in the words of the then Vice-Chancellor of the University of Science and Technology, to '. . . extend the university's third role: that of service to the community.' It was designed to '. . . serve as an effective interface between the R&D activities taking place at the university and the Ghanian public' and this '. . . involved the use of available expertise from the faculties for undertaking consultancy work; the transfer of technologies for industrial development through the establishment and coordination of campus-based production units; and the use of the Centre as a clearing house for technical information and services to and from the university' (quoted in Smillie, 1986). The history of the TCC has been vividly portrayed in the memoir of Ian Smillie.

The bulk of the Centre's expenditures have always been allocated to establishing pilot production units utilizing techniques which can be adopted by new firms operating on a small scale (see Table 3.14). To the extent that there *are* new and novel manufacturing techniques which can be adopted by firms operating at a small scale, the Centre builds equipment that incorporates these and demonstrates them to potential entrepreneurs. When the potential entrepreneurs indicate an interest in adopting the new techniques, the Centre assists them in importing and purchasing the equipment and in applying to banks for funding.

Much of the remainder of the resources available to the Centre are allocated to the Intermediate Technology Transfer Units (ITTUs). The first of the ITTUs was established in 1980 in Ghana's largest industrial area, near Kumasi, called the Suame Magazine, where there are approximately 30,000 workers engaged in small scale enterprises in the mechanical industries – such as metal machining, sheet metal fabrication, woodworking, and automobile repairs. In fulfilling its functions, the Intermediate Technology Transfer Unit created workshops in the industrial centre, in order to provide on-the-job training for craftsmen and managerial education for entrepreneurs.

This, the first of the International Technology Transfer Units, has been so successful that additional ones have been established in all of Ghana's ten regions; but only the initial one falls within the administrative control of the Technology Consultancy Centre. The data which we present in Table 3.14 therefore include only the unit in Suame Magazine. The construction of Table 3.14 is somewhat different from that of the previous tables; figures on development (capital) expenditures are available only for the years 1989 and 1990. It appears as if the foreign loans in those two years more than exceeded the amount of capital expenditures undertaken. If we can assume that most of the development items were financed from abroad, then Table 3.14, columns 7 and 8, which list foreign grants and loans from the year of the establishment of the Technology Consultancy Centre, provide a fair measure of the capital expenditure undertaken. That does not mean that the Ghanaian government is relieved of the bulk of the financing, for in those two years we see from the data on recurrent expenditures that this item consumed 63 million Cedis, whereas only 11 million Cedis were allocated to capital expenditures. As in all the research institutes, wages and salaries comprise the largest single component, and these are financed almost entirely by the Ghanaian government.

In examining the sources of external grants and loans we observe an interesting pattern. Initially, foreign exchange is provided in the form of grants given mainly by charitable agencies. Of the five grantors in 1972, three of them – the Rockefeller Brothers' fund, OXFAM and the World Council of Churches – provided approximately 70 per cent; the balance was contributed by Barclays Overseas Development Corporation and the Ghana Commercial Bank. Four years later, in 1976, OXFAM remained one of the contributors but rather more was given by the Canadian International Development Research Centre and United States Agency for International Development. For the next ten years the aid agencies of the developed countries provided almost all funds, but in 1987 a source shifted from the aid agencies to the World Bank, and the type of funds from grants to loans. Since then, 90 per cent of the Technology Consultancy Centre's foreign assistance has arisen within the World Bank, and has been in the form of loans. The Centre continues to draw upon foreign assistance, but is now committed to repaying the monies received. Moreover, the World Bank's loan in 1988 was not to the Technology Consultancy Centre for its own work, but was for assistance in implementing a project in the Intermediate Means of Transport, on behalf of the Ministry of Transport and Communication.

Table 3.14 Ghana: Technology Consultancy Centre (TCC) requests for funds and actual expenditures 1972–1990

Year	Recurrent items financed by the central government (millions current Cedis)			Development items (millions current Cedis)			Foreign assistance (thousands US dollars)		Ratios: expenditures as a percentage of requests	
	Requests by TCC	Approvals by Finance Ministry	Release for expenditure	Requests by TCC	Approvals by Finance Ministry	Release for expenditure	Grants	Loans	Recurrent	Development
1972	n.a.	0.005	0.005	n.a.	n.a.	n.a.	a	0	n.a.	n.a.
1973	n.a.	0.035	0.035	n.a.	n.a.	n.a.	a	0	n.a.	n.a.
1974	n.a.	n.a.	n.a.	n.a.	n.a.	n.a.	a	0	n.a.	n.a.
1975	n.a.	n.a.	n.a.	n.a.	n.a.	n.a.	a	0	n.a.	n.a.
1976	n.a.	n.a.	n.a.	n.a.	n.a.	n.a.	a	0	n.a.	n.a.
1977	n.a.	n.a.	n.a.	n.a.	n.a.	n.a.	a	0	n.a.	n.a.
1978	n.a.	n.a.	n.a.	n.a.	n.a.	n.a.	a	0	n.a.	n.a.
1979	n.a.	n.a.	n.a.	n.a.	n.a.	n.a.	a	0	n.a.	n.a.
1980	n.a.	0.18	0.18	n.a.	n.a.	n.a.	a	0	n.a.	n.a.
1981	n.a.	0.33	0.33	n.a.	n.a.	n.a.	a	0	n.a.	n.a.
1982	n.a.	0.22	0.22	n.a.	n.a.	n.a.	a	0	n.a.	n.a.
1983	0.80	0.65	0.65	n.a.	n.a.	n.a.	a	0	81	n.a.
1984	n.a.	1.5	1.5	n.a.	n.a.	n.a.	a	0	n.a.	n.a.
1985	6.8	4.4	4.4	n.a.	n.a.	n.a.	a	0	45	n.a.
1986	8.2	6.0	6.0	n.a.	n.a.	n.a.	a	0	73	n.a.
1987	12.6	9.2	9.2	n.a.	n.a.	n.a.	a	83	73	n.a.
1988	13.9	11.9	11.9	n.a.	n.a.	n.a.	12	83	84	n.a.
1989	22.7	18.0	18.0	27.1	7.0	7.0	10	83	79	26
1990	63.3	44.9	44.9	13.2	4.0.	4.0.	n.a.	n.a.	71	30

Source: Technology Consultancy Centre

Note: a: Various unspecified amounts whose donors are identified in the text

It will be asked how effective the Technology Consultancy Centre has been in inspiring Ghana's industrial growth. We should say at the outset that we are not able to provide any assured answer. Those who work for the Technology Consultancy Centre (see, e.g. the paper by Buatsi, 1991) provide a considerable list of accomplishments, ranging from the education of entrepreneurs and workers, through the establishment of small industrial firms, to the increases in output and employment that these firms have provided. Particular emphasis is placed upon the workshops established in industrial locations, as providing the training for those who subsequently become entrepreneurs and a model for them to imitate. The advocates of the Centre also emphasise the external economies secured, through the generation of employment in activities that supply the newly created industrial firms, and in the distribution of their products. The data on new firms established, on output produced and on employment generated are necessarily fragmentary, but the numbers appear to be quite high relative to the totals for all Ghanaian industry. Finally, one cannot be certain of the extent to which the efflorescence of small manufacturing firms in Ghana can be attributed to the Technology Consultancy Centre: other enabling institutions such as local banks, Chambers of Commerce, and the Ministry of Industry, Science and Technology may all have contributed.

When it comes to the studies of industry in Ghana, particularly that comprised by firms operating on a small scale, there is a large amount of evidence (one recent study, by Steel and Webster (1990) lists in its bibliography 39 previous studies), yet contributions by the Technology Consultancy Centre, as well as those by other enabling bodies, are seldom mentioned. Steel and Webster's own study, which is an inquiry in detail into the response of small firms to the rigours of structural adjustment, does not mention the Technology Consultancy Centre at all.

Our own impression, based upon systematic interviews at the Centre and casual impressions of Ghanaian industrial firms, is that, to the contrary, the Centre has been very effective. It seems to have been one of the forces leading to the very rapid growth of small industrial firms in Kumasi and its surroundings. It also seems, through the network of Intermediate Technology Transfer Units, of which it was the originator, to have stimulated industrial growth elsewhere in Ghana. Our impression is supported, somewhat, by the evidence of substantial and continued grants of funds by various foreign donors to the Centre, at least over its first 15 years of operation. That the Centre has now had to turn to the World Bank for loans may signify that grants are being given to the establishment of other institutions, and that foreign donors consider the Centre to be well established.

Institutions that provide only education seldom give rise to such questions of effectiveness. The presumption in all countries is that education, particularly university education, be it technical or in arts subjects, should be provided on as large a scale as the country can afford. The sorts of questions that arise when education is concerned are not whether or not it is effective but rather whether, given the needs of the country and the demands of its young citizens and their parents for education, the government is providing sufficient opportunities. Unlike such institutions as the Technology Consultancy Centre, the needs facing the universities can be expressed numerically, in terms of numbers of applicants; as can the output, expressed in terms of numbers of graduates. Statistics on educational attainment at secondary and university level in Technical subjects, have been assembled by UNESCO and the World Bank and will be presented on a comparative basis in Chapter 7 (see also Lall *et al.*, 1994; Tables 2.5, 2.6).

The published figures give an apparent picture of stability, if not progress. But when we come to the universities in practice, we find a much less happy situation. To the observer, the lack of resources for technical education in Ghana is quite apparent. The facilities on the campus – buildings, laboratories, libraries etc. – are dilapidated and poorly equipped; enrolments are stagnant; and the fraction of those enrolled who complete their courses has fallen. Employment in the teaching faculties at the universities offers little inducement to apply for jobs, and many of those who are employed are in constant search of jobs elsewhere. Emigration of trained people, particularly in the early and middle years of their careers, is chronic, and there is no replenishment from abroad.

But this is a general condemnation; the experience of individual faculties is not identical. The University of Science and Technology as a whole receives fairly generous treatment from the Ghanaian government, but some departments, such as those of Agricultural Engineering and Mechanical Engineering, fare better, in large part because they have attracted foreign donations. Others, particularly the Faculty of Science (which excludes Engineering and Agricultural Science) are distressed. We shall now consider one of its most distressed departments, that of Mathematics, in relation to the rest of the university.

Over the years 1988–1991 the portions of the total funds for current expenditures received relative to the University's requests, were 0.63, 0.90, 0.83 and 0.74 respectively, averaging 0.78; in brief three Cedis were expended for each four Cedis requested. The fraction received by the Mathematics Department was considerably less, probably below 0.50. Of the 20 staff members permitted within the University's table of organization, the funds provided permitted employing only just over half: 11 in each academic year 1988 and 1989–90. Moreover, in these and the preceding eight years there was substantial turnover of staff, many of the senior members (those with PhDs) leaving (two to Nigeria) and being replaced by local graduates completing the MSc degree.

Moreover, the Mathematics Department has fared much less well in its applications for foreign assistance. From 1980/1 to 1985/6, none of its requests for foreign assistance was approved by the University; from 1985/6 to 1989/90 the approval of the University was secured for approximately 25 per cent of the amounts requested for current expenditures and 10 per cent for capital expenditures, but practically no grants were received from abroad. Current requests for foreign assistance (to the Dutch and Japanese governments) seem pitifully small – 50 new books and six journals per year, plus funds for exchange scholarships for three persons. Lacking the appeal of the applied sciences, Mathematics in Ghana is a neglected subject.

GHANA'S TOTAL EXPENDITURES ON THE PURSUIT OF SCIENCE AND TECHNOLOGY

We shall now try to construct estimates of Ghana's annual expenditures on advancing science and technology, moving from those of the public research institutes to those of the public sector as a whole, and finally to those of the country as a whole.

Some of the figures for the public research institutes, operating under the umbrella of the Council for Scientific and Industrial Research, are given in Table 3.16; they cover the years 1974–81, the only ones for which summaries have been made. Moving back to Table 3.15, we see from the figures on total expenditures on science and technology for Ghana's public sector (in the penultimate column) that the fraction accounted for by the public research institutes is approximately 10 per cent.

The other 90 per cent of Ghana's public expenditures on science and technology are accounted for by bodies outside the purview of the CSIR, namely the faculties, research institutes, centres and stations of the universities of Ghana, the scientific and technical departments of government Ministries, and the research departments of government-owned (parastatal) firms. Breakdowns of these different organizations' expenditures are not available.

Looking at the figures in the last column of Table 3.17 we see that public expenditures on advancing science and technology in Ghana have fluctuated considerably as a percentage of total government expenditures. Apart from the year of 1983, one of particular austerity, the range within which fluctuations occurred has been 2–6 per cent with an arithmetic average of

Table 3.15 Ghana: compilation of expenditures (or approvals) on R&D by a sample of organizations, and comparison with estimates of total public expenditure on R&D, 1980–1992 (millions current Cedis)

| | Sample of organizations | | | | | | | Council of Scientific and Industrial Research[a] | Estimated expenditures of the SCIR[b] | Estimated total expenditure on R&D | Ratio of sample sub-total to total expenditure | Estimate of total based on sample ratio of 0.2 |
Year	IRI	SIC	FRI	TTC	CRIG	TCC	Sub-total					
1980	0.80	n.a.	n.a.	n.a.	10.7	0.18	11.7	19.1	19	400	0.03	–
1981	1.16	0.2	2.2	n.a.	18.4	0.33	22.3	37.2	37	260	0.09	–
1982	1.51	1.0	3.8	n.a.	25.6	0.22	32.1	n.a.	53	n.a.	n.a.	–
1983	1.55	1.4	n.a.	n.a.	31.4	0.65	35.1	n.a.	59	110	0.32	–
1984	2.17	9.1	4.0	n.a.	58.5	1.5	75.3	n.a.	123	1,300	0.06	–
1985	6.86	27.5	n.a.	n.a.	133	4.4	172	n.a.	286	2,860	0.06	–
1986	16.5	33.5	25.8	n.a.	377	6.0	459	n.a.	760	3,600	0.13	–
1987	22.6	27.9	33.3	n.a.	1,046	9.2	1,139	n.a.	1,900	2,510	0.45	–
1988	41.7	11.5	55.2	3.7	715	11.7	839	n.a.	1,400	n.a.	n.a.	4,200
1989	115	n.a.	77.4	20.2	1,607	25.0	1,845	n.a.	3,100	n.a.	n.a.	9,200
1990	90	34.8	126	29.1	1,185	48.9	1,514	n.a.	2,500	n.a.	n.a.	7,600
1991	n.a.	n.a.	89.5	55.8	978	n.a.	1,123+	n.a.	1,900+	n.a.	n.a.	5,600+
1992	n.a.	n.a.	n.a.	n.a.	n.a.	n.a.	n.a.	n.a.	n.a.	n.a.	n.a.	n.a.

Sources: Tables 3.9–3.14 for sample. (Figures are of expenditures, where available, and include both recurrent and development items. Table 3.16 for R&D expenditure by the CSIR; and Table 3.17 for estimates of total expenditure, public and private

Notes: a: Excludes expenditures by the Cocoa Research Institute of Ghana (CRIG)
b: At a ratio of 0.60 for the sample sub-total to 1.00 for the total of the CSIR

Table 3.16 Ghana: R&D expenditures by the Council for Scientific and Industrial Research (CSIR) 1974–1981 (millions current Cedis)

Year	Total (personal emoluments and other expenditure)	Other expenditures alone	Other expenditure as a percentage of total expenditure
1974	3.2	0.4	11.9
1975	6.2	0.4	6.5
1976	6.1	0.3	5.1
1977	7.4	0.3	4.4
1978	14.7	0.3	2.4
1979	17.7	0.5	2.9
1980	19.1	1.3	6.7
1981	37.2	1.0	2.7

Source: Goka *et al.*, 1990, Table 6.4, p. 37

Note: Other expenditures consist of development expenditures plus the non-salary and wages component of recurrent expenditures

3.8 per cent. We shall in later chapters compare the average from Table 3.17, and a second average to be computed, with the other countries in our sample.

The second average to be estimated for Ghana is the percentage of the country's total economic activity devoted to pursuing science and technology. We do not know by what amount Ghana's private sector – chiefly private firms – augments public expenditures, but we believe it to be relatively small. The ratio of private to public expenditures in Kenya is known; it is 9.5: 90.5, or between one to nine and one to ten. Assuming the larger of these ratios to be appropriate for Ghana, which has a larger scientific and engineering base than Kenya, the estimates for total expenditures on science and technology appear in Table 3.18, column 3.

The figures in Table 3.17 cease in 1987, yet we need a series up to 1992 if we are to make comparisons, for more recent years, with expenditures on science and technology by Kenya, Tanzania and Uganda. To extend Ghana's series beyond 1987 we will make use of the financial data that we have collected on the expenditures of R&D institutions, inflating these data to allow for expenditures of three unidentified institutions. The estimates have been made in Table 3.15; in the next to last column there are listed the fractions of the identified R&D institutions' expenditures to Gioka, Mikyo and Osumbor's totals for Ghana, throughout the period for which they

Table 3.17 Ghana: trends in public expenditure on science and technology
1974–1987

Year	Estimated S&T expenditures by the public sector (million Cedis)	Total government expenditure (recurrent and development) (billion Cedis)	Expenditures on S&T as a percentage of total government expenditures
1974	30	1.16	2.6
1975	39	1.44	2.7
1976	53	1.95	2.7
1777	138	3.02	4.6
1978	213	4.09	5.2
1979	175	4.67	3.7
1980	362	7.72	4.7
1981	240	8.84	2.7
1982	n.a.	n.a.	n.a.
1983	100	14.8	0.6
1984	1,170	26.7	4.4
1985	2,580	45.8	5.7
1986	3,230	70.7	4.6
1987	2,262	102	2.2

Source: Goka *et al.*, 1990. Table 6.3, p. 36

overlap (1980–1987). Taking an average fraction of 0.2, the total expenditures of the identified R&D institutes are then multiplied by 1: 0.2 (i.e. by five) to obtain the estimates of Ghana's total expenditures on science and technology for 1988–1991. Combined with the estimates for 1974–1987 (in Table 3.18) these give us a continuous series from 1974 to 1991).

Table 3.18, on total expenditures, completes our study of expenditures for advancing science and technology in Ghana. Given their dubious accuracy, we can do little more than say that, as a fraction of all economic activity, the amount spent on science and technology out of the country's resources is no higher, and may well be lower, since the beginning of Structural Adjustment. What has entered the country as donations from abroad is unknown: for estimates of foreign contributions to the pursuit of science and technology we shall have to await the next chapter, where we can observe their impact, not on Ghana, but on Kenya.

Table 3.18 Ghana: estimated expenditures on science and technology, totals and relative to GDP, 1974–1991

Year	Expenditures on science and technology (billions of current Cedis)			R&D as a percentage of GDP
	Public sector	Estimated private sector	Total estimate	
1974	0.03	0.00	0.03	0.6
1975	0.04	0.00	0.04	0.6
1976	0.05	0.01	0.06	0.6
1977	0.14	0.01	0.15	1.3
1978	0.21	0.02	0.23	1.1
1979	0.18	0.01	0.19	0.7
1980	0.36	0.04	0.40	0.9
1981	0.24	0.02	0.26	0.4
1982	n.a.	n.a.	n.a.	n.a.
1983	0.10	0.01	0.11	0.0
1984	1.18	0.12	1.30	0.5
1985	2.60	0.26	2.86	0.8
1986	3.27	0.33	3.60	0.6
1987	2.28	0.23	2.51	0.3
1988	4.20	0.40	4.60	0.4
1989	9.20	0.90	9.90	0.7
1990	7.60	0.80	8.40	0.4
1991	5.60	0.60	6.20	0.3

Sources: Column 1, 1974–1987: Table 3.17, column 1, 1988–1991; Table 3.15, final column
Column 2: see text
Column 3: columns 1 plus 2
Column 4: statistics on GDP from Table 3.1, column 1

4 Kenya

INTRODUCTION

The second of the countries whose undertakings in science and technology were studied is Kenya. With approximately 25 million inhabitants, each enjoying on the average a yearly income of nearly US$400, Kenya is both the most populous and the least poor of the countries in our sample.

Our purposes in this chapter are, first, to describe briefly Kenya's recent economic history, up to and including its adoption of Structural Adjustment Programmes under the guidance of the IMF and World Bank. The narrative will be backed by appropriate statistics, drawn from published sources. The specific topics upon which emphasis will be placed are those that theory suggests to be the most important; these will relate chiefly to Kenya's responses, at the overall level of the economy, to the stringencies of the adjustment programmes.

Secondly, we shall report the results of our survey of institutions active in the realms of science and technology, plus any corroborating material. The data we generated were both quantitative – concerning the institutions' budgets and personnel – and qualitative – concerning their aims, resources, conduct, accomplishments and impediments. In our survey, we encountered five institutions, one located in the agricultural sector, one in the industrial, two on the boundary of the two sectors, and one in education.

After the last of the case studies will come a short summary, whose purpose is solely to record our general impressions of Kenya's recent progress in advancing science and technology, and its potential for still further advance. All substantive work will be left until Part III, where the data from Kenya, both quantitative and qualitative, will be added to those from the other three countries, and analyzed.

RECENT ECONOMIC HISTORY

At the time Kenya secured its independence, in 1962, the country contained approximately nine million inhabitants, the vast majority of whom lived in the countryside and supported themselves by farming. (A description of the economy and polity from this time till the early 1970s can be found in Leys, 1975; the subsequent period is covered in Mosley, 1991.)

In 1969, the Kenyan economy generated a total output valued at US$1.4 billion, in terms of the prices current in that year. This output provided an income for each Kenyan, on the average, of US$130 per year (see Tables 4.1 and 4.2). The structure of the economy, in the same year, is indicated by the proportion of the total marketed income arising in agri- culture (35 per cent), industry (20 per cent), and services (46 per cent) (see Table 4.3): by the standards of developing countries with similar per capita incomes the proportion of income accruing to those in the service sector (primarily government) was rather high.

Thereafter, for the next ten years, the Kenyan economy grew quite rapidly. By 1979, average income per capita had risen to $370 in current US dollars; a better measure of the increase in the average is provided by data on GDP per capita in constant Kenyan Shillings (of 1987) from column 2 of Table 4.2; here the increase was from Kshs 4,400 in 1969 to Kshs 5,980 in 1979, an average yearly rate of growth of a little over 3 per cent. Surprisingly this welcome increase took place with little change in the relative size of the three different sectors; in terms of the incomes their participants earned, all sectors grew at approximately equal rates (see Table 4.3).

The decade of the 1980s was very different for Kenya. A succession of changes, some evident towards the end of the previous decade (a deterior- ation of prices for coffee and tea in world markets), others emerging only in the 1980s (the second oil price rise and the subsequent recession in the world at large; the expansion of petroleum refining in the Arabian Gulf at the expense of Kenya's refined exports; and the cutting off of trade with Tanzania and Uganda – all events beyond Kenya's control) harmed Kenya's economy. For a few years until 1982, the country was able to finance deficits in its balance of payments and accompanying shortages of foreign exchange by borrowing abroad (see Table 4.4), but by late 1981 external sources both private and governmental had been exhausted.

Short-term debt, particularly to the private sector, reached a peak in 1980, and the servicing of the debt, both short- and long-term, was ap- proaching the level of annual borrowings, so that there was no longer a substantial net inflow of foreign funds (see Table 4.5, column 1). The

Table 4.1 Kenya: GDP 1969–1991

Year	GDP (billions current KSh)	GDP deflator (1987=100)	GDP (billions KSh at constant 1987 prices)	Official exchange rate (annual average conversion factor, KSh per $US)	GDP (billions current $US)
1969	10	21.4	49	7.14	1.4
1970	11	24.7	46	7.14	1.5
1971	13	22.4	57	7.14	1.8
1972	15	22.4	67	7.14	2.1
1973	18	24.7	71	7.00	2.6
1974	21	28.8	74	7.14	2.9
1975	24	32.1	75	7.34	3.3
1976	29	38.2	76	8.37	3.5
1977	37	44.6	83	8.28	4.5
1978	41	46.1	89	7.73	5.3
1979	47	48.7	96	7.48	6.3
1980	54	53.5	100	7.42	7.3
1981	62	59.1	105	9.05	6.8
1982	70	65.8	107	10.92	6.4
1983	80	73.5	108	13.31	6.0
1984	89	81.0	110	14.41	6.1
1985	101	87.6	115	16.43	6.1
1986	117	95.4	123	16.23	6.7
1987	130	100.0	130	16.45	7.9
1988	149	109.1	137	17.75	8.4
1989	170	119.1	143	20.75	8.2
1990	199	131.3	152	24.08	8.3
1991	227	147.4	154	28.07	8.1

Sources: 1969–1989: World Bank, World Tables 1991, 1993
1990–1991: Republic of Kenya, Economic Survey, 1992

Table 4.2 Kenya: GNP per capita 1969–1991

	Population (millions)	GDP per capita (KSh at constant 1987 prices)	GNP per capita (current US dollars)	Average rate of growth of GDP (% per year)	Consumer Price Index (1987 = 100.0)
1969	11.1	4,400	130	n.a.	15.5
1970	11.5	4,000	130	-4.7	15.8
1971	11.9	4,800	160	22.5	16.4
1972	12.3	5,500	180	18.3	17.3
1973	12.8	5,500	180	5.8	19.0
1974	13.2	5,600	210	3.6	22.3
1975	13.7	5,500	230	1.3	26.6
1976	14.3	5,300	240	2.2	29.6
1977	14.8	5,600	270	9.4	34.0
1978	15.4	5,800	310	6.8	39.8
1979	16.0	6,000	370	7.5	43.0
1980	16.6	6,000	420	5.4	48.9
1981	17.3	6,000	430	4.1	54.7
1982	18.0	6,000	400	1.9	65.9
1983	18.6	5,800	350	1.5	73.4
1984	19.4	5,700	330	1.7	80.9
1985	20.1	5,700	310	4.3	91.5
1986	20.9	5,900	330	7.1	95.1
1987	21.6	6,000	340	5.9	100.0
1988	22.4	6,200	370	6.0	108.3
1989	23.3	6,200	370	4.6	118.9
1990	24.0	6,300	370	4.2	146.8
1991	24.5	6,200	330	2.2	175.7

Sources: 1969–1989: All columns except column 2: World Bank, *World Tables 1991, 1993*
Column 2: GDP at constant 1987 prices (from Table 4.1) divided by population in column 1

Table 4.3 Kenya: GDP by sector 1964–1991

	GDP (at factor cost, billions of current KSh)	Agricultural product (at factor cost, billions current KSh)	Share of agriculture in GDP (%)	Industrial product (at factor cost, billions current KSh)	Share of industry in GDP (%)	Manufacturing product (at factor cost, billions current KSh)	Share of manufacturing in GDP (%)	Services (at factor cost, billions current KSh)	Share of services in GDP (%)
1964	n.a.	n.a.	42	n.a.	n.a.	n.a.	n.a.	n.a.	n.a.
1965	n.a.	n.a.	37	n.a.	n.a.	n.a.	n.a.	n.a.	n.a.
1966	n.a.	n.a.	40	n.a.	n.a.	n.a.	n.a.	n.a.	n.a.
1967	n.a.	n.a.	38	n.a.	n.a.	n.a.	n.a.	n.a.	n.a.
1968	n.a.	n.a.	36	n.a.	n.a.	n.a.	n.a.	n.a.	n.a.
1969	9.53	3.22	35	1.88	20	1.14	12	4.43	46
1970	10.38	3.46	33	2.06	20	1.24	12	4.86	47
1971	11.40	3.58	31	2.32	20	1.43	13	5.50	48
1972	13.78	4.85	35	2.81	20	1.56	11	6.12	45
1973	15.79	5.60	35	3.28	21	1.89	12	6.92	44
1974	18.78	6.64	35	3.89	21	2.39	13	8.25	44
1975	21.14	7.22	34	4.28	20	2.54	12	9.64	46
1976	25.56	9.69	38	4.76	19	2.88	11	11.12	43
1977	32.81	13.77	42	5.90	18	3.60	11	13.15	40
1978	35.60	13.14	37	7.15	20	4.39	12	15.31	43
1979	40.66	14.07	35	8.07	20	5.00	12	18.52	46
1980	45.97	14.98	33	9.58	20	5.90	13	21.40	47
1981	53.19	17.29	33	10.78	20	6.56	12	25.12	47
1982	60.99	20.35	33	12.16	20	7.45	12	28.48	47
1983	69.47	23.77	34	13.46	19	8.16	12	32.24	47
1984	77.46	26.27	34	14.66	19	9.22	12	36.53	47
1985	88.37	28.73	32	16.88	19	10.37	12	42.76	49
1986	102.30	33.80	33	19.01	19	12.17	12	49.49	48
1987	112.25	35.64	32	20.89	19	13.05	12	55.72	49
1988	127.82	40.78	32	24.67	19	15.06	12	62.38	49
1989	146.61	45.43	31	29.25	20	17.11	12	71.94	49
1990	170.81	47.7	27	34.0	20	20.0	12	89.1	52
1991	196.00	53.0	27	39.2	20	23.4	12	104.8	53

Sources: 1964–1968: Van der Hoeven and Vandermoortele, 1987, Table 2, p. 42
1969–1989: World Bank, *World Tables 1991, 1993*
1990–1991: Republic of Kenya, *Economic Survey, 1992*

Table 4.4 Kenya: debt and debt servicing 1970–1991

Year	Total debt outstanding (millions current US dollars)	Official debt (millions current US dollars)	Debt to IMF (millions current US dollars)	Debt to Wold Bank (IBRD/IDA) (millions current US dollars)	Private debt (millions current US dollars)	Total debt as a percentage of GDP	Service of total debt, annual total (millions current US dollars)	Service of official debt (millions current US dollars)	Service of private debt (millions current US dollars)	Total debt service as a percentage of GDP	Total debt service as a % of total exports	Service of official debt, as a % of government current revenue
1970	406	n.a.	n.a.	n.a.	n.a.	n.a.	n.a.	n.a.	n.a.	n.a.	n.a.	n.a.
1971	421	n.a.	n.a.	n.a.	n.a.	n.a.	n.a.	n.a.	n.a.	n.a.	n.a.	n.a.
1972	493	n.a.	n.a.	n.a.	n.a.	n.a.	n.a.	n.a.	n.a.	n.a.	n.a.	n.a.
1973	723	n.a.	n.a.	n.a.	n.a.	n.a.	n.a.	n.a.	n.a.	n.a.	n.a.	n.a.
1974	999	n.a.	n.a.	n.a.	n.a.	n.a.	n.a.	n.a.	n.a.	n.a.	n.a.	n.a.
1975	1,108	n.a.	n.a.	n.a.	n.a.	n.a.	n.a.	n.a.	n.a.	n.a.	n.a.	n.a.
1976	1,304	n.a.	n.a.	n.a.	n.a.	n.a.	n.a.	n.a.	n.a.	n.a.	n.a.	n.a.
1977	1,746	n.a.	n.a.	n.a.	n.a.	n.a.	n.a.	n.a.	n.a.	n.a.	n.a.	n.a.
1978	2,323	n.a.	n.a.	n.a.	n.a.	n.a.	n.a.	n.a.	n.a.	n.a.	n.a.	n.a.
1979	2,887	n.a.	n.a.	n.a.	n.a.	n.a.	n.a.	n.a.	n.a.	n.a.	n.a.	n.a.
1980	3,530	n.a.	n.a.	n.a.	n.a.	n.a.	n.a.	n.a.	n.a.	n.a.	n.a.	n.a.
1981	3,366	1,715	204	586	1,652	46	n.a.	n.a.	n.a.	5.7	23	n.a.
1982	3,798	2,068	342	742	1,730	51	n.a.	n.a.	n.a.	5.9	27	n.a.
1983	3,909	2,278	417	840	1,631	51	427	142	285	5.5	28	11.4
1984	3,927	2,569	380	1,032	1,361	50	489	188	301	6.3	29	14.9
1985	4,501	2,968	486	1,124	1,533	56	520	230	290	6.4	33	18.6
1986	4,665	3,237	431	1,179	1,428	55	564	279	285	6.7	30	18.8
1987	5,730	3,475	401	1,681	n.a.	73	792	354	n.a.	10.0	46	20.0
1988	5,757	3,476	455	1,646	n.a.	68	887	388	n.a.	10.5	44	20.2
1989	5,783	3,270	415	1,782	n.a.	69	862	500	n.a.	10.5	45	25.2
1990	7,006	3,657	482	2,056	n.a.	84	868	394	n.a.	10.5	84	19.9
1991	7,014	3,897	493	2,153	n.a.	89	566	385	n.a.	7.0	49	18.8

Sources: Column 1: 1970–1980, 1987–1991: World Bank *World Tables 1991, 1993*
Column 1: 1981–1986, and Columns 2–11: Strack and Schönherr, 1989
Columns 2, 3, 6, 7: 1987–1991: World Bank, *World Debt Tables, 1993–4*,
Column 12: column 8 divided by column 1, Table 4.8 (converted to US dollars by the exchange rate in column 4, Table 4.1)

private sector's account had turned negative by 1983, indicating that on balance the private sector was exporting capital. In 1980, the total foreign debt was US$3.5 billion; its service in 1981 consumed 5.7 per cent of GDP, and 23 per cent of export earnings.

In 1980 the Kenyan government was forced to turn to the World Bank for its first Structural Adjustment loan, amounting to US$70 million, bringing the country's indebtedness to the World Bank to nearly half a billion US$, or three-quarters of a billion when combined with that owed to the IMF (see Table 4.4). (This and succeeding programmes of stabilization are described in van der Hoeven and Vandemoortele, 1987, and in Mosley, 1991. The various conditions imposed on the Kenyan government from the first Structural Adjustment by the World Bank through the Financial Sector Adjustment Credit of July 1989 are listed in Mosley, 1991: 277–82, Table 16.4). In order to conserve foreign exchange the government increased controls on imports, restrained credit, and partially devalued the Kenyan Shilling. These measures enabled the country to cut the deficit on current account of its balance of payments by nearly US$300 million between 1980 and 1981, and by another US$250 million between 1981 and 1982 (approximately 4 per cent of GDP in each year). Nonetheless, the crisis continued and in 1983 Kenya found it necessary to accept the IMF's strictures, involving further reductions in the budget deficit and bank lending, increased agricultural prices and a successive, sharper devaluation. The IMF continued to advance loans, as did the World Bank, with its second structural adjustment loan of US$131 million, and subsequent sectoral loans: for agriculture, for US$60 million in 1986; for industry, for US$112 million in 1988; and for finance, for US$120 million in 1989 (World Bank, May 1990, Annex IIa). In line with these loans, other official loans were granted to Kenya, so that its current indebtedness is mainly of long-term liabilities assumed by the government of Kenya (see Table 4.5). The total debt, official and private, as of the end of 1989, was US$5.7 billion, representing 70 per cent of the annual value of GDP; public sector debt was US$5.0 billion.

Servicing the total debt in 1989 consumed US$490 million, almost exactly 40 per cent of total export earnings for the year (see Table 4.6); servicing the official debt consumed US$316 million, 17 per cent of the government's total revenues for the year. Loans and grants from abroad were considerably less than these sums; in total there was a net outflow from Kenya in 1989 of US$286 million, of which US$150 million was the contribution of Kenya's private sector to foreign creditors and US$139 the contribution of Kenya's government (see Table 4.6).

It is not easy for the citizens of a country, developing or developed, to

Table 4.5 Kenya: net transfers from abroad 1981–1990 (millions current US dollars)

Year	Total net transfers	Net transfers to official suppliers	Net transfers to private suppliers	Total flow of funds into country	Non-debt creating flows	Official grants	Direct investment	Total interest payments	Interest payments on official debt
1981	n.a.	n.a.	n.a.	219	143	77	8.3	n.a.	n.a.
1982	n.a.	n.a.	n.a.	234	131	78	3.4	n.a.	n.a.
1983	70	140	−70	236	172	121	9.2	166	77
1984	51	298	−248	220	170	144	3.9	170	92
1985	−63	19	−82	119	178	140	12.7	182	107
1986	69	6	64	274	190	150	27.8	206	133
1987	−111	66	−177	n.a.	n.a.	n.a.	n.a.	202	133
1988	−231	−61	−171	n.a.	n.a.	n.a.	n.a.	192	132
1989	−286	−139	−150	n.a.	n.a.	n.a.	n.a.	180	127
1990	−347	−213	−134	n.a.	n.a.	n.a.	n.a.	164	120

Sources: Strack and Schönherr, 1989

Table 4.6 Kenya: balance of payments 1964–1991

Year	Total exports of goods and services (millions current US dollars)	Total imports of goods and services (millions current US dollars)	Balance on current account (after transfers, private and official) (millions current US dollars)	Net exports of oil and refined products (millions current US dollars)	Share of coffee in exports (% of total earnings)	Share of tea in exports (% of total earnings)	Share of oil and refined products in exports (% of total earnings)
1964	n.a.	n.a.	n.a.	n.a.	32.7	13.0	4.7
1965	n.a.	n.a.	n.a.	n.a.	29.9	12.9	10.0
1966	n.a.	n.a.	n.a.	n.a.	32.3	14.9	10.1
1967	n.a.	n.a.	n.a.	n.a.	29.5	13.9	13.5
1968	n.a.	n.a.	n.a.	n.a.	22.1	17.3	10.9
1969	n.a.	n.a.	n.a.	n.a.	26.5	17.9	12.0
1970	506	580	-49	32	31.1	17.7	11.5
1971	529	699	-112	38	26.6	16.3	12.2
1972	581	687	-68	42	27.4	18.1	9.8
1973	706	862	-126	44	29.2	13.9	7.7
1974	971	1,311	-308	51	23.6	11.9	16.1
1975	1,011	1,280	-218	116	16.4	10.7	22.7
1976	1,143	1,282	-124	133	29.3	10.0	18.1
1977	1,594	1,633	28	171	42.5	14.9	15.1
1978	1,544	2,295	-661	205	33.7	17.1	16.3
1979	1,629	2,219	-498	185	28.7	16.3	17.7
1980	2,061	3,095	-886	223	22.2	11.9	31.1
1981	1,799	2,575	-558	445	21.3	11.9	30.7
1982	1,630	2,068	-302	375	26.5	14.2	26.0
1983	1,525	1,753	-45	263	25.3	19.5	19.6
1984	1,663	1,966	-123	206	27.0	25.1	17.4
1985	1,607	1,911	-110	199	29.7	24.7	14.0
1986	1,902	2,148	-37	156	n.a.	n.a.	n.a.
1987	1,739	2,447	-494	155	n.a.	n.a.	n.a.
1988	1,880	2,680	-454	175	n.a.	n.a.	n.a.
1989	1,935	2,905	-587	173	n.a.	n.a.	n.a.
1990	24.88b	50.91b	-11.84b	2.80b	17.9	25.5	11.4
1991	32.59b	52.92b	-6.35b	5.10b	13.6	23.7	15.8

Sources: 1964–1968: Van der Hoeven and Vandermoortele, 1987, Table 2, p. 42 and Table 4, p. 44
1969–1989: World Bank, World Tables 1991
1990, 1991: Republic of Kenya, Economic Survey, 1992

Note: b signifies billions of Kenya Shillings

change the structure of its economy while making such substantial contributions to foreigners. The resources that are needed for internal adjustment – be they adjustment from the public sector to the private; or from industry to agriculture; or within industry; or within agriculture; or wherever – cannot also, at the same time, be devoted to satisfying the claims of outsiders. It is in the framework of competition for Kenya's scarce resources, and the pressure that this competition imposes on its government, that the pursuit of science and technology will have to be placed.

INVESTMENT FOR THE FUTURE

In our economic descent from the general to the particular we shall use investment as our vehicle. The exposition will involve two different modes, the first a disaggregation of overall statistics on investment, the second an assembly of statistics on the pursuit of science and technology.

The figures that will be disaggregated are those on gross domestic fixed investment (see Table 4.7). Adjusting by GNP deflator (see Table 4.1) yields the figures in the third column. Ratios against GDP indicate that investment in Kenya was high, at approximately 25 per cent, in the generation after independence, and has been sustained at approximately 20 per cent of GDP in the last decade. In this latter period, and for a developing country as heavily indebted as Kenya, to have allocated a fifth of its annual output to investment is a considerable achievement.

The next task is to disaggregate investment into its components. For the shorter period 1979 to 1985 Kenyan government figures reveal the percentage breakdown in Table 4.8 and Table 4.9 (accumulated by van der Hoeven and Vandemoortele, 1987). The data in the latter table reveal declines in the portion of total capital formation directed towards manufacturing and transport, without any compensating rise in the portion directed to agriculture. (The rise in investment in the traditional sector is attributed by van der Hoeven and Vandemoortele to increases in the construction of traditional dwellings, in response to population increase: *ibid.*: 23.) So far as investment is concerned, what reallocation has taken place has been from manufacturing and transport to finance and other services; whether or not this reallocation was beneficial to the economy as a whole is arguable.

The only other aggregated statistics for Kenya relevant to our enquiry are those produced in two surveys of science and technology in all of Africa. One is of potential scientific and technological inputs, the other of outputs. The results of the first, conducted by UNESCO, and shown in Table 4.10, indicated that in 1982 there were in Kenya 16,241 scientists and engineers, and 45,952 technicians. Kenya's ratios of scientists, engineers

Table 4.7 Kenya: public, private and total investments in absolute amounts and as a percentage of GDP, 1969–1991

Year	Absolute amounts (billions of 1987 KSh)			% of GDP		
	Public	Private	Total	Public	Private	Total
1969	n.a.	n.a.	19.6	n.a.	n.a.	n.a.
1970	n.a.	n.a.	27.0	n.a.	n.a.	24.4
1971	n.a.	n.a.	27.4	n.a.	n.a.	23.9
1972	n.a.	n.a.	25.2	n.a.	n.a.	22.3
1973	n.a.	n.a.	30.4	n.a.	n.a.	25.8
1974	n.a.	n.a.	28.8	n.a.	n.a.	25.8
1975	n.a.	n.a.	19.7	n.a.	n.a.	18.1
1976	n.a.	n.a.	22.1	n.a.	n.a.	20.2
1977	n.a.	n.a.	30.0	n.a.	n.a.	23.7
1978	n.a.	n.a.	37.1	n.a.	n.a.	29.8
1979	n.a.	n.a.	28.0	n.a.	n.a.	22.3
1980	n.a.	n.a.	37.7	n.a.	n.a.	29.2
1981	n.a.	n.a.	36.6	n.a.	n.a.	27.7
1982	n.a.	n.a.	28.1	n.a.	n.a.	21.8
1983	n.a.	n.a.	24.3	n.a.	n.a.	20.8
1984	n.a.	n.a.	25.5	n.a.	n.a.	20.7
1985	n.a.	n.a.	32.1	n.a.	n.a.	25.5
1986	n.a.	n.a.	27.3	n.a.	n.a.	21.8
1987	9.3	16.4	25.7	7.2	12.6	19.8
1988	12.5	17.8	30.3	8.4	11.9	20.3
1989	13.9	19.3	33.2	8.2	11.4	19.5
1990	19.1	21.5	40.6	9.6	10.8	20.4
1991	19.1	23.7	42.8	8.4	10.4	18.9

Soures: Total investment in absolute amounts and as a percentage of GDP: World Bank, *World Tables 1991*

and technicians per million of the population were then compared to the same ratios for eight other Sub-Saharan nations. Kenya's proportions were three times those of the next most well-endowed country, Senegal, and of an order of magnitude greater than the remainder.

The same conclusion can be drawn from the second survey, conducted by the World Bank (Zymelman, 1990), which measures an output of

Table 4.8 Kenya: government revenues, expenditures and investment 1964–1991

Year	Government current revenue (billions current KSh)	Government current expenditure (billions current KSh)	Government surplus (+) or deficit (−) (billions current KSh)	Government capital payments (billions current KSh)	Government consumption (billions of current KSh)	Government gross investment (% of total investment)
1964	n.a.	n.a.	n.a.	n.a.	n.a.	25.3
1965	n.a.	n.a.	n.a.	n.a.	n.a.	26.3
1966	n.a.	n.a.	n.a.	n.a.	n.a.	32.0
1967	n.a.	n.a.	n.a.	n.a.	n.a.	35.0
1968	n.a.	n.a.	n.a.	n.a.	n.a.	37.1
1969	n.a.	n.a.	n.a.	n.a.	1.7	33.0
1970	n.a.	n.a.	n.a.	n.a.	1.9	30.6
1971	n.a.	n.a.	n.a.	n.a.	2.3	38.9
1972	2.7	2.4	−0.6	0.9	2.7	38.5
1973	2.8	2.6	−0.9	1.1	2.9	45.3
1974	3.7	3.1	−0.6	1.2	3.6	45.2
1975	4.5	4.0	−1.2	1.7	4.4	41.9
1976	5.3	4.8	−1.7	2.2	5.1	42.2
1977	6.4	5.5	−1.3	2.2	6.4	42.3
1978	9.4	5.5	−1.3	2.2	8.0	37.7
1979	10.1	9.4	−3.0	3.7	9.0	46.0
1980	12.2	10.5	−2.4	4.2	10.7	45.2
1981	14.0	12.9	−4.0	5.1	11.5	44.5
1982	15.3	16.4	−5.5	4.3	13.0	45.0
1983	16.6	17.0	−3.8	4.5	14.7	38.0
1984	18.2	19.3	−4.3	3.2	15.5	37.7
1985	20.3	21.8	−6.2	4.2	17.6	41.8
1986	24.1	25.1	−5.1	4.2	21.5	n.a.
1987	29.1	30.0	−8.3	7.5	24.3	n.a.
1988	34.1	34.2	−6.3	6.2	25.8	n.a.
1989	41.0	44.2	−3.2	1.2	32.7	n.a.
1990	47.9	53.4	−5.5	3.2	11.0	n.a.
1991	57.6	60.8	−3.3	1.8	8.2	n.a.

Sources: 1964–1968: Van der Hoeven and Vandermoortele, 1987, Table 2, p. 12
1969–1991: World Bank, *World Tables, 1991, 1993*

Table 4.9 Kenya: share of total investment (%) by sectors 1979–1985

Sector	1979	1980	1981	1982	1983	1984	1985
Traditional economy	7.3	7.0	7.0	8.1	9.2	9.3	10.1
Agriculture	7.8	7.5	7.5	7.7	7.7	6.8	7.9
Forestry	0.1	0.2	0.1	0.0	0.0	0.0	0.0
Mining	0.7	0.8	0.7	0.6	0.7	0.9	0.5
Manufacturing	16.4	12.4	12.2	9.9	15.5	11.9	11.8
Construction	4.8	5.4	4.5	4.3	8.3	7.9	3.8
Trade and tourism	3.2	4.5	3.0	3.6	4.1	3.7	4.7
Transport	18.8	16.5	15.7	15.2	15.4	15.7	13.8
Ownership of dwelling	10.2	10.1	9.7	10.9	6.7	6.2	7.1
Electricity	5.9	6.6	9.0	11.3	7.9	5.5	5.9
Finance	1.5	1.6	3.3	1.4	2.3	2.2	2.0
Other services	5.9	6.6	6.8	7.9	8.1	7.0	10.0
Government	17.3	20.7	20.5	18.9	17.6	22.6	22.2

Source: Reproduced from Van der Hoeven and Vendermoortele 1987, Table A.4, p. 74

scientific and technological activity (defined as scientific papers published in over 3,000 scientific journals, for which the Institute of Scientific Information compiles a 'Science Citation Index'). Over the period 1981–1986, the order of standing, with numbers of articles per country in parenthesis, was Nigeria (4,529), Kenya (1,454), Sudan (558), Zimbabwe (407), Tanzania (393), Senegambia (358), Côte d'Ivoire (209), Ethiopia (219), Zambia (172) and Zaire (119) (*ibid.*, I-4: p. 14). Lest too much emphasis be placed on Kenya's high standing, the author of the study reports that there is a very strong correlation ($R^2 = 0.95$) between the measures of scientific and technological output, on the one hand, and measures of GDP, on the other (*ibid.*: p. 7). But this is to be expected, since progress in science and technology is closely associated, in the long run, with economic growth.

R&D INSTITUTIONS

Let us move now from aggregated data, to data from individual entities, most of which we shall ultimately consolidate. Our procedure will be, first, to present the material for the institutions we studied, one by one. Next we will add any material available on the institutions that did not enter into our sample of cases. Finally we will combine all the data so as to obtain a synthetic measure of the intensity of Kenya's pursuit of science and

Table 4.10 Kenya: scientists, engineers and technicians in the labour force 1982

	Total number of scientists and engineers	Total number of technicians	Total	Scientists and engineers per million of the population	Technicians per million of the population	Total per million of the population
Kenya	16,241	45,962	62,203	901	2,551	3,451
Burkina Faso	n.a.	n.a.	n.a.	170	206	376
Cameroon	n.a.	n.a.	n.a.	93	n.a.	n.a.
Côte d'Ivoire	n.a.	n.a.	n.a.	306	209	515
Guinea	n.a.	n.a.	n.a.	253	121	374
Mali	n.a.	n.a.	n.a.	344	187	531
Mauritania	n.a.	n.a.	n.a.	194	324	618
Niger	n.a.	n.a.	n.a.	114	248	362
Senegal	n.a.	n.a.	n.a.	453	618	1,071

Source: UNESCO, 1990. *Statistical Yearbook 1990*, Tables 5.2 and 5.17

technology. (One last indicator of the country's endeavour – university education in science and technology, will be left until later in this chapter.)

The first three entities that we will describe are R&D institutions, the first in the field of agriculture, the second in the field of industry, and the third in both (or neither). The government R&D institutions in agriculture are described in three papers by Simons (Simons 1989a (January), Simons 1989b (July) and Simons and Gitu, 1989), but the agricultural R&D institute that we studied lay outside the government: it is the Coffee Research Foundation, a component of the para-statal Coffee Board of Kenya.

With an annual budget of approximately KShs 80 million the Coffee Research Foundation is the largest non-governmental R&D institution in Kenya. Established during the colonial period and staffed initially by foreign scientists, the Coffee Research Foundation was transferred at the time of independence to the newly formed government. The government, in turn, in 1963 leased the land, buildings and equipment to the para-statal Coffee Board of Kenya, under which the Research Foundation operates and for which the Foundation undertakes all Kenya's R&D in coffee. Over the years, Kenyans have replaced foreign scientists and administrators, and have taken over running the research programmes, stations, and commercial plantations.

The Coffee Research Foundation has its laboratories at Ruiru, 17 kilometres to the west of Nairobi, as well as a plantation, 'Azania' (in Juja, in a coffee-growing zone on the eastern escarpment of the Rift Valley), four sub-stations and several demonstration plots. Activities are divided into seven main divisions: Plant Pathology (coffee berry disease, leaf rust and bacterial blight), Coffee Breeding, Agronomy, Chemistry and Processing, Crop Physiology, Entomology and Agricultural Economics. The breeding of new varieties of coffee for disease resistance is a continuing challenge; one particularly successful new variety, Ruiri 11, has proven itself impervious to coffee berry disease.

Three-quarters of the income of the Coffee Research Foundation is derived from a levy of 1 per cent on the sales of Kenya's coffee through the Coffee Board. The Coffee Board augments the levy with smaller amounts for specific projects (another one-sixth of the total) and the Foundation itself makes up the balance through sales of coffee beans from its plantation and charges to coffee planters for special services. Table 4.11 provides some data on the Foundation's revenues and costs for the five fiscal years 1987/8–1991/2. From 1987/8–1989/90 revenues rose by less than, and costs by more than, the rate of inflation, so that the budget moved from being in surplus to being in deficit. The estimated deficit of KSh10 million for 1989/90 compares with the Coffee Research Foundation's

Table 4.11 Kenya: budgets for the Coffee Research Foundation, 1987/8–1991/2 (millions of current KSh)

Budget item	1987/8 (actual)	1988/9(a) (actual)	1989/90 (actual)	1990/1 (budget)	1991/2 (estimates)
Revenues					
Coffee Board subvention	41.1	55.3	65.4	n.a.	n.a.
Other Coffee Board payments for special projects	14.1	15.1		21.0(c)	30.4(c)
Proceeds from sale of coffee beans	12.4	5.3	7.6	17.3	15.3
Other revenues	1.7	2.0	2.0	1.5	1.0
Total revenues	69.4	76.7	75.0	101.4(d)	127.2(d)
Expenditures					
Recurrent(b)	42.7	46.5	55.5	60.8	64.3
Capital	n.a.	6.4	9.9	7.6	16.5
Expenditures					
Special projects	14.2	15.0	19.6	21.0	30.4
Total expenditures	n.a.	68.0	85.0	89.4	111.2
Surplus or (deficit)	n.a.	8.7	(10.0)	(12.0)d	(15.0)d

Sources: 1987/8–1988/9: Coffee Research Foundation, Annual Report and Accounts 1988–1989
1989–1991/2: Government of Kenya, Programme Review and Forward Budget, 1990/1–1992/3

Notes: (a) There is a typographical mistake of 1 million Shillings in one of the revenue items. The total revenue is correct
(b) Recurrent expenses include, in 1987/8 and 1988/9, miscellaneous expenses and audit fees
(c) It is assumed that revenues granted for special projects will equal budgeted expenditures
(d) Estimated

Director's subsequent estimates of KSh12 million, for the same year 1989/90, KSh15 million for the following year 1990/1, and KSh37 million for 1991/2, given current commitments and anticipated revenues.

Increasing deficits are not surprising, in light of the secular fall in the price of coffee, *vis à vis* other traded products. With a fixed levy of 1 per cent of the Coffee Board's revenues from the sale of coffee, the Foundation's revenues will fall *pari pasu*. The Foundation is therefore in a quandary; it must either reduce expenditures or seek additional income. Assuming the latter course is preferred, additional income could come from a transfer of 'Regular' projects to the category of 'Special' projects, for which specific funds are allocated by the Coffee Board itself, or by the Government of Kenya. Income could also come from foreign donors, whose assistance has not yet been sought. Finally, additional funds could be raised by increasing the levy to, say, 1.5 per cent: it could be argued that this percentage is still less than the figure of 2 per cent of revenues which Kenya's National Council for Science and Technology has set as its goal for the country's R&D efforts.

That the Coffee Research Foundation's income is short of what is needed can be seen from another two sets of data; the one on turnover of scientific personnel and the other from a partial list of underfunded projects. In 1988/9, four scientists left (Coffee Research Foundation, 1989: 4); over the ten years 1981–1991 resignations of scientists were 39 in number (interview 18 September 1991). Half those leaving had served for several years or more, the other half only long enough – two to three years – to complete their advanced degrees or win study tours abroad, or both. The majority of those who left took equivalent positions at higher salaries in Kenya, or emigrated, chiefly to Zambia and Botswana, at still higher salaries.

The other indication of insufficient funds for R&D is a list, obtained during interview, of shortfalls in the funds granted in response to project requests. Still needed, in 1991, were KSh2 million for seed multiplication in the plant breeding programme; KSh8 million for equipment in the pest control project; KSh2 million for equipment and KSh3 million for annual expenses in the soil and leaf analysis; KSh3 million for basic equipment in the coffee processing machinery workshop (the workshop itself was funded in 1988/9 within the capital budget: see Table 4.11); and KSh2 million for coffee testing: in total KSh20 million, or roughly one-fifth in addition to what was spent in the year.

The second R&D organization that constituted one of our case studies is the Kenya Industrial R&D Institute (abbreviated KIRDI). Like the Coffee Research Foundation, KIRDI's origin lies in the colonial period, when in 1942, the East African Industrial Research Organization was established to develop local industries, with the objective of relieving shortages brought about by World War II. After the collapse of the East African Community in 1977, the Kenyan government first transferred the Organization to the Ministry of Commerce and Industry, and then, two years later, gave it autonomy.

KIRDI employes approximately 270 persons in Nairobi, the facilities consisting of several workshops, laboratories and offices. Its statutory duties include:

1 identifying and developing appropriate process and product technologies to suit the local market and export potential;
2 exploring the possibilities of substituting imported raw materials and intermediate goods with indigenous materials
3 designing, developing and adapting machinery, tools, equipment and instruments and processes suitable for introduction and use in the rural areas:
4 developing suitable treatment/recovery processes and devices to reduce environment hazard created by industrial wastes and effluents;
5 setting up pilot plants where necessary to demonstrate the efficacy of industrial technology; and
6 acting as consultants to industry in the provision of industrial information and technical services, and if necessary to commercialize the relevant research findings.

For more detail, see Mwamadzingo, 1991: 50–9.

In fulfilment of these duties, KIRDI divides itself into four divisions: Analytical and Testing, Design and Engineering, Process and Product Development, and Project Studies and Development (primarily market research). A better idea of the work undertaken can be gathered from a description of KIRDI's workshops and laboratories: there is a mechanical workshop, a leather technology laboratory, a ceramics laboratory and workshop, a microbiology laboratory and a chemical laboratory.

Funding for KIRDI comes from two major and one minor sources; the Government of Kenya and foreign donors, in roughly equal amounts, and, in much lesser amount, KIRDI's own consulting fees and charges. Expenditures for the seven fiscal years 1986/7–1991/3 are given in Table 4.12; revenues are approximately equal to expenditures. The first observation from the data in the table is that the three years 1986/7–1988/9 display capital expenditures that are falling steadily in nominal terms and at an even greater rate in real terms. Recurrent costs, typically 85 per cent of which are wages and salaries (personal emoluments, gratuities and pensions, housing allowance, and travel to and from work) rise in line with

Table 4.12 Kenya: budgets of the Kenya Industrial Research and Development Institute (KIRDI) 1986/7–1992/3 (millions of current KSh)

Budget Item	Expenditure 1986/7	Expenditure 1987/8	Expenditure 1988/9	Expenditure 1989/90	Expenditure 1990/1	Estimates 1991/2	Estimates 1992/3
Recurrent costs	13.9	16.2	22.7	22.5	25.6	28.3	29.8
Development (Capital) Expenditures							
Project Studies and Research	0.1	0.0	0.0	0.0	0.2	0.0	0.0
Plant and Equipment	0.2	0.1	0.9	0.6	0.2	1.2	1.4
Construction of Research Labs.	10.5	10.3	7.0	4.0	2.5	10.0	10.0
Leather Pilot Project	0.2	0.0	1.4	2.6	0.1	0.2	0.2
Mechanical Engineering Project	0.4	0.0	0.2	0.0	0.1	0.2	0.2
Technical Engineering Project	–	–	0.3	0.2	0.1	0.2	0.2
Power Alcohol Project	–	–	0.3	0.2	0.2	0.3	0.4
Technical Advisory Mission	–	–	–	0.0	76.3	12.0	12.0
Total	11.4	10.4	10.1	7.6	79.4	24.1	24.6
Total Expenditures	25.3	26.6	32.8	30.1	105.0	52.4	54.4

Source: Kenya Industrial Research and Development Institute

the cost of living. In the next year, 1989/90, even recurrent costs fell chiefly through a reduction in laboratory equipment and supplies. Capital expenditures continued their fall.

It was in fiscal year 1990/1 that KIRDI's finances turned around, with an injection of KSh20 million from UNDP. This was the largest given by foreign donors, and was part of a sizeable grant of US$4 million from UNDP, extending over several years, and financing a new engineering workshop and equipment. In addition, UNIDO and the German Trust Fund supplied US$0.2 million for the leather project, most of which was spent in 1989/90; and the Canadian IDRC Can$70,000, expended in 1990/91. All together, foreign donations amounted to US$4.25 million, much of which was committed to the years 1989/90–1992/3. In the same four years, the Government of Kenya's total expenditure on KIRDI amounted to approximately US$5 million. (Total expenditures of KSh189.3 million, from Table 4.12, converted to US$ at an average exchange rate of KSh25 to US$1, less some US$2.5 million for that part of the foreign donations expended in those years.) This very rough calculation suggests that foreign donors are currently matching the expenditures of the Kenyan government on KIRDI. Another way of measuring the input of foreign donations is to notice, in Table 4.12, that it was only in 1990/1 that KIRDI's development (capital) expenditures once again nearly equalled KIRDI's current expenses. Properly equipped, as well as staffed, KIRDI can now hope to resume fulfilling its obligations.

The third R&D institution that it was hoped to study was the Agricultural Implements Manufacturers Ltd, located in Nakuru, a town in the Rift Valley 60 kilometres northwest of Nairobi. This enterprise was established in the mid-1980s with funds contributed by private firms; its function was to develop agricultural machinery which could be manufactured within the country and which would be appropriate for Kenyan farmers and processors. From the beginning the funds were inadequate, but with the recession in Kenyan industry (following the reduction of industrial exports to Tanzania and Uganda, and the increase in imports from the rest of the world), funds dried up completely, and the enterprise was abandoned. This terminated Kenya's first endeavour in privately sponsored R&D on appropriate technology.

SCIENCE AND TECHNOLOGY AT THE KENYAN UNIVERSITIES

Public R&D in the realm of appropriate technology is concentrated in a different sort of institution, the Appropriate Technology Centre (ATC) of Kenyatta University. Initially a section within the Physics Department, in

1980 the ATC became a separate department within the Faculty of Science. There it received substantial funds from foreign agencies such as the Intermediate Technology Development Group, GTZ and UNICEF, and developed a famous cooking stove, the Kenya Ceramic Jeko, as well as other, minor products. Internally the ATC is divided into seven subject areas, viz. agriculture, manufacturing, renewable energy, construction, water technologies, biomass and stove testing, and transport. Over the last four years, 1988/9–1991/2, its staff has varied from a low of 25, of whom 14 were technically trained, to a high of 42, of whom 25 were technically trained. Recent fluctuations in staffing numbers are high, in large part because of a dearth of financing: foreign assistance has ceased, so that the ATC has received funds only from Kenyatta University (KSh171,685 in 1988/9, of which 96 per cent was expended on wages and salaries; and KSh94,075 in 1989/90, of which 95 per cent was expended on wages and salaries). Operating under such constraint, the ATC's further contribution to the development of appropriate technologies has been minimal.

Science and technology continue to be pursued in Kenya's major institution of higher learning, the University of Nairobi. Inspecting the budgets of the University and of the institutes as a whole (see Table 4.13) one sees that funds for recurrent expenditures (primarily wages and salaries) approximate closely the sums authorized, whereas capital (development) expenditures often fall short of those authorized. One also sees that the University of Nairobi draws the largest proportion of foreign support.

Moving on to the internal budgets of the University of Nairobi, we find data under different headings, 'Estimates' and 'Actual'. It appears that the former refers to requests made by the University to the Ministry of Education, the latter to the funds expended during the year. The relation between the two provides an indication of the extent to which the relevant faculty of department is able to meet its needs, through financial subventions from the Kenyan government and from abroad.

Within the University of Nairobi it is probably the Science Faculty (including Veterinary Agriculture) and Medicine (including the College of Health Sciences) that have closest links with foreign institutions and that receive the largest donations. The generosity of foreigners has enabled the first of these faculties to expand to the point where it has 13 departments, and the second to the point where it has 16.

Table 4.14 gives the average ratio of expenditures to requests for two faculties, the Faculty of Engineering and the Faculty of Science, and for the latter's least favoured department, Mathematics. The mathematicians receive somewhat less than half the funds the University requests on their behalf, the scientists as a whole a little over two-thirds, and the engineers a

Table 4.13 Kenya: budgets for university education and for the University of Nairobi (millions of K£)[a], 1986/87–1992/93

	1986/87	1987/88	1988/89	1989/90	1990/91	1991/92	1992/93
All universities:							
Recurrent expenditures							
Approved estimates	38.4	51.8	71.9	91.9	n.a.	n.a.	n.a.
Actual expenditures	38.1	54.8	73.3	84.4	n.a.	n.a.	n.a.
Development expenditures							
Approved estimates	12.1	20.7	47.1	53.7	n.a.	n.a.	n.a.
Actual expenditures	10.2	14.6	38.3	23.1	n.a.	n.a.	n.a.
Foreign assistance received	0.8	0.1	0.3	0.3	n.a.	n.a.	n.a.
University of Nairobi:							
Recurrent expenditures							
Approved estimates	16.9	20.3	26.3	23.4	31.5	33.0	34.7
Actual expenditures	16.4	20.3	25.8	21.9	n.a.	n.a.	n.a.
Development expenditures							
Approved estimates	2.8	1.2	0.4	11.2	7.1	1.7	1.4
Actual expenditures	2.0	0.8	4.4	5.9	n.a.	n.a.	n.a.
Foreign assistance received	0.6	0.1	0.3	0.3	2.7	1.7	1.4

Source: University of Nairobi; 1990/1–1992/3 are projections

Note: [a] Units of currency are Kenyan pounds, in each of which there are twenty shillings

Table 4.14 Kenya: actual expenditure on recurrent items as a fraction of requests, Faculties of Engineering and Science, and Department of Mathematics of the University of Nairobi, 1988/9–1990/91 (absolute figures in thousands of K£)[a]

Branch of the University of Nairobi	Actual expenditures as a fraction of requests		
	1988/1989	*1989/1990*	*1990/1991*
Faculty of Engineering	746/1,227 = 0.61	789/1,230 = 0.64	887/1,281 = 0.69
Faculty of Science	1,711/2,450 = 0.70	1,748/2,470 = 0.71	1,853/2,695 = 0.69
Department of Mathematics	150/321 = 0.47	168/330 = 0.51	165/348 = 0.47

Source: University of Nairobi

Note: [a] Units of currency are Kenyan pounds, in each of which are twenty shillings

little less than two-thirds. These are for recurrent expenditures; funds for capital expenditures are relatively even more generously supplied to the Engineering Faculty, in part through foreign donations.

ESTIMATING KENYA'S TOTAL EXPENDITURES ON ADVANCING SCIENCE AND TECHNOLOGY

We now wish to estimate the total amounts of money spent in Kenya on the pursuit of science and technology, and to discern any change in these amounts during the course of Structural Adjustment.

Besides the public institution (KIRDI), which we have already described there are six other government R&D organizations for which statistical summaries are available. Published in various public documents are the figures appearing in Table 4.15, in the three categories Recurrent Expenditure, Development Expenditure and foreign contributions ('Foreign Aid'). The figures in the last category, like those in the proceeding two, are of expenditures: funds appropriated by foreign donors are substantially larger, but many have not yet been utilized.

With the data available in Tables 4.12, and 4.15 we can begin to accumulate estimates of the total amount expended in Kenya on R&D. Expenditures by government institutions are summarized in Table 4.16, where the figures are denominated in Kenyan shillings at current prices.

Table 4.15 Kenya: budgets of other public R&D institutions, 1986/7–1990/1 (millions of KSh at current prices)

Year	Budget item	KARI	KEFRI	KEMFRI	KEMRI	KETRI	NCST	TOTAL
1986/1987	Recurrent expenditure	54.7	19.7	22.3	49.1	20.0	3.8	169.6
	Development expenditure	2.0	0.6	5.6	28.2	16.0	6.0	58.4
	Total expenditure	56.7	20.3	27.9	77.3	36.0	9.8	228.0
	Foreign aid	5.3	0.2	1.4	0.1	0.0	–	7.0
1987/1988	Recurrent expenditure	144.3	26.7	21.9	59.1	20.3	3.6	275.9
	Development expenditure	40.1	11.4	11.3	25.0	14.0	3.6	104.4
	Total expenditure	184.4	38.1	33.2	84.1	34.3	7.2	381.3
	Foreign aid	22.2	0	11.3	0.2	0.0	–	33.7
1988/1989	Recurrent expenditure	252.5	33.1	32.0	75.6	24.3	5.1	422.6
	Development expenditure	21.4	12.5	–	12.3	6.4	3.9	56.5
	Total expenditure	273.9	45.6	32.0	87.9	30.7	8.9	479.0
	Foreign aid	14.6	0	1.7	0.0	0.2	–	16.5
1989/1990	Recurrent expenditure	207.5	46.7	39.5	84.0	23.6	8.3	409.6
	Development expenditure	92.7	13.6	2.9	14.3	5.1	2.5	131.1
	Total expenditure	300.2	60.3	42.4	98.3	28.7	10.8	540.7
	Foreign aid	58.2	13.6	0.2	0.2	0.0	–	72.2
1990/1991	Recurrent expenditure	232.6	60.5	46.7	88.0	29.4	7.8	465.0
	Development expenditure	285.3	14.0	1.3	38.0	2.0	0.6	341.2
	Total expenditure	517.9	74.5	48.0	126.0	31.4	8.4	806.2
	Foreign aid	49.8	–	–	19.0	–	–	68.8

Key: KARI = Kenya Agricultural Research Institute KEFRI = Kenya Forestry Research Institute
KEMFRI = Kenya Marine and Fisheries Research Institute KEMRI = Kenya Medical Research Institute
KETRI = Kenya Trypanosomiasis Research Institute NCST = National Council for Science and Technology

Sources: 1986/7 to 1989/90: Republic of Kenya, *The Appropriation Accounts, Other Public Accounts and the Account of the Funds:* Nairobi, Office of the Auditor General, various issues
1990/91: Republic of Kenya, 1990. *Programme Review and Forward Budget, 1990/91–1992/93.* Nairobi, Office of the Vice President and Ministry of Finance

Next we add in R&D expenditures by non-governmental organizations. The one set of figures we have collected, for the Coffee Research Foundation, are reported in Table 4.11; they add roughly 15 per cent to the total of government expenditure. For the other para-statal firms we have no evidence, although their number is substantial, as are their expenditures on science and technology. Many of them – namely the Tea Research Foundation, the Kenya Seed Company, the National Irrigation Board, the Lake Basin and the Kerio Valley Development Authorities, the High Level Research Station and the National Horticultural Station (both at Thika), the Kenya Industrial Training Institute, Kenya Industrial Estates, and the Industrial and Commercial Development Corporation – devote their efforts almost entirely to advancing science and technology. Others, existing within government ministries – the Kenya Bureau of Standards, the Forestry Inspectorate in the Ministry of Labour, a group in the Ministry of Industry, the Kenya Industrial Property Office, and the Kenya–Railway Workshops – are also engaged. Although their expenditures, individually, are considerably less than those of the Coffee Research Foundation, collectively they amount to rather more. If we augment the total figures for governmental R&D institutions (from Table 4.16) by 40 per cent (15 per cent for the

Table 4.16 Kenya: budgets of all public R&D institutions 1986/7–1990/1 (millions of KSh at current prices)

Governmental R&D institutes' expenditures[a]	1986/7	1987/8	1988/9	1989/1	1990/1
KIRDI	25.3	26.6	32.8	30.1	52.4
KARI[b]	56.7	184.4	273.9	300.2	468.1
KEFRI	20.3	38.1	45.6	60.3	72.4
KEMFRI	27.9	33.2	32.0	42.4	54.7
KEMRI	77.3	84.1	87.9	98.3	91.2
KETRI	36.0	34.3	30.7	28.7	34.6
NCST	9.8	7.2	8.9	10.8	8.4
Total Expenditures	253.3	407.9	511.8	570.8	781.8

Sources: Table 4.12 (KIRDI) and Table 4.15 (Other Public Institutions)

Notes: [a] For key, see Table 4.15
[b] R&D expenditures of KARI in the 11 years 1972/3–1982/3 appear in Simon and Gitu, 1989 (Table 4, p. 15); in millions K£ they are 1.40, 2.13, 2.40, 2.93, 3.67, 5.73, 6.37, 7.01, 8.95 and 9.40 respectively. As a percentage of GDP originating in agriculture expenditures rise from 0.60% in 1972/73 to 1.03% in 1982/3. In those years personal costs represented half to two-thirds of total recurrent expenditures

Coffee Research Foundation plus 25 per cent for the other para-statal organizations) we can obtain an estimate of the total R&D expenditures of the public sector: these appear in the third row of Table 4.17. In the fourth row are estimates of the expenditures on the pursuit of science and technology by the universities: these are drawn primarily from the figures on the budgets of Faculties of Engineering and Science of the University of Nairobi in Table 4.14 (converted from K£ to KSh), with added allowance for the greater expenditures in agriculture and medicine, and the lesser expenditure of scientific and technical faculties in other universities. The fifth row of the table aggregates all public sector expenditure.

There are three further rows in Table 4.17, whose purpose is to put public expenditures on advancing science and technology in perspective. The first of these three gives the percentages of total public sector expenditure devoted to advancing science and technology. (The figures on total government expenditures come from Table 4.8, columns 2 and 4.) The second gives those devoted to reporting foreign contributions to the public R&D institutes, in absolute amounts, and the final row gives those to expressing foreign contributions as a fraction of total expenditures on advancing science and technology.

At this point, we might say a word about the source of statistics on foreign contributions to the pursuit of science and technology. For Ghana, there were no compilations available, but for Kenya and Tanzania there are. In both these countries, UNDP collects statistics on the volume of foreign aid, which it has begun to publish in reports entitled *Development Cooperation: Kenya* and *Development Cooperation: Tanzania*. It is from the former of these that we have abstracted the figures in Table 4.18 in this chapter. Notice how rapidly foreign donations rose! The fall since 1990 has been almost equally rapid, as foreign donors have curtailed contributions following the breakdown of negotiations with Kenya in Paris in 1991 (UNDP, 1993: 49).

To the expenditures of the public sector on advancing science and technology we must finally add estimates of concomitant expenditures by the private sector. These have been determined accurately for one year, 1985/6, by B.F. Makau (1988), who compiled a list of 32 private firms with research establishments, employing 90 scientists full-time, 9.1 per cent of the country's total of 986 engaged full-time in R&D. These private firms spent KSh 47,560,000 in that year, 9.5 per cent of the total of about KSh 500 million estimated by Makau as the total for Kenya as a whole.

Assuming that the ratio of private to public sector expenditures has remained the same throughout the period since 1985/6, we can augment the figures in Table 4.17, row 4 by 9.5: 90.5, yielding the totals for the entire

Table 4.17 Kenya: estimate of total expenditures by the public sector on the pursuit of science and technology, 1986/7–1990/1 (millions of KSh, excepting rows 6 and 8)

Item	1986/7	1987/8	1988/9	1989/90	1990/1
Expenditures by public R&D institutes	253	408	512	571	781.8
Expenditures on R&D by para-statal bodies	101	163	205	228	390.9
Total public expenditures on R&D institutes	354	571	717	799	1,172.7
Expenditures in science & technology by the universities	97	139	212	185	233
Total public sector expenditures in advancing science & technology	451	710	929	984	1,306
Public sector expenditures on advanced science & technology (% total government expenditures)	1.5	1.9	2.3	2.2	2.3
Contributions of foreign aid to advancing science & technology	7.0	33.7	87.5	654	1,218
Foreign aid (% public sector expenditures on Advancing Science & Technology)	1.6	4.7	9.4	66.5	93.5

Sources: Row 1: the sum of the final row in Table 4.12 (total expenditures of KIRDI) and the final column in Table 4.15 (total expenditures of other public R&D institutes), less foreign aid

Row 2: see text

Row 3: the sum of rows 1 and 2

Row 4: Recurrent and development expenditures of all universities (Table 4.13, rows 2 and 4) multiplied by 0.10, the fraction of university expenditures devoted to science and technology (1987/8 estimated as 10%; 1988/9 as 9.5%; 1989/90 as 11.6%, the last two percentages calculated from figures in Tables 4.13 and 4.14)

Row 5: the sum of rows 3 and 4

Row 6: Total government expenditures for the earlier of the two (calendar) years are the sum of government current expenditure and capital payments (Table 4.8, columns 2 and 4)

Row 7: 1986/7 and 1987/8; see Tables 4.12 and 4.15 1988/9–1990/1; see Table 4.18; conversion from US dollars to KSh at the exchange rates in Table 4.1

Row 8: row 7 divided by row 5

Table 4.18 Kenya: estimate of total expenditures on the pursuit of science & technology and their percentages of GDP, 1986/7–1990/1 (billions KSh, excepting rows 5 and 8)

Item	1986/7	1987/8	1988/9	1989/90	1990/1
Expenditures of the public sector in the pursuit of science & technology	0.45	0.71	0.93	0.98	1.31
Expenditures of the private sector	0.05	0.07	0.09	0.10	0.124
Total expenditures by the country as a whole	0.50	0.78	1.02	1.08	1.43
GDP	117	130	149	170	199
Total Kenyan expenditures (% GDP)	0.4	0.6	0.7	0.6	0.7
Foreign donations	0.01	0.04	0.09	0.65	1.22
Total Kenyan plus foreign expenditures	0.51	0.82	1.11	1.73	2.65
Total Kenyan plus foreign expenditures (% GDP)	0.4	0.6	0.7	1.0	1.3

Sources: Row 1: Table 4.17, row 5
Row 2: see text
Row 3: the sum of rows 1 and 2
Row 4: Table 4.1, column 1 (the previous calendar year figures; e.g. GDP in 1988 for 1988/9's expenditures
Row 5: row 3 divided by row 4
Row 6: Table 4.17, row 7
Row 7: row 3 plus row 6
Row 8: row 7 divided by row 4

Table 4.19 Kenya: foreign donations aiding the pursuit of science & technology, 1988–1992 (millions current US dollars)

Year	*Technology policy and planning*	*Technical and managerial education and training*	*Agricultural R&D*	*Industrial technological R&D*	*Total*
		Category of Donation			
1988	–	3.17	1.70	0.06	4.93
1989	0.49	20.84	10.15	0.00	31.48
1990	0.03	31.02	16.33	3.14	50.52
1991	0.19	15.75	21.34	0.61	36.89
1992 (planned)	–	4.71	11.54	–	16.25

Source: UNDP, 1993, Table A.1, pp. 62–5

country in Table 4.18, row 2. Compared to Kenya's GDP (row 4) these represent between 0.5 and 1 per cent over the years, comparing favourably with UNESCO's estimates for all of Africa of 0.34 per cent in 1970 and 0.36 per cent in 1980 (UNESCO, 1990). Thanks to foreign contributions, the percentages for years after 1988 were substantially higher, reaching a peak of 1.3 per cent in 1990/1 (see Table 4.19).

5 Tanzania

INTRODUCTION

When it attained its independence in 1961, Tanzania was one of the poorest countries in the developing world, dependent almost entirely on agriculture for its national income. For the first several years of its independent existence, Tanzania lacked any overall direction; but, in 1967, it chose to establish a socialist society. The programme annunciated in the Arusha Declaration decreed that the direction of the economy should be under public control. Agriculture was to be run on a communal basis, but industry, trade and commerce were to be the province of state activities. Some of these activities were to be undertaken within the existing ministries; others were to be the responsibility of new, para-statal bodies, existing outside the narrow confines of government but subject to its overall direction.

During the next decade in Tanzania substantial progress was made in the social sector, in such fields as education, health and infrastructure. Industry advanced relatively rapidly, stimulated by public investment, particularly in the new para-statal firms. But the modest advances were brought nearly to a halt by the dissolution of the East African Community in 1977 and the war in Uganda in 1978–1979: the economy was unable to absorb these adverse forces. Perhaps most damaging was the fall in agricultural output, particularly output destined for exports, which reduced Tanzania's earnings of foreign exchange and resulted in a substantial reduction in imports of capital goods, spares and raw materials. Government revenues, equally dependent upon the maintenance of agricultural output, fell so that the economy was constrained both in the amounts of foreign exchange it could allocate to imports and the amounts of domestic resources it could allocate to maintenance and expansion. Immediate efforts to replenish agricultural exports, aided in 1981 by a loan from the

World Bank in the amount of US$50 million, failed to reverse the unfavourable trend. Several years of further deterioration led the country, finally, to embark upon a profound adjustment of its structure, designed at first by the Tanzanian government, but augmented by the World Bank in the course of negotiating its two subsequent loans. These negotiations took place over a few years, and resulted in an allotment of US$96.2 million by the World Bank in 1987 for rehabilitation of the entire economy, and of US$135 million in 1989 for the privatization of industry and the liberalization of trade. These programmes are still in force; compliance has been both difficult and slow. (For extended studies of recent changes in the Tanzanian economy see Ndulu, 1988; Berg-Schlösser and Siegler, 1990.)

In this chapter, we shall follow the same order that we have in the preceding two on Ghana and Kenya: first we shall examine the statistics on the entire Tanzanian economy, concentrating on total output and its division among the different sectors, upon government expenditures, upon borrowings by Tanzanians and the annual service of those borrowings, upon imports and exports, and upon the Structural Adjustment Programmes. After examining the Tanzanian economy in its totality, we shall shift our focus to that of individual R&D institutions. Those institutions engaged in agricultural R&D will be the first to be surveyed, followed by those working in industry, and by those engaged in developing appropriate technologies. Next, we will examine those activities in pursuit of science and technology carried out within colleges and universities, both their teaching and their own R&D. Finally, we shall attempt to aggregate statistics on all expenditures on science and technology in Tanzania, selecting first those that are under government aegis, and subsequently adding foreign donations. At the very end of the chapter, there will be a brief summary.

MACRO-ECONOMIC TRENDS IN THE TANZANIAN ECONOMY

The recent economic history of Tanzania can best be seen in the light of its growing population. From a total of approximately 9 million people at the time of independence in 1961, the population of Tanzania has been growing inexorably at a rate of over 3 per cent per year, until it has reached at the present a figure of nearly 27 million. This is a trebling in population: the economy must have trebled in order simply to have maintained income per capita.

Maintaining income per capita is all the Tanzanian economy has been capable of doing. Initially, in its first decade, the economy was able to expand at a rate faster than the population grew (see Table 5.1), so that GDP per capita (Table 5.2, column 2) rose, in terms of constant prices of 1987, from approximately TSh900, to a peak, in the years 1975/6, of TSh985 per year. At the present, income per capita is back at its original level. There are three times as many Tanzanians as at the time of independence, but individual Tanzanians, on the average, enjoy no higher a standard of living. In per capita terms, Tanzania's is not a growing but a static economy.

Other economic data, appearing in Tables 5.1–5.3, reveal that the era of rising incomes per capita, from independence until the mid-1970s, coincided with a growth of the industrial sector, whose share of GDP

Table 5.1 Tanzania: GDP 1971–1991

Year	GDP at market prices (billions current TSh)	GDP deflator (1987=100)	GDP (billions TSh constant prices of 1987)	Exchange rate (annual average conversion factor, TSh per $US)	GDP (billions current $US)
1971	9.8	7.8	126	7.14	1.37
1972	11.2	8.3	135	7.14	1.57
1973	13.1	9.1	144	7.02	1.87
1974	16.0	10.9	147	7.14	2.28
1975	19.0	12.5	152	7.37	2.58
1976	24.4	15.5	157	8.38	2.90
1977	28.9	18.3	158	8.29	2.48
1978	32.2	20.0	161	7.71	4.15
1979	36.3	22.0	165	8.22	4.41
1980	42.1	24.9	169	8.20	5.12
1981	45.6	26.7	171	8.28	5.90
1982	53.7	31.3	171	9.28	6.25
1983	64.4	37.8	170	11.14	6.32
1984	79.7	46.5	171	15.29	5.79
1985	105	59.0	178	17.47	6.81
1986	140	76.2	184	32.70	4.79
1987	193	100.0	193	64.26	3.20
1988	279	137.3	203	99.29	2.93
1989	369	175.2	211	143.38	2.60
1990	451	206.6	218	195.06	2.30
1991	600	265.0	226	219.16	2.74
1992	745p	318p	234p	n.a.	n.a.
1993	935p	383p	244p	n.a.	n.a.

Source: 1971–1991: World Bank, *World Tables 1991, 1993*
1992, 1993: Planning Commission/Ministry of Finance, n.d. Table 4.5, p. 19 and Table 4.2, p. 15
Note: ᵖ preliminary

Table 5.2 Tanzania: GNP per capita 1971–1991

Year	Population (millions)	GDP per capita (TSh at 1987 prices)	GNP per capita (current US dollars)	Average rate of growth of GDP
1971	13.9	905	100	3.9
1972	14.2	950	110	7.1
1973	14.6	985	120	6.2
1974	15.0	980	140	2.1
1975	15.4	985	160	4.0
1976	15.9	985	180	3.3
1977	16.4	968	190	0.0
1978	17.0	950	220	2.1
1979	17.5	944	250	2.5
1980	18.1	933	280	2.7
1981	18.7	915	300	–1.0
1982	19.3	885	310	–0.3
1983	19.9	853	320	–0.5
1984	20.5	835	310	4.6
1985	21.2	840	310	1.5
1986	21.8	843	270	5.4
1987	22.4	860	200	4.1
1988	23.0	880	150	5.2
1989	23.8	885	120	4.3
1990	24.5	890	94	4.5
1991	25.2	860	108	3.9
1992	25.9	904	n.a.	3.6
1993	26.6	915	n.a.	4.3

Sources: 1971–1991: World Bank, *World Tables 1993*
1992, 1993: author's estimates

reached a peak of nearly 13 per cent during the same period. Over the next ten years, industry declined in absolute amount: it is only in the latter half of the 1980s that the output of the industrial sector resumed its rise, although it has still to reach its peak of the mid-1970s as a proportion of GDP.

The decline of industry is one reason; many other reasons are given for Tanzania's relative decline since the mid-1970s, and some of them are quite obvious – a relative fall in the prices of Tanzania's agricultural exports, particularly that of coffee; the sudden eruption of war with Uganda in

Table 5.3 Tanzania: GDP by sector 1971–1991

Year	GDP (at factor cost, billions constant TSh 1987)	Agricultural product (at factor cost, billions constant TSh 1987)	Share of agriculture in GDP (%)	Industrial product (at factor cost, billions constant TSh 1987)	Share of industry in GDP (%)	Manufacturing product (at factor cost, billions constant TSh 1987)	Share of manufacturing in GDP (%)	Services (at factor cost, billions constant TSh 1987)	Share of services in GDP (%)
1971	130	84	64.6	17	13.1	9	6.9	31	23.8
1972	138	91	66.0	17	12.3	10	7.2	33	23.9
1973	143	92	64.4	18	12.6	11	8.0	35	24.5
1974	146	88	61.3	18	12.3	11	7.5	40	27.4
1975	155	96	61.9	18	11.6	11	7.1	42	27.1
1976	157	91	58.0	20	12.8	13	8.3	45	28.7
1977	158	92	58.2	19	12.0	12	7.6	46	29.1
1978	161	90	56.0	19	11.8	12	7.4	49	30.4
1979	165	91	55.0	20	12.1	13	7.9	51	30.9
1980	170	94	55.2	20	11.8	12	7.1	52	30.5
1981	169	95	56.2	18	10.7	11	6.5	53	31.4
1982	170	97	57.0	18	10.6	10	5.9	53	31.2
1983	166	99	59.7	15	9.0	9	5.4	52	31.3
1984	172	103	59.8	16	9.3	10	5.8	53	30.8
1985	179	110	61.5	16	8.9	9	5.0	53	29.6
1986	186	116	62.4	16	8.6	9	4.8	54	29.0
1987	193	121	62.8	16	8.3	9	4.7	56	29.1
1988	243	148	61.0	16	6.6	15	6.2	79	32.5
1989	310	193	62.4	16	5.2	15	4.8	101	32.4
1990	368	220	60.0	20	6.4	17	4.6	128	34.8
1991	487	296	60.9	25	5.1	20	4.1	165	33.9
1992	n.a.	152p	n.a.	n.a.	n.a.	n.a.	n.a.	n.a.	n.a.
1993	n.a.	159p	n.a.	n.a.	n.a.	n.a.	n.a.	n.a.	n.a.

Source: 1971–1991, columns 1, 2, 4, 6, 8: World Bank, World Tables, 1991, 1993
1992, 1993: column 2: Tanzania, Ministry of Agriculture, Livestock and Cooperatives, 1991

Note: P preliminary

1978/9 and the continued claims of the expanded Tanzanian army upon the output of the country; and the shortages, particularly of imported raw materials and spare parts, accompanying the reduction in foreign earnings. But, even severally, these explanations do not appear to be completely adequate; some blame must be levelled at the transfer of resources into the meeting of social needs, particularly that of employment in the cities. Here the figures in Tables 5.4–5.6 are revealing, for they show that an ever-increasing fraction of government expenditures are devoted to meeting current consumption. It is not that government expenditures as a whole have risen rapidly, nor that the government's budget deficits have increased substantially, but that increasing amounts of what the government is able to raise and to expend are devoted to meeting the costs of ever-expanding employment in the public and para-statal sectors. That these expenditures are at the expense of the development of the Tanzanian economy can be seen both in the total figures on gross investment (the final column of Table 5.4) and in the shares of total government expenditures allocated to those activities which raise productivity (the columns headed Agriculture, Education and Health in Table 5.6). Focusing on government expenditures, the shares of the total represented by expenditures on agriculture and education have both fallen proportionally by nearly half, from 14 per cent to 7 per cent and from 14 per cent to 8 per cent respectively. The main increases are in Defence expenditures and in the 'Other' in Table 5.6, which includes the wages and salaries of most civil servants and the amounts by which the para-statals fail to cover their wage and salary bills.

Tanzania's external accounts reveal the difficulties already mentioned. Looking at imports and exports (see Table 5.7) we see that exports in terms of current US dollars rose year by year to 1981. Simultaneously, imports rose, and by a much more rapid rate, so that in the year in which imports peaked, 1980, the country's balance of payments deficit was US$628 million, 75 per cent of export earnings. Thereafter, export earnings declined from the peak of US$809 million to a low of half that amount in 1985; subsequent years have shown little real improvement. Imports contracted by a lesser amount, but have resumed their rise and are now at their highest level ever. In spite of growing remittances from abroad, the deficit in the balance of payments seems inexorably to rise.

To explain why imports have been able to rise more rapidly than exports, and particularly why they rose again after 1983 when exports were barely increasing, one must turn to Tanzania's foreign borrowings and repayments. The deficit in the balance of payments over the years has been financed almost entirely by long term borrowings. These borrowings have been mainly official, through the offices of the international financial

Table 5.4 Tanzania: public, private and total investment as a percentage of GDP 1964/5–1991

Year	As a percentage of GDP		
	Public	*Private*	*Total*
1964/65	2.3	4.7	7.0
1966/69	5.6	4.7	10.3
1970	n.a.	n.a.	25.5
1971	15.9	2.9	26.4
1972	n.a.	n.a.	21.8
1973	n.a.	n.a.	21.1
1974	n.a.	n.a.	22.0
1975	13.4	7.3	21.1
1976	n.a.	n.a.	22.9
1977	n.a.	n.a.	26.1
1978	n.a.	n.a.	25.2
1979	14.6	12.9	26.1
1980	n.a.	n.a.	23.0
1981	n.a.	n.a.	20.6
1982	n.a.	n.a.	21.0
1983	n.a.	n.a.	13.6
1984	n.a.	n.a.	15.3
1985	n.a.	n.a.	15.7
1986	n.a.	n.a.	19.5
1987	n.a.	n.a.	22.8
1988	n.a.	n.a.	21.2
1989	n.a.	n.a.	n.a
1990	n.a.	n.a.	n.a.
1991	n.a.	n.a.	n.a.

Source: Public and private, as a percentage of GDP: Ndulu, 1988, Table 2, p. 46
Total, as a percentage of GDP: World Bank, *World Tables 1991, 1993*

agencies and developed countries (see Tables 5.8 and 5.9). The IMF has accounted for a very small portion of this; the World Bank for a larger portion, averaging approximately one-fifth. The remainder of the borrowings have been primarily bilateral, at least a substantial portion which have been in the form of export credits. External debt continues to rise, standing now at nearly US$7 billion. This represents roughly three times Tanzania's GDP. Relative to total exports, the servicing of Tanzania's debt comes out at approximately one-half, a figure higher than that of the other countries

Table 5.5 Tanzania: government revenues, expenditures, and total investment 1971–1991

Year	Government current revenue (billions current TSh)	Government current expenditure (billions current TSh)	Government surplus (+) or deficit (−) (billions current TSh)	Government capital payments (billions current TSh)	Government consumption (billions of current TSh)	Total gross domestic investment (billions of current TSh)	Total gross domestic investment (billions of TSh at 1987 prices)
1971	n.a.	n.a.	n.a.	n.a.	1.14	2.59	52
1972	1.8	1.6	−0.6	0.7	1.40	2.44	41
1973	2.3	2.1	−0.7	1.0	1.91	2.76	43
1974	3.2	2.9	−0.9	1.2	2.76	3.52	49
1975	4.2	4.4	−1.9	1.8	3.28	4.00	45
1976	4.4	4.3	−1.5	1.6	3.99	5.60	50
1977	5.9	5.2	−1.5	2.2	4.31	7.52	59
1978	6.8	5.9	−2.4	3.3	5.58	8.09	57
1979	7.4	8.2	−5.4	4.5	5.96	9.46	59
1980	8.5	7.5	−3.5	4.5	5.49	9.69	55
1981	10.3	9.0	−3.3	4.6	5.80	10.4	53
1982	n.a.	n.a.	n.a.	n.a.	7.1	11.7	58
1983	n.a.	n.a.	n.a.	n.a.	8.7	10.9	40
1984	20.1	18.5	−5.5	7.1	11.6	11.6	46
1985	n.a.	n.a.	n.a.	n.a.	16.2	16.3	50
1986	n.a.	n.a.	n.a.	n.a.	21	25.1	51
1987	n.a.	n.a.	n.a.	n.a.	25	50.0	50
1988	n.a.	n.a.	n.a.	n.a.	31	85.1	60
1989	n.a.	n.a.	n.a.	n.a.	41	106.1	72
1990	n.a.	n.a.	n.a.	n.a.	49	124.8	n.a.
1991/92	n.a.	n.a.	n.a.	n.a.	94	131.2	n.a.
1992/93	164	279	n.a.	n.a.	n.a.	n.a.	n.a.
1993/94	236	384	n.a.	n.a.	n.a.	n.a.	n.a.

Sources: 1969–1989: World Bank, World Tables, 1991, 1993
1992/93, 1993/94: Planning Commission/Ministry of Finance, n.d., Table 12.1, p. 99

Table 5.6 Tanzania: central government expenditures, share of total expenditures (%) by function 1976–1985

Year	Agriculture, forestry, fishing	Mining, manufacturing, construction	Transport and communication	Education	Health	Defence	Other	Total expenditures (millions of current TSh)
1976	14.0	2.0	6.3	14.0	7.1	12.1	45	5,969
1977	11.6	7.4	6.6	13.5	7.0	12.2	42	7,404
1978	9.3	8.7	5.5	14.5	7.3	14.8	40	9,131
1979	7.4	6.8	7.6	12.3	5.7	25.8	34	12,756
1980	10.9	11.6	9.2	13.3	6.0	9.2	40	12,102
1981	11.1	9.6	9.4	13.3	6.0	12.3	38	13,096
1982	7.0	8.5	8.1	12.4	5.4	12.5	46	18,427
1983	6.4	7.3	7.5	13.2	5.1	13.2	47	19,289
1984	7.4	6.3	6.0	11.7	5.5	12.8	50	21,461
1985	7.1	6.3	7.2	8.3	5.7	15.8	50	23,178

Source: IMF, 1990, *Government Finance Statistics Yearbook 1990*, Washington DC International Monetary Fund

Table 5.7 Tanzania: balance of payments 1971–1991

Year	Total exports of goods and services (millions of current US dollars)	Total imports of goods and services (millions of current US dollars)	Balance on current account (before official transfers) (millions of current US dollars)
1971	350	455	–102
1972	412	473	–76
1973	456	568	–127
1974	488	823	–346
1975	491	824	–321
1976	633	722	–78
1977	656	843	–167
1978	625	1,263	–614
1979	697	1,219	–492
1980	762	1,412	–628
1981	809	1,346	–514
1982	530	1,173	–617
1983	491	899	–389
1984	506	1,024	–455
1985	437	1,178	–506
1986	446	1,242	–545
1987	448	1,421	–742
1988	507	1,504	–765
1989	538	1,549	–825
1990	548	1,667	–955
1991	535	1,775	–832

Sources: 1971–1991: World Bank, *World Tables 1993*

we have studied; relative to GDP to over 10 per cent (see Table 5.9), again higher than comparable countries.

If the servicing of its debt is one of Tanzania's main problems, the relation that this bears to the inflow of capital to the country is another. On balance, as Table 5.10 reveals, capital continued to flow into the country until 1986. In the following year, there was a reversal, so that capital flowed out of the country in almost exactly the same amounts as had flowed inwards in previous years. This reversal of capital flow has occurred on both official and private transactions. Instead of Tanzania, a country in which capital is scarce, receiving capital from abroad, it became and has continued to be up to the present a net exporter of capital. In meeting its international financial obligations, Tanzania is acting as a good citizen of

Table 5.8 Tanzania: debt 1971–1991 (millions of current US dollars outstanding at end of year)

Year	External debt total	Long term debt total	Short term debt total	Private sector debt, total (Including non-guaranteed debt)
1971	258	258	0	20
1972	360	360	0	30
1973	495	495	0	46
1974	703	703	0	52
1975	889	889	0	57
1976	1,058	1,058	0	64
1977	1,448	1,289	159	65
1978	1,806	1,523	253	70
1979	2,101	1,851	250	80
1980	2,476	2,170	306	107
1981	2,622	2,321	301	94
1982	2,915	2,506	409	100
1983	3,136	2,675	461	94
1984	3,385	2,775	611	94
1985	3,752	3,034	718	50
1986	4,295	3,941	355	47
1987	5,142	3,654	488	56
1988	5,409	4,880	529	46
1989	5,349	4,993	356	45
1990	6,129	5,750	380	43
1991	6,460	5,941	519	42

Source: 1971–1991: World Bank, *World Tables 1993*

the world; in supplying capital to capital-rich institutions in the developed countries, Tanzania is perverting the world's allocation of resources.

THE STRUCTURAL ADJUSTMENT PROGRAMMES

There have been four distinct stages in Tanzania's attempts to improve the structure and performance of its economy: the National Economic Survival Programme (established in 1981), the Structural Adjustment Programme (1982), the Economic Recovery Programme (ERPI, 1986) and the Economic and Social Action Programme (ERPII, 1989).

The first major attempt by the Government to deal with unprecedented economic difficulties facing the country was the formulation of the National Economic Survival Programme (NESP) in 1981. The objectives of NESP

Table 5.9 Tanzania: debt servicing 1981–1990

Year	Official debt (millions of current US dollars)	Debt to IMF (millions current US dollars)	Debt to World Bank (IBRD/IDA) (millions current US dollars)	Total debt as a % of GDP	Service of debt, annual total (millions current US dollars)	Service of official debt (millions current US dollars)	Service of private debt (millions current US dollars)	Total debt service as a % of GDP	Total debt service as a % of total exports	Service of official debt, as a % of government expenditures
1981	1,850	99	529	53	n.a.	n.a.	n.a.	2.0	11.7	n.a.
1982	1,945	81	626	61	n.a.	n.a.	n.a.	1.6	15.7	n.a.
1983	2,208	51	699	68	77	47	28	1.5	15.8	n.a.
1984	2,201	24	749	68	68	54	14	1.3	14.2	n.a.
1985	2,509	21	818	75	65	55	10	1.2	15.0	2.9
1986	3,314	45	894	72	69	69	0	1.3	15.2	4.5
1987	n.a.	n.a.	n.a.	161	275	238	37	8.6	61.5	21.0
1988	n.a.	n.a.	n.a.	185	332	258	74	11.4	65.6	22.9
1989	n.a.	n.a.	n.a.	206	335	275	61	12.9	62.4	27.9
1990	n.a.	n.a.	n.a.	267	271	220	51	11.8	49.5	n.a.

Sources: Columns 1–3, 5–7: Strack and Schönherr, 1989
Column 10: for Government expenditures see Table 5.25, column 2; conversion to US dollars official rates of exchange (Table 5.1)

Table 5.10 Tanzania: net transfers from abroad 1981–1990 (millions of current US dollars)

Year	Total net transfers	Net transfers to official suppliers	Net transfers to private suppliers	Total flow of funds into country	Interest payments, as % of exports
1981	n.a.	n.a.	n.a.	293	n.a.
1982	n.a.	n.a.	n.a.	316	n.a.
1983	294	273	22	329	35
1984	162	127	35	190	29
1985	115	111	5	137	22
1986	116	116	1	143	26
1987	–114	–78	–36	n.a.	100
1988	–229	–155	–74	n.a.	130
1989	–264	–204	–61	n.a.	121
1990	–225	–174	–51	n.a.	111

Source: 1981–1990: Strack and Schönherr, 1989

included mounting an aggressive export drive in order to increase substantially foreign exchange earnings; saving on imports; eliminating food shortages; controlling of public spending in both government and para-statals; formulating development plans emphasizing consolidation of existing activities, in contrast to extension into new activities; and raising the productivity of the workers and farmers through appropriate incentive schemes. As a follow-up to these efforts, the government, with the help of an Independent Advisory Group, prepared a three-year Structural Adjustment Programme (1982/3–1984/5).

The main elements of the Structural Adjustment Programme could be said to comprise the provision of incentives and support for exporters of both traditional and non-traditional products; an articulation of specific priorities for cutbacks in the composition of future government recurrent and development expenditures; a reduction in the rate of monetary expansion through measures to restore overall economic balance, as well as strict financial controls of public sector expenditures; an improvement of efficiency in the para-statal sector, in some cases through the device of privatization; the rationalization of agricultural producer and ultimate consumer pricing policies; an increase in efficiency of transport, marketing and distribution services; and the effective use of external assistance, taking into consideration the nation's objectives as well as its investment priorities. In order to implement this programme, the government began to take measures at macro and sectoral levels, aimed primarily at consolidating and rehabilitating the national economy. The later programmes (ERPI and ERPII) have tended to repeat the elements in the original Structural Adjustment Programme.

Comprehensive as the measures in all the programmes may seem, from the point of view of the advancement of science and technology there are no instructions. That R&D should be conducted with more efficiency, both in governmental and para-statal enterprises, is implied, but no specific guidance is to be found. For that, one must turn to proposals for the furthering of R&D in the individual sectors of the Tanzanian economy.

The most impressive of the sectoral R&D programmes is that for agriculture (see Tanzania, Ministry of Agriculture, Livestock and Cooperatives, 1991, subsequently referred to as the *Masterplan*). Formulated by a 'Task Force' recruited from Tanzania's Ministry of Agriculture, the Planning Commission, the Treasury and the Civil Service, Sokoine Agricultural University and abroad (with a ratio of approximately two Tanzanians to each foreigner) the *Masterplan* is addressed to the difficulties facing agricultural R&D in Tanzania and to their elimination. It admits that the research system is run-down, and that substantial efforts will be needed to rehabilitate it, and recognizes that the Tanzanian government alone cannot accomplish the task. Foreign donors must be sought; their funding to be geared exclusively to the implementation of the *Masterplan* (*ibid*.: xii).

The *Masterplan* sets priorities for research. 'Due to the importance of agricultural export earnings for financing national development, research in export commodities was given special attention' (*ibid*.: xi, xii). With the emphasis placed on traditional exports, three of the commodities appearing in the set given highest priority are not surprising: they are coffee, cotton and tea. Completing the set of commodities given highest priority are rice and meat. Assigned to the second set are some of Tanzania's main food crops – maize, roots and tubers (cassava, sweet and round potatoes), beans, legumes, vegetables and oil seeds. The remaining main food crops – sorghum, bananas and wheat – appear in the third priority set.

In its discussion of financing, the *Masterplan* reveals the function of the priority sets: they are to determine the future allocation of resources to agricultural research. Research on crops in the first category will be rationalized and expanded, those in the second will continue at the present level, and those in the third will be '. . . de-emphasized, and resources currently applied to them might be re-allocated' (*ibid*.: x).

The resources applied to research in agriculture and livestock in Tanzania by the Ministry of Agriculture, at the time of the formulation of the *Masterplan*, comprised 50 research institutes, staffed by 3,375 employees, of whom 350 were scientists, 550 technicians and 760 assistants. Within the research institutes there were 22 crop commodity programmes, five livestock programmes, and six special programmes. In the interval between 1981 and the present, the numbers of institutes, employees and programmes have increased, as the Ministry has absorbed the research establishments of para-statal firms disbanded or privatized (e.g. coffee and tea). Ultimately, all public research in agriculture will be concentrated within the Ministry (with one exception, to which we shall shortly come).

The financial resources necessary to implement the *Masterplan* were estimated to be an injection of US$10 million for rehabilitation plus annual expenditures of US$7 million per year over the first seven-year period. Of the annual expenditures, a little over half (US$3.66 million, or TSh651 million at 1981 prices) were to be allocated to maintenance, supplies, publications, training and other non-wage current costs; and a little less than half (US$3.34 million, or TSh651 million) to the payments of salaries and wages. It was the first two items (rehabilitation and non-wage current costs) that had been beyond the ability of the Tanzanian government to finance; prior to the formulation of the *Masterplan* the government was hard pressed to meet even the salary and wage bill for the existing number of workers.

No such masterplan exists for research in any other sectors of the Tanzanian economy, probably because so little research has been undertaken there (either public or private). To be sure, there are development programmes for the industrial, transport, health and other sectors, but the attention devoted to research in these programmes is negligible. Our own sample of research institutions will not reflect the proportions in which R&D is carried out in the different sectors, however, since we covered only three institutes, out of the many whose activities fall within the agricultural sector, whereas we covered two industrial institutes, out of that sector's four.

R&D INSTITUTIONS

We shall now report on those R&D institutes which we visited: the first is the Tropical Pesticides Research Institute (abbreviated TPRI).

When Tanzania, Kenya and Uganda were British colonies, the colonial power established several research institutes, whose aim was to increase the production of exportable commodities. These research institutes continued to operate on an East African basis until the break-up of the Community in 1977, when the individual member nations took over the responsibility for those establishments physically located in their own country. The Tropical

Pesticides Research Institute was one such institute, and its control descended to the Tanzanian government.

Having acquired an agricultural research institute of a size previously sufficient for three countries, the Tanzanian government continued to operate it at the same scale: by the same scale is meant with the same staff, but not with the same intensity of effort. As time passed and the Tanzanian government's revenues fell, relative to the needs of the expanded population, the amounts allocated to research institutes fell in line. From supporting not only the staff but a full range of activities, the Tanzanian government's contributions to TPRI reached the stage by 1985/6 where they were capable of meeting little more than the bill for wages and salaries. Almost all other activities had ceased: subscriptions to foreign journals and books were allowed to lapse, capital expenditures were minimal and current expenditures for such items as maintenance, laboratory supplies and travel were severely curtailed.

In these senses TPRI was typical of the research institutes designated for rehabilitation under the agricultural *Masterplan*. Under the terms of the *Masterplan*, 'TPRI should retain responsibility for research work in bird pests, rodents and weeds. It should also continue work on the pathology of stored products and seeds, in particular research on control of large grain borer' (*ibid.*: 24, 5). Other work on etymology and pathology of crops, as well as research on ticks and the tsetse fly, is scheduled to be transferred to the appropriate crop and animal research institutes. These transfers will free resources at TPRI, resources which may then be re-assigned, either at TPRI to increased work screening, registering and testing new pesticides, or to employment at other research institutes.

TPRI is not typical of Tanzanian agricultural research institutes in that it was semi-autonomous, drawing public funds and conforming generally to governmental rules and regulations but, alone of all the rest, administratively outside the Ministry of Agriculture. This status, which is confirmed in the *Masterplan*, enables its Director General to solicit donations from abroad; it also confers on its organization a certain flexibility and on its planning a certain autonomy, attributes which are appreciated and which lead to greater productivity.

Nonetheless, given the financial constraints under which TPRI, like the other research institutes, operates, it is very difficult for the scientists and technicians to maintain current programmes, let alone undertake research in new areas. With minimal regular contact with the outside world, either through published material or through official exchanges of personnel, the chief way in which the scientists obtain knowledge of research conducted outside TPRI is through their own personal contacts. These are broader than might be expected, for many of the former employees of TPRI have taken jobs abroad, the majority in those other African countries which devote greater amounts of money to agricultural research, the minority to research organizations in the developed countries. With their former colleagues, the scientists at TPRI maintain close ties. In addition to personal contacts, there is some information gained in attending conferences within Tanzania, for whose attendance some funds are allocated.

The existence of a research institute staffed with well-educated people and the inheritor of a large amount of previous research on the pests and diseases that afflict African agricultural commodities has been observed by foreign assistance organizations. Wishing to encourage research into pesticides, and reassured by Tanzania's acquiesence to the conditions imposed by the IMF and the World Bank, foreign donors are helping to finance research undertaken at TPRI. Table 5.11 identifies foreign donations, commencing in 1985/6, as well as Tanzanian government contributions, among TPRI's budgets for the last several years.

Tanzanian government funds are identified, under the headings of 'Recurrent' and 'Development': recurrent expenditures are those allocated to the hiring or purchase of current inputs, of which in recent years nearly 90 per cent has been for wages and salaries. Development expenditures are primarily those devoted to the acquisition of buildings and equipment; most foreign donations are also for developmental purposes. So long as foreign donations continue to be received by TPRI, its future is secure. If foreign donations continue at their present rate, TPRI may be able to rebuild its library, to re-institute the programme of advanced studies abroad for its members, purchase modern analytical equipment and increase its contacts with those who apply pesticides in agriculture.

Unlike TPRI, the Centre for Agricultural Mechanization and Rural Technology (CAMARTEC), the second research institute studied, is a creation of the Tanzanian government, with the directive to develop machinery and other artifacts useful in, and appropriate for, Tanzania's agricultural sector. Employing approximately ten engineers and 30 technicians, as well as an administrative staff of equal numbers, CAMARTEC is organized so as to undertake R&D projects, the emphasis being on development rather than research. Within each project, its activities fall into two categories, the first being the development of the technology underlying the product, and the second being the manufacture of a sufficient number of products in order to disseminate the results. The projects undertaken by CAMARTEC lie in the fields of agricultural mechanization, water supply, building construction, sanitation, rural transport and energy conservation. A typical project is the two-wheeled cart, whose specifications are

Table 5.11 Tanzania: budgets for the Tropical Pesticides Research Institute (TPRI) 1983/4–1993/4 (millions TSh)

| Year | Public expenditures of the government of Tanzania (current TSh) ||||||| Foreign donors (current TSh) || Total expenditures ||
| | Recurrent expenditures ||| Development expenditures ||| Total public expenditures | Requests | Actual | (Current TSh) | (Constant TSh)[a] |
	Requests	Approved	Actual	Requests	Approved	Actual					
1983/4	13	12	12	54	7	5	17	–	–	17	45
1984/5	20	17	16	7	4	7	23	–	–	23	49
1985/6	24	20	18	14	8	3	21	n.a.	6	27	46
1986/7	27	21	21	22	20	10	31	n.a.	15	46	60
1987/8	60	33	33	34	34	35	68	n.a.	1	69	69
1988/9	84	80	82	46	29	–	82	n.a.	–	82	60
1989/90	161	151	151	46	10	–	151	–	7	158	90
1990/1	167	152	151	71	5	–	151	13	9	160	78
1991/2	181	185	179	115	38	32	211	6	14	225	85
1992/3	273	191	n.a.	96	41	71	260p	29	10	270p	85
1993/4	170	195	n.a.	n.a.	n.a.	n.a.	n.a.	n.a.	n.a.	n.a.	n.a.

Notes: p Preliminary
a Current TSh converted to constant prices by the GDP deflator (Table 5.1)

that it be capable of hauling heavy agricultural produce over rough ground, that its manufacture uses materials available locally, and that its sale be at a price lower than that for imported carts. The design and construction of prototypes has occupied CAMARTEC a considerable time; the most unusual element in the design being the hub of the cart's two wheels, comprised of a basin-like plate of steel (instead of spokes) and a simple set of bearings constructed locally. Combined with used car tyres and a wooden frame, both materials available locally, and an axle constructed out of tubular steel, the cart was complete. A few finished carts have been sold locally, and as the technology improves, a larger number will be manufactured. Since CAMARTEC is located on the main railway line to the coast, physical distribution within northeastern Tanzania will be relatively inexpensive.

Like TPRI, CAMARTEC has had some success in attracting foreign donations. These have taken the form chiefly of equipment, each foreign donor giving items manufactured in its own country. The pieces of foreign equipment are relatively simple and are divided roughly half and half between those useful in testing new products and those useful in their manufacture. A continued flow of funds from foreign donors will be necessary in order to maintain CAMARTEC's competence, and much of the success in securing these funds will depend upon the efforts of CAMARTEC's Director.

Differing markedly from TPRI and CAMARTEC, and from the two industrial research institutes still to be described, is the Village Oil Press Project. It lies outside the orbit of public research, being the creation of two American charitable bodies, Lutheran World Relief (New York) and Appropriate Technology International (Washington, DC). Operating under their benign authority, it has a tiny staff, comprising only of six persons (the Director, Lynn Schleuter; the Senior Field Manager, Dallas Granima; three Field Managers and a secretary), all of whom are talented, versatile, mobile and dedicated to the project. It concentrates on the production, sale and use of a single commodity – a cheap, portable hand-operated press for oil-bearing crops, with potentially universal application in rural communities; it devotes as much attention to the operation of the presses in the villages as to their design, manufacture and distribution (i.e. it carries out the functions of product design and promotion; market research and testing; equipment purchasing and sub-contracting; and quality control, as well as conventional R&D); and it is, by any measure, a splendid success. Its success is evident from reading its progress reports (see, e.g. Schleuter, 1993), and has been celebrated extensively in print (Hyman, 1993). The project is to be replicated in Uganda, and most likely other Sub-Saharan African countries.

Table 5.12 Tanzania: budgets for the Centre for Agricultural Mechanization and Rural Technology (CAMARTEC) 1983/4–1993/4 (millions TSh)

| | Public expenditures of the government of Tanzania (current TSh) | | | | | | | | | Total expenditures | |
| | Recurrent expenditures | | | Development expenditures | | | Total governmental expenditures | Foreign donors | | | |
Year	Requests	Approved	Actual	Requests	Approved	Actual		Requests	Actual	Current TSh	Constant TSh at 1987 prices
1983/4	4	4	4	10	25	10	14	n.a.	1	15	40
1984/5	5	4	5	4	28	4	9	n.a.	2	11	24
1985/6	13	9	7	26	8	7	14	n.a.	–	14	24
1986/7	12	10	9	42	23	19	28	n.a.	–	28	37
1987/8	18	13	12	52	21	21	33	n.a.	n.a.	33+	33+
1988/9	15	18	19	103	22	24	43	n.a.	21	64	46
1989/90	50	24	24	160	32	22	46	n.a.	40	86	49
1990/1	51	27	25	130	46	38	63	n.a.	40	103	50
1991/2	n.a.	31	18	n.a.	28	28	46	n.a.	69	115	43
1992/3	n.a.	41	n.a.	n.a.	65	n.a.	106p	n.a.	n.a.	106+	33+
1993/4	n.a.	37	n.a.	n.a.	40	n.a.	77p	n.a.	n.a.	77+	20+

Source: CAMARTEC (except for foreign donations for 1991/2, for which the source is UNDP 1993, Table C.3, p. 108)

Notes: p = preliminary
+ = greater than the amount listed, by the (unknown) amounts of foreign donations

One of the Tanzanian government's two research institutes directed towards industry is the Tanzanian Industrial R&D Organization (TIRDO). Like CAMARTEC, TIRDO was established by the Tanzanian government itself, after it secured its independence. TIRDO therefore has a much shorter history than TPRI, and a more tentative place among Tanzania's public research institutes. Located in a tranquil setting outside the city of Dar es Salaam, in buildings half-completed, TIRDO is a relatively small institution with relatively little support. As can be seen from Table 5.13 the resources which TIRDO has at its disposal each year, for nearly all of industry, amount to no more than TPRI has at its disposal for research into pesticides alone. The number of industrial research projects undertaken by TIRDO is, therefore, relatively few. Like TPRI and CAMARTEC, TIRDO is dependent upon foreign donations for much of its capital expenditures; unlike these two, TIRDO's receipts from foreign bodies are very small, except for the year 1988/9. The Director of TIRDO, like his counterpart at TPRI, is permitted to approach foreign assistance bodies personally, but he has found a less encouraging welcome than have directors of the agricultural research institutes. It appears that foreign donors prefer to support R&D in agriculture rather than in industry.

The other research institute directed towards industry is the Tanzania Engineering and Manufacturing Design Organization (TEMDO). Located not in Dar es Salaam but in Arusha, TEMDO is of comparable size to TIRDO, employing a staff of 70, including 11 mechanical engineers, three draughtsmen, and 14 technicians. Its income is also comparable to TIRDO's, although half of TEMDO's is earned through the sale of wood joinery and the provision of technical designs and training for outside organizations, whereas TIRDO has no commercial undertakings. TEMDO's involvement in commerce has the merit of keeping it alert to the practicality of its R&D work.

TEMDO's budgets for the most recent 11 years are shown in Table 5.14. The amounts of foreign assistance are not available, being included within the general figures for the Ministry of Industries and Trade, but it is known that the Swedish International Development Agency (SIDA) has provided outside financial support, and that a German assistance agency is currently involved in negotiations over the establishment in TEMDO of educational and training programmes emphasizing the role of maintenance in Tanzanian industry, a much neglected activity (Mjema and Kundi, 1993).

This completes our brief studies of a sample of Tanzanian R&D organizations. The four public research institutes that we investigated represent a fairly substantial sample of the total in Tanzania. The industrial research organizations (TIRDO and TEMDO) and the research institute

Table 5.13 Tanzania: budgets for the Centre for the Tanzanian Industrial Research Organization (TIRDO) 1983/4–1993/4 (millions TSh)

Public expenditures of the government of Tanzania (current TSh)

Year	Recurrent expenditures			Development expenditures			Total public expenditures	Foreign donors		Total expenditures	
	Requests	Approved	Actual	Requests	Approved	Actual		Requests	Actual	Current TSh	Constant TSh
1983/4	n.a.	n.a.	3	25	–	–	3	n.a.	–	3	8
1984/5	n.a.	3	3	32	20	20	23	n.a.	–	23	49
1985/6	n.a.	4	4	n.a.	10	13	17	n.a.	1	18	31
1986/7	n.a.	6	4	55	47	49	53	n.a.	3	56	73
1987/8	n.a.	7	8	55	33	33	41	n.a.	3	44	44
1988/9	n.a.	13	13	68	42	12	25	n.a.	56	81	59
1989/90	n.a.	21	21	77	45	45	66	n.a.	3	69	40
1990/1	n.a.	25	26	84	38	28	54	n.a.	–	54	26
1991/2	n.a.	31	31	n.a.	67	n.a.	98p	n.a.	–	98	37
1992/3	n.a.	39	n.a.	n.a.	85	n.a.	124p	n.a.	–	124	39
1993/4	n.a.	45	n.a.	n.a.	90	n.a.	n.a.	n.a.	–	n.a.	n.a.

Source: Tanzanian Industrial Research Organization (except for 1991/2, whose source is UNDP, 1993, Table C.3, p. 115)

Table 5.14 Tanzania: budgets for the Tanzanian Engineering and Manufacturing Design Organization (TEMDO) 1983/4–1993/4 (millions TSh)

Public expenditures of the government of Tanzania (millions of current TSh)

| Year | Recurrent expenditures | | | Development expenditures | | | Total public expenditures | Foreign donors | | Total expenditures | |
	Requests	Approved	Actual	Requests	Approved	Actual		Requests	Actual	Current TSh	Constant TSh
1983/4	n.a.	2	v2	n.a.	4	v4	v6	–	–	v6	v16
1984/5	n.a.	3	v3	n.a.	3	v3	v6	–	–	v6	v13
1985/6	n.a.	4	v4	n.a.	20	v20	v24	–	–	v24	v41
1986/7	n.a.	5	v5	n.a.	38	v38	v43	–	–	v43	v56
1987/8	n.a.	7	v7	n.a.	37	v37	v44	–	–	v44	v44
1988/9	n.a.	n.a.	n.a.	n.a.	n.a.	n.a.	n.a.	–	–	n.a.	n.a.
1989/90	21	10	v10	139	55	v55	v65	n.a.	n.a.	65+	37+
1990/1	21	12	v12	115	48	v48	v60	n.a.	n.a.	60+	29+
1991/2	30	14	v14	184	44	v44	v58	n.a.	n.a.	58+	22+
1992/3	52	18	n.a.	147	55	n.a.	73p	n.a.	n.a.	73+	23+
1993/4	45	19	n.a.	210	70	n.a.	89p	n.a.	n.a.	89+	23+

Source: TEMDO

Notes: The symbols: v signifies 'approximately'
                     p signifies 'preliminary'
                     + signifies 'more than'

devoted to developing appropriate technology (CAMARTEC) are under the authority of the Ministry of Industry and Trade; their number is augmented by two others – the Institute of Production Innovation (attached to the University of Dar es Salaam) and the Tanzania Bureau of Standards. The pesticides research institute (TPRI) is one of many research institutes in the field of agriculture, the remainder now within the purlieu of government. There are two more public R&D institutes in the field of health, and equal numbers in natural resources and construction. As in Kenya, there is also an umbrella organization, the Tanzania Commission for Science and Technology (COSTECH), which oversees the country's R&D and helps to coordinate activities (see Goka *et al.* 1990: 206–314).

From the macro-economic statistics and from our remarks on the conduct of R&D, one would infer that R&D in Tanzania is not flourishing. Yet, two independent studies of Tanzania's relative achievements in conducting R&D suggest that Tanzania's contributions are relatively greater than our evidence indicates. Both studies are attempts to measure the output of R&D, rather than, as in our case, the inputs to R&D. The first is that of Manuel Zymelman (Zymelman, 1990). Zymelman reported the results of a study conducted at the World Bank on education in, and the pursuit of, science and technology in Sub-Saharan Africa. Combing through published research findings, a feat involving considerable effort, he was able to produce an index of scientific and technological research output. The source of the data was the Science Citation Index, published by the Institute of Scientific Information. (The Index covers eight major areas: Clinical Medicine, Bio-medical Research, Biology, Chemistry, Physics, Earth and Space, Engineering and Technology, and Mathematics.) An Activity Index was calculated on the basis of the share in the total of scientific publications accruing to each country.

In the overall compilation, Tanzania stood fifth among Sub-Saharan African countries, with 4 per cent of the total. Within its total, Tanzania ranked above average in clinical medicine and biology; equal in engineering and technology; and lower than average in the other five areas. When allowance is made for its level of GDP, Tanzania excelled in R&D in clinical medicine, biology and engineering and technology; but was lower in the other areas.

The second survey of achievements in R&D was conducted by the United Nations Industrial Development Organization (UNIDO, 1988 and 1990 as reported in Saha, 1991: 2759, Table 4). From among the 26 Sub-Saharan African countries for which data were gathered, and in both the years surveyed, 1970 and 1987, Tanzania achieved the second highest 'Technology Score', exceeded only by Angola. In UNIDO's method of measuring the overall output of science and technology – 'Lines of Engineering Production' – Tanzania again stood second, with eight 'lines' in 1970, eight also in 1980, and 13 in 1987. Again, only Angola exceeded Tanzania among Sub-Saharan African countries in the numbers of types of capital goods manufactured. These independent studies seem to agree that advances in science and technology in Tanzania are greater than economic statistics would suggest.

EDUCATION IN SCIENCE AND TECHNOLOGY

Education in science and technology is provided at three different levels: university, technical college and vocational courses. In Tanzania there are two universities, one at Dar es Salaam with multiple faculties, and one at Sokoine, in the central part of the country, devoted entirely to agriculture. Together they graduate approximately 1,700 engineers and scientists each year (COSTECH, 1990: 18, Table 5.1). Of technical colleges there are four, one each in Dar es Salaam, Arusha, Mbeya and Zanzibar. Their graduates number some 1,900 annually. Vocational courses are provided in a range of institutes, of which the largest number are post-primary technical training centres, simple establishments teaching crafts to children who have terminated their formal schooling (see Table 5.15 for a list of institutions and enrolments, as of 1986). They currently turn out around 12,000 graduates

Table 5.15 Tanzania: numbers of vocational training establishments and enrolments (as of 1986)

Type of institution	Number of establishments	Enrolments (number annually)	Graduations (number annually)
Local post-primary technical training centres	313	4,200	3,570
Technical secondary schools	10	790	790
Tanzania Parents Association Technical Schools	35	2,000	1,700
Mission/church trade schools	n.a.	700	665
Company/para-statal training programmes	n.a.	210	200
Folk development centres	52	2,600	2,210
Government vocational training centres	17	2,250	2,140
Totals	527+	12,750	11,625

Source: Mlawa and Sheya, 1990, Table 4.1, p. 56

per year, with quite varied levels of technical skills. All told, Tanzania adds to its workforce approximately 16,000 technically trained people annually.

Compared to its needs, the country's provision of technically and scientifically skilled persons is inadequate. Estimates made in 1986 of shortfalls in the graduation of scientists, engineers, technicians and craftsmen (corresponding to graduates of universities, technical colleges and vocational training establishments) for the four categories were 70 per cent, 59 per cent, 65 per cent and 58 per cent respectively, for an average over all the skills of 60 per cent (*ibid.*: 66, Table 6.3). The situation is no better today; it may be worse, because of the emigration of Tanzanian scientists, engineers and technicians to neighbouring countries offering higher wages.

It was within this context that the data on the budgets of the two universities (Tables 5.16 and 5.17 for the University of Dar es Salaam and Sokoine Agricultural University) and, collectively, the four technical colleges (Table 5.18) were gathered. The figures for government expenditures, both Recurrent and Development, both Approvals and Actual, are reasonably accurate, but the figures for foreign donations are woefully understated.

The reason for the understatements is that most of the funds granted by foreign donors are directed to, and expended by, individual faculty members – scientists, engineers, economists and others – or teams of such faculty members. The administrations of the universities are not informed of the sums involved, and so cannot include them in their annual budgetary submissions. Figures on total foreign donations, assembled from data provided by the donors themselves, indicate that receipts are of the order of ten to 20 times the amounts listed in Tables 5.16 and 5.17. According to the budgets in Tables 5.16 and 5.17, the University of Dar es Salaam and Sokoine Agricultural University together received TSh59 million in the fiscal year 1989/90, TSh480 in 1990/1, and TSh430 million in 1991/2. According to the donors, they gave US$15,224,000 in the calendar year 1989 for tertiary education and US$22,963,000 for technical and managerial education and training, or a total of US$38,187,000 (UNDP, 1992: 42, Table 4.1). Totals for 1990 and 1991 were US$48,861,000 and 36,687,000 respectively. Converting the US$ to TSh at the average exchange rates in Table 5.1 yields donations of TSh4,230 million for 1989, TSh9,550 million for 1990, and TSh8,050 million for 1991. These make the universities' budgetary totals of TSh59 million, TSh480 million and TSh430 million seem very paltry: the conclusion is that most foreign donations to universities and their members are unrecorded in official statistics. To be sure, the donors figures include money destined for technical colleges and vocational programmes (within UNDP's category 'technical and managerial education and training'), but the amounts the

Table 5.16 Tanzania: budgets for the University of Dar es Salaam 1983/4–1993/4 (millions of TSh)

Public expenditures of the government of Tanzania (current TSh)

Year	Recurrent expenditures			Development expenditures			Total public expenditures	Foreign donors (current TSh)		Total expenditures	
	Requests	Approved	Actual	Requests	Approved	Actual		Requests	Actual	Current TSh	Constant TSh
1983/4	n.a.	n.a.	294	n.a.	n.a.	13	307	n.a.	14	321	850
1984/5	376	272	302	n.a.	9	8	310	8	16	326	648
1985/6	419	326	340	n.a.	n.a.	17	357	n.a.	59	416	705
1986/7	503	446	467	n.a.	32	32	499	103	76	575	755
1987/8	822	501	562	n.a.	39	n.a.	v600	96	n.a.	v650	v650
1988/9	1,235	801	775	n.a.	23	n.a.	795	211	n.a.	v895	v652
1989/90	2,418	1,303	1,510	n.a.	51	49	1,559	26	18	1,577	892
1990/1	4,802	2,004	1,061	n.a.	114	106	1,167	504	470	1,637	789
1991/2	n.a.	2,641	3,259	n.a.	213	116.	3,375	500	430	3,805	1,437
1992/3	n.a.	3,711	n.a.	n.a.	177	n.a.	3,888p	880	n.a.	4,768p	1,499p
1993/4	n.a.	3,066	n.a.	n.a.	124	n.a.	3,190p	1,016	n.a.	4,206p	1,100p

Sources: 1983/4–1991/2: University of Dar es Salaam
1992/3, 1993/4: Government of Tanzania, Annual Budgets

Notes: v signifies 'approximately'
p signifies preliminary

Table 5.17 Tanzania: budgets for the Agricultural University of Sokoine 1983/4–1993/4 (millions of TSh)

Public expenditures of the government of Tanzania (current TSh)

Year	Recurrent expenditures			Development expenditures			Total public expenditures	Foreign donors (current TSh)		Total expenditures	
	Requests	Approved	Actual	Requests	Approved	Actual		Requests	Actual	Current TSh	Constant TSh
1983/4	n.a.	n.a.	–	n.a.	n.a.	13	13,307	–	22	35	93
1984/5	n.a.	96	5	n.a.	11	10	15	33	18	33	66
1985/6	n.a.	136	127	n.a.	n.a.	10	137	n.a.	44	181	307
1986/7	n.a.	168	n.a.	n.a.	11	9	v160	59	39	v199	v262
1987/8	n.a.	256	267	n.a.	41	n.a.	v300	40	n.a.	v320	v320
1988/9	n.a.	374	327	n.a.	90	n.a.	v370	222	n.a.	v510	v371
1989/90	n.a.	491	601	n.a.	60	111	712	1	41	753	430
1990/1	n.a.	666	353	n.a.	114	n.a.	v440	n.a.	10	v450	v218
1991/2	n.a.	889	1,017	n.a.	141	104	1,121	–	–	1,121	420
1992/3	n.a.	1,210	n.a.	n.a.	230	n.a.	1,440p	–	–	1,440p	456p
1993/4	n.a.	1,520	n.a.	n.a.	116	n.a.	1,636p	648	n.a.	2,284p	597p

Source: Government of Tanzania, Annual Budget

Notes: v signifies 'approximately'
  p signifies preliminary

Table 5.18 Tanzania: budgets for the technical colleges 1983/4–1993/4 (millions of TSh)

Public expenditures of the government of Tanzania (current TSh)

Year	Recurrent expenditures			Development expenditures			Total public expenditures	Foreign donors (current TSh)		Total expenditures	
	Requests	Approved	Actual	Requests	Approved	Actual		Requests	Actual	Current TSh	Constant TSh
1983/4	n.a.	n.a.	18	n.a.	n.a.	42	60	n.a.	–	60	159
1984/5	n.a.	n.a.	18	n.a.	n.a.	63	81	n.a.	1	82	163
1985/6	n.a.	n.a.	31	n.a.	n.a.	52	83	n.a.	1	84	142
1986/7	n.a.	n.a.	42	n.a.	92	92	134	29	29	163	214
1987/8	n.a.	n.a.	57	n.a.	100	100	157	1	1	158	158
1988/9	n.a.	n.a.	73	n.a.	130	130	203	13	13	216	157
1989/90	n.a.	n.a.	140	n.a.	240	240	380	4	4	384	219
1990/1	n.a.	n.a.	97	n.a.	295	220	317	28	24	341	165
1991/2	n.a.	789	407	n.a.	100	100	507	50	–	507	192
1992/3	n.a.	998	n.a.	n.a.	132	n.a.	1,130p	–	n.a.	1,130p	349p
1993/4	n.a.	1,159	n.a.	n.a.	167	n.a.	1,326p	12	n.a.	1,338p	350p

Source: Technical College, Arusha, and Government of Tanzania, Annual Budgets

Note: p signifies 'preliminary'

secondary level institutions receive is far less than that received by the tertiary level institutions, as the data in Tables 5.16, 5.17 and 5.18 reveal. We must conclude that the Tanzanian universities' financial position is considerably better than indicated by their recorded income figures, at least so far as their individual faculty members are concerned.

Unfortunately for us, foreign donations are not broken down by faculty or department, neither in the universities' budgets nor by the donors. Our disappointment arises because we would like to have comparable figures for the engineering and 'hard' science departments, in the one hand, and for the 'soft' science departments, on the other. Denied these, we cannot document with statistics our impression that financing the universities partly with foreign donations leads to a very uneven allocation of funds among departments. Receiving the favourable attentions of foreign donors, the Engineering Faculty of the University of Dar es Salaam has prospered in several ways: the salaries of its staff have been augmented, raising them above the abysmal levels of those dependent entirely on Tanzanian government's emoluments; new laboratories have been built and equipment procured; foreign publications have been subscribed to; and foreign study leave granted. Within the Faculty of Science, the Chemistry Department has also been well-favoured.

The Mathematics Department has received none of these supplements. Dependent solely upon funds received through Tanzania's government budget, the Mathematics Department has not been able to maintain its numbers, let alone prosper. (In 1991/2, Mathematics' approved estimates for other than wage costs was one-fifth, in 1992/3 one-seventh, that of Chemistry's.) Over the nine years 1983–1991, eight professional mathematicians resigned from the department (out of a total of 93 departures from the university as a whole during the same period); of the 14 established posts within the Mathematics Department, only seven are currently occupied.

From the University of Dar es Salaam, academic mathematicians leave in two directions: some find academic posts in universities abroad, chiefly in other Sub-Saharan African countries such as Zambia and Botswana; others move into the private sector, where they find employment as applied mathematicians, usually in accountancy. Those remaining at the university are overloaded, for mathematics continues to be one of the basic subjects in all scientific fields, and they teach ever-larger classes. An increasing number of the lectures are delivered by graduate students. Looking at the university as a whole, one concludes that teaching of science and technology is advancing in the applied areas, but suffering in the theoretical areas. Among those foreigners who make donations to the university, it appears as if the contributions which science and engineering can make to

Tanzania's economy are appreciated, but the contributions made by those who teach scientists and engineers are not. Whether or not science and technology will advance faster, if larger numbers of less well-taught scientists and engineers are graduated, is a moot point.

ESTIMATES OF THE RESOURCES DEVOTED TO THE PURSUIT OF SCIENCE AND TECHNOLOGY

We are now in a position to estimate the expenditures in Tanzania devoted to advancing science and technology. We shall proceed by aggregation: first we will add up the Recurrent Expenditures of government institutions, both R&D institutes and universities and the technical colleges. Our aggregations, covering the years since 1983/4 to the present will then be spliced to COSTECH's, covering the years 1978/9–1988/9, yielding a continuous and quite accurate series from the first of these years, 1978/9, to the current year 1993/4. Table 5.19 provides Recurrent Expenditures on science and technology for the universities and technical colleges: the main assumptions are that 70 per cent of the University of Dar es Salaam's expenditures are on science and technology (this being the percentage of 'other costs' spent on the Engineering and Science Faculties) and that all of Sokoine Agricultural University's and the technical colleges' are.

The universities' and technical colleges' recurrent expenditures are carried over to Table 5.20, where they are joined with those of the R&D institutes which we visited. The totals can be compared with COSTECH's, which purport to cover the universities, the technical colleges and all R&D institutes. Since ours are higher for all but one of the comparable years (1983/4–1988/9) we prefer them. (Ours for the R&D institutes are biased downwards because not all institutes are covered in our sample; but the figures for the universities and technical colleges may be biased upwards, because of our questionable allocation of most of the total expenditures of the University of Dar es Salaam to science and technology.)

The final column of Table 5.20 gives total Recurrent Expenditures on science and technology financed by the Tanzanian government in terms of constant prices; i.e. in real terms (the conversion is carried out by application of the GDP deflator in Table 5.1, and by assumption that the 1987 value of 100 applies to the fiscal year 1987/8). Looking at the series, we see that expenditures have approximately doubled in real terms, from an average of roughly TSh500 million (in 1987 prices) in the late 1970s to twice that at the end of the 1980s. The prospect for the early 1990s is a further increase.

When we add in to public expenditures on Recurrent items those on Development items as well, we produce the figures in Tables 5.21 (for the

Table 5.19 Tanzania: total expenditures of universities and technical colleges on science and technology 1983/4–1993/4 (millions of current and constant TSh)

| Year | Universities' income from government (current TSh) | | | | | | | Estimate of technical colleges' recurrent plus development expenditures | Total government expenditures on S&T in higher education | | Foreign donors' support, total (current TSh) | Total expenditures on S&T in higher education | |
| | University of Dar es Salaam recurrent expenditures | | Sokoine Agricultural University recurrent expenditures on S&T | Total university recurrent expenditures on S&T | Development expenditures | | Total of universities' recurrent plus development expenditures | | | | | | |
	Total	on S&T			University of Dar es Salaam	Sokoine			Current TSh	Constant TSh of 1987		Current TSh	Constant TSh of 1987
1983/4	307	214	–	214	13	13	240	60	300	794	96	396	1,048
1984/5	310	216	5	221	8	10	239	81	320	688	116	436	938
1985/6	357	249	127	376	17	10	403	83	486	825	187	673	1,048
1986/7	499	349	160	509	32	9	550	134	684	899	278	962	1,262
1987/8	600	420	267	687	38	33	758	157	915	915	n.a.	915+	915+
1988/9	795	555	327	882	20	43	945	203	1,148	835	n.a.	1,148+	835+
1989/90	1,559	1,090	601	1,691	49	111	1,841	380	2,221	1,268	4,230	6,451	3,680
1990/1	1,167	817	353	1,170	106	87	1,363	317	1,680	814	9,550	11,230	5,440
1991/2	3,375	2,360	1,017	3,377	116	104	3,597	507	4,104	1,550	8,050	12,154	4,580
1992/3	3,711p	2,595p	1,210p	3,805p	177p	230p	4,212p	1,130p	5,342p	1,680	n.a.	5,342+	1,680+
1993/4	3,066p	2,170	1,520p	3,690p	124p	116p	3,930p	1,326p	5,256p	1,373	n.a.	5,256+	1,373+

Sources: Tables 5.16–5.18: for foreign donations in 1989, 1990 and 1991, see text

Notes: p signifies 'preliminary'
+ signifies 'more than'

Table 5.20 Tanzania: estimates of recurrent expenditures on science and technology 1978/9–1993/4 (millions of TSh)

	Recurrent expenditures on science and technology (millions of current TSh)						Total recurrent expenditures (millions of constant TSh of 1987)
	Enumerated institutions' recurrent expenditures			Recurrent expenditures as derived by COSTECH	Ratio of COSTECH to total for enumerated institutions	Estimates of total: COSTECH till 1982/3; own thereafter	
Year	R&D institutes	Universities and technical colleges	Total				
1978/9	n.a.	n.a.	n.a.	97	n.a.	97	465
1979/80	n.a.	n.a.	n.a.	85	n.a.	85	390
1980/1	n.a.	n.a.	n.a.	136	n.a.	136	546
1981/2	n.a.	n.a.	n.a.	145	n.a.	145	544
1982/3	n.a.	n.a.	n.a.	200	n.a.	200	640
1983/4	21	232	253	228	0.90	253	668
1984/5	27	239	266	284	1.07	266	570
1985/6	33	407	440	288	0.65	440	745
1986/7	39	551	590	532	0.90	590	775
1987/8	60	744	804	600	0.74	804	804
1988/9	123	955	1,078	931	0.86	1,078	785
1989/90	206	1,831	2,037	n.a.	n.a.	2,037	1,160
1990/1	214	1,267	1,481	n.a.	n.a.	1,481	718
1991/2	240	3,784	4,024	n.a.	n.a.	4,024	1,510
1992/3	289	4,803 p	5,092 p	n.a.	n.a.	5,092 p	1,600 p
1993/4	296	4,849 p	5,145 p	n.a.	n.a.	5,145 p	1,340 p

Sources: Table 5.19 and COSTECH

Note: p signifies 'preliminary'

R&D institutes) and 5.22 (for the universities and technical colleges too). The third column of Table 5.22 displays figures on total government funding of science and technology in current Tanzanian shillings, the fourth column total government funding in constant Tanzanian shillings (in 1987 prices). Looking again at changes in real funding, we see that the conclusion is identical, namely a rough doubling in the decade of the 1980s.

There are two further additions to be made before we reach grand totals for expenditures on the pursuit of science and technology in Tanzania: these are expenditures by the private sector and foreign donations. Let us take foreign donations first, since we have two conflicting sets of observations. As we mentioned when considering the budgets of the University of Dar es Salaam, the figures on foreign donations reported in the budget statistics are only a small fraction of those acknowledged by donors. Does the same disparity exist over the entire area of science and technology? Table 5.23 gives total donations for science and technology, according to the donors. A rough comparison with the totals in Table 5.22, column 3 (total government expenditures on science and technology in current TSh) for the same years 1989, 1990 and 1991 suggests that foreign donations exceeded the Tanzanian government's total financial contributions by a very large amount, say, by twice as much. (In 1989 foreign donations were half as much again as government's funding; in 1990 nearly four times as much; and in 1991 nearly twice as much.) Not only has the Tanzanian government been increasing its contributions to science and technology, but foreign bodies have been augmenting the contributions still further.

Much the same story emerges if we narrow our focus to the furtherance of science and technology in agriculture. Table 5.24 provides the figures, with government expenditures on agricultural R&D reported in the first two columns, and the government's figures on foreign donations towards agricultural R&D in the next two columns. In the final column are the donors' figures (taken from the preceding table); these are seen to be two to three times the government's own contributions and one-and-a-half times the sum of foreign donations reported by the government. These are smaller multiples than for the previously cited differences in science and technology as a whole, but still indicative of a substantially greater R&D effort in agriculture than generally believed. Things are better than they appear.

The final allowance to be made is for expenditures on advancing science and technology in Tanzania's para-statal firms and private sector. Here we must admit almost complete ignorance, but it is most surely ignorance of small numbers rather than ignorance of large numbers. So far as agricultural R&D is concerned, all public sector research is now administered in the Ministry of Agriculture: there is a little R&D carried on in the private

Table 5.21 Tanzania: total expenditures of R&D institutes 1983/4–1993/4 (millions of current TSh)

	Agricultural institutes				Industrial institutes				Total R&D institutes	
	TPRI		CAMARTEC		TIRDO		TEMDO			
Year	Government	Total	Governmental	Total	Governmental	Total	Governmental	Total	Governmental	Total
1983/4	17	17	14	15	3	3	6	6	40	41
1984/5	23	23	9	11	23	23	6	6	61	63
1985/6	21	27	14	14	17	18	24	24	76	83
1986/7	31	46	28	28	53	56	43	43	155	173
1987/8	68	69	33	33	41	44	44	44	186	190
1988/9	82	82	43	64	25	81	n.a.	n.a.	200	277
1989/90	151	158	46	86	66	69	65	65+	328	378+
1990/1	151	140	63	103	54	54	60	60+	328	377+
1991/2	211	225	46	46+	98	98+	58	58+	413	427+
1992/3	260p	270p	106p	106+p	124p	124+	73p	73+p	563p	573+p
1993/4	195+	195+p	77	77+p	135p	135p	89p	89+p	496p	496+p

Sources: Tables 5.11–5.14

Notes: + signifies 'more than'
p signifies 'preliminary'

Table 5.22 Tanzania: estimates of total public expenditures and total foreign donations for science and technology 1978/8–1993/4 (millions of current TSh)

Year	Total government expenditures				Total foreign donations (current TSh)			
	Research institutes	Universities and technical colleges	Total (current TSh)	Total (constant TSh)	Research institutes	Universities and technical colleges	Total	Total (current TSh)
1978/9	n.a.	n.a.	97	465	n.a.	n.a.	n.a.	97+
1979/80	n.a.	n.a.	85	388	n.a.	n.a.	n.a.	85+
1980/1	n.a.	n.a.	136	546	n.a.	n.a.	n.a.	136+
1981/2	n.a.	n.a.	145	544	n.a.	n.a.	n.a.	145+
1982/3	n.a.	n.a.	200	630	n.a.	n.a.	n.a.	200+
1983/4	40	300	340	895	1	96	97	437
1984/5	61	320	381	815	2	116	118	499
1985/6	76	486	562	950	7	187	194	756
1986/7	155	684	839	1,100	18	278	296	1,135
1987/8	186	915	1,001	1,001	4	n.a.	4+	1,005+
1988/9	200	1,148	1,348	985	77	n.a.	77+	1,425+
1989/90	328	2,221	3,549	2,030	50+	4,230+	4,280+	7,779+
1990/1	328	1,680	2,008	970	49+	9,550+	9,599+	11,607+
1991/2	413	4,104	4,517	1,710	14+	8,050+	8,064+	12,571+
1992/3	563p	5,342p	5,905p	1,850p	10p	n.a.	n.a.	5,905+
1993/4	496p	5,256p	5,752p	1,495p	n.a.	n.a.	n.a.	5,752+

Source: Tables 5.15–5.19

Notes: + signifies 'more than'
p signifies preliminary

Table 5.23 Tanzania: foreign assistance for science and technology 1988–1991

	Expenditure Items (millions US dollars)			Total	
Year	Agricultural R&D	Industrial technological R&D	Technical and managerial education and training	(current US dollars)	(current TSh)
1988	7.8	1.8	11.8	21.4	2,130
1989	10.5	1.4	23.0	34.9	5,020
1990	13.7	1.4	26.0	41.1	7,910
1991	10.4	1.7	27.9	40.0	8,750
1992	1.8	0.9	12.5	15.2	n.a.

Sources: UNDP, May 1991, Table A.1, pp. 46–49; August 1992, Table A.1, pp. 42–44; and October 1993, Table A.1, pp. 35–41

Table 5.24 Tanzania: expenditures on agricultural science and technology 1978/9–1993/4 (millions of current TSh)

Year	Government expenditures		Foreign donations		
	Recurrent	Total	Enumerated R&D institutions	Total, according to government	According to donors
1978/9	28	28	n.a.	n.a.	n.a.
1979/80	19	19	n.a.	n.a.	n.a.
1980/1	57	57	n.a.	n.a.	n.a.
1981/2	53	53	n.a.	n.a.	n.a.
1982/3	93	93	n.a.	n.a.	n.a.
1983/4	120	148	23	n.a.	n.a.
1984/5	153	174	20	n.a.	n.a.
1985/6	177	197	50	n.a.	n.a.
1986/7	276	314	54	n.a.	n.a.
1987/8	386	482	n.a.	n.a.	n.a.
1988/9	611	725	21+	n.a.	780
1989/90	776	909	224	1,510	2,419
1990/1	529	681	98	2,680	3,361
1991/2	1,214	1,378	14+	920	2,280
1992/3	1,442	1,808+	10+	n.a.	n.a.
1993/4	1,752	1,808+	600+	n.a.	n.a.

Sources: Government Expenditures: Recurrent – 1978/9–1988/9: COSTECH, 1990, Table 3(a), p. VI-1
1989/90–1991/4: the sum of expenditures by TPRI, CAMARTEC and Sokoine Agricultural University
Total 1978/9–1988/9: COSTECH (idem) plus development expenditures of TPRI, CAMARTEC and Sokoine Agricultural University
1989/90–1993/4: as for recurrent expenditures
Foreign donations: enumerated institutions – the sum of receipts by TPRI, CAMARTEC and Sokoine Agricultural University
Total, according to Donors – UNDP May 1991, p. 46; August 1992, p. 43, and October 1993, p. 37

sector, chiefly in tea, but the monetary amounts are small. The same holds for industry and the other production activities; para-statal and private firms do no formal R&D, and little of what would classify as informal R&D. All one encounters in conversations and plant visits are laments that none is done, and that the few scientists and larger number of engineers employed are engaged in expediting production under existing technology, rather than advancing it. In the case of Kenya, we augmented public sector expenditures on advancing science and technology by 50 per cent to allow for the para-statal firms' expenditures and approximately 10 per cent to allow for private firms; in the case of Tanzania, whose para-statal firms' scope is being reduced and whose private firms do no more R&D than Kenya's, we shall augment the government's total by one-fifth, to cover both. The figures in Table 5.25, column 4 include the augmentation, and are labelled 'National Expenditures on S&T'. In the last column they are related to Tanzania's GDP, providing a measure of the nation's own contribution to furthering science and technology.

This can be seen to have increased in two surges, the first in the early 1980s and the second in the late 1980s. As a percentage of GDP, Tanzanians are now, after this second surge, spending a little more than twice as much on the pursuit of science and technology as they did 15 years ago.

As we have discovered, foreign donations add markedly to national expenditures; the problem arises as to how to combine the two sources of funds. If we use the government's budget statistics, we will gravely underestimate foreign donations; if we use the donors' figures, we will limit our statistical series of total expenditures to the four years 1988–91. The figures in Table 5.24, columns 4 and 5 illustrate this dilemma.

What we have done is to retain both series, that for national expenditures (Table 5.25) and that for national expenditures plus foreign donations (Table 5.22, final column).

We should stress that great confidence cannot be given to this final, most highly aggregated, set of figures, for our accuracy has fallen as we have moved from government research institutes to those of the para-statals, and from the public sector to the private, and from national contributions to foreign. Nonetheless, the figures in Table 5.22 do give some indication of the overall commitment of Tanzania to advancing science and technology: they show that, thanks in part to their own efforts, and in part to the contributions of foreigners, Tanzania is allocating a creditable portion of its GDP to the task. They also permit some comparison with the other countries in our sample: a comparison that will occupy us in Chapter 7. In the meantime, we will move on to Chapter 6, in which the efforts of Uganda are described.

Table 5.25 Tanzania: public and national expenditures on advancing science and technology, and their relation to total public expenditures and GDP 1978/9–1993/4

	Public expenditure			National expenditures on advancing S&T	
Year	on S&T (millions of current TSh)	Total public expenditures (billions of current TSh)	S&T as % of total public expenditures	(millions of current TSh)	as % of GDP
1978/9	97	6.8	1.4.	117	0.36
1979/80	85	7.4	1.1	102	0.28
1980/1	136	8.5	1.6	164	0.39
1981/2	145	10.3	1.4	174	0.38
1982/3	200	n.a.	n.a.	240	0.45
1983/4	340	n.a.	n.a.	408	0.64
1984/5	381	n.a.	n.a.	457	0.57
1985/6	562	33.1	1.7	675	0.64
1986/7	839	49.7	1.7	1,008	0.72
1987/8	1,001	73.3	1.4	1,202	0.63
1988/9	1,348	112.2	1.2	1,620	0.58
1989/90	3,549	141.2	2.5	4,275	1.15
1990/1	2,008	n.a.	n.a.	2,420	0.54
1991/2	4,517	223.5	2.0	5,430	0.90
1992/3	5,905p	278.8p	2.1p	7,110p	0.97p
1993/4	5,752p	384.8p	1.5p	6,900p	0.74p

Sources: Table 5.22 and text

Note: p = preliminary

6 Uganda

INTRODUCTION

The last of the countries whose undertakings in science and technology were studied is Uganda. With a population of nearly 18 million, Uganda is approximately the same size as Ghana; with an average yearly per capita income of approximately US$200, Uganda is on approximately the same level as Tanzania. Even more than both these countries, Uganda has suffered during the 1980s: the economy that has emerged from this period of hardship is one that is only just beginning to function again.

Our purposes in this chapter are, first, to describe briefly Uganda's recent economic history, up to and including its adoption of restoration programmes under the guidance of the IMF and World Bank. The description will be backed by macro-economic statistics, drawn almost entirely from published sources. The nature of the restoration programme will be described, as will Uganda's responses, at the overall level of the economy.

Secondly, we shall report the results of our survey of institutions active in the realms of science and technology. Our own survey covered five institutions: one located in the agricultural sector, one in the industrial, one on the boundary of the two sectors, and two in education and planning. The data that we collected were in part quantitative – relating to the budgets and personnel of the institutions – and in part qualitative – relating to their aims, resources, conduct, accomplishments and impediments. In addition, we shall draw upon whatever corroborating material we can; although it must be admitted that both our material and that of others is scanty.

Thirdly, after the last of the case studies will come a short summary, whose purpose is solely to record our general impressions of Uganda's recent progress on advancing science and technology, and its potential for still further advance. This summary will be discursive; quantitative analyses will be left for Part III, where the data from Uganda, both quantitative and qualitative, will be added to those from the other three countries and subjected to systematic study.

RECENT ECONOMIC HISTORY

At the time of its independence, in 1962, Uganda contained approximately 8 million inhabitants, each of whom enjoyed an income per capita of a little less than US$200, giving them on that crude measure approximately the same standard of living as the inhabitants of Kenya and Tanzania, their two neighbours; and approximately one half of that of each Ghanaian. National income in that year of promise was about USh160 billion, expressed in constant prices of 1987.

Since then, the Ugandan economy has fluctuated widely. GDP rose in 1971 to a height of USh208 billion (at 1987 prices – see Table 6.1), fell to a low of USh152 billion in 1980: the fall from the peak of 1971 to the trough of 1980 was approximately 25 per cent. The subsequent rise has been slightly higher, to an estimated USh300 billion in the latest year.

Had the population of Uganda remained constant, income per capita would have followed the same path; but from the initial population of approximately 8 million the number of Ugandans has more than doubled to the present total of a little less than 18 million (see Table 6.2). Income per capita, again expressed in constant prices of 1987, declined from the peak of a little over USh20,000 in 1971 to the minimum of USh12,000 in 1980. In that awful decade, the Ugandans' standard of living, as measured by GDP per capita, fell by 40 per cent. Since then, although the economy has started to recover in both absolute terms and in terms of income per capita, the current figure is still below that attained at the time of independence.

That the economy of Uganda should have been in eclipse during the 1980s is quite understandable, when one recalls the military incursion into Tanzania, occurring just before the decade began, and the subsequent civil unrest within Uganda itself. By 1982, the foreign adventure had terminated, and Uganda was in a position to receive US$70 million from the World Bank as the first of its loans under the Economic Recovery programme. A second loan was advanced by the World Bank in 1984 in the amount of US$50 million. The state of the Ugandan economy in the early 1980s was so fragile that the Economic Recovery loans were at their best stabilizing; they helped solely to prevent a further deterioration. It was only towards 1990, with the arrival of the third Economic Recovery loan from the World Bank, that Uganda was able to contemplate economic advance. The sum of money, US$65 million, was no larger than the previous amounts, but the economy was in a better position to take advantage of it.

Table 6.1 Uganda: GDP (at market prices) 1969–1991

Year	GDP (billions current USh)	GDP deflator (1987=100)	GDP (billions USh at constant 1987 prices)	Exchange rate (annual average conversion factor, USh per $US)	GDP (billions current US dollars)
1969	0.08	0.04	193.1	0.050	1.6
1970	0.10	0.05	195.6	0.050	2.0
1971	0.11	0.05	208.2	0.050	2.2
1972	0.11	0.05	205.9	0.050	2.2
1973	0.13	0.07	199.8	0.060	2.2
1974	0.16	0.08	202.9	0.070	2.3
1975	0.23	0.12	192.1	0.090	2.5
1976	0.27	0.14	197.1	0.100	2.7
1977	0.54	0.27	200.1	0.170	3.2
1978	0.59	0.32	186.8	0.230	2.6
1979	0.88	0.55	159.2	0.400	2.2
1980	1.26	1.2	151.6	1.00	1.3
1981	2.30	1.5	163.0	2.00	1.2
1982	3.32	2.1	182.1	2.00	1.7
1983	5.01	2.9	206.5	3.00	1.7
1984	10.5	4.9	216.4	4.00	2.1
1985	26.5	12.6	213.2	11.00	2.4
1986	61.9	29.9	209.6	16.00	3.9
1987	220	100.0	222.5	51.00	4.3
1988	613	260.8	237.7	250.8	2.5
1989	1,153	455.8	256.4	396.1	2.9
1990	1,560	588.9	270.2	570.1	2.7
1991	2,158	795.7	281.0	832.5	2.6
1992	n.a.	n.a.	286.0	n.a.	n.a.
1993	n.a.	n.a.	306.1	n.a.	n.a.

Sources: 1969–1991: World Bank, *World Tables 1991, 1993* (figures for the GDP Deflator for the period 1969–1980 are calculated by dividing GDP at current prices by GDP at constant 1987 prices)
1992, 1993: Fitzgerald, 1993

Table 6.2 Uganda: GDP per capita 1969–1991

Year	Population (millions)	GDP per capita (thousand USh at constant 1987 prices)[a]	GDP per capita (current US dollars)	Average rate of growth of GDP (% p.a.)
1969	9.4	21	180	
1970	9.8	20	190	1.3
1971	10.1	21	200	6.4
1972	10.4	20	210	−1.1
1973	10.7	19	210	−3.0
1974	10.9	19	220	1.6
1975	11.2	17	220	−5.3
1976	11.5	17	270	2.6
1977	11.9	17	280	1.5
1978	12.2	16	280	−6.6
1979	12.5	13	290	−14.8
1980	12.8	12	280	−4.8
1981	13.1	13	220	7.5
1982	13.3	14	240	11.7
1983	13.6	15	120	11.8
1984	13.9	16	170	4.8
1985	14.1	15	170	−1.5
1986	14.5	14	200	−1.7
1987	14.8	15	240	6.2
1988	15.3	16	240	6.8
1989	15.8	16	210	7.9
1990	16.3	17	180	5.4
1991	16.9	17	170	4.0
1992	17.4	16	n.a.	1.8
1993	17.8	17	n.a.	7.0

Note: [a]: GDP per capita calculated by dividing GDP at constant Ugandan shillings (Table 6.1, column 3) by population.

Although its command over the economy in 1988 was quite meagre, the Ugandan government was in a better position than it had been in the immediate past to exert some influence. Realizing this, the World Bank imposed conditions upon the granting of the Economic Recovery loan. These conditions were necessarily less severe than those imposed upon countries with stable regimes, but they still included typical pledges: a reduction in government deficit, preferably by a reduction in government expenditures; a bringing of the exchange rate into alignment with the rate existing in the parallel markets; reduction of government involvement in industry and trade; and a freeing of prices, particularly those received by farmers.

In the three previous countries we have studied, the civil service of each has been sufficiently numerous and skilled to be able to plan for the meeting of the World Bank's conditions. In Uganda, such governmental resources did not exist, and could be provided only by expatriates. The Ugandan government has welcomed such people, who have augmented the staff of the Economic Planning Commission and organized its work. As a result, the attainment of the conditions imposed by the World Bank, a foreign institution, is largely in the hands of another group of foreigners. One need not doubt the objective of each of these two groups, which is to improve the performance of the Ugandan economy; but it does seem rather strange that one foreign group should be setting the standards of performance, and a second foreign group ensuring that those standards are met.

The movements in the overall level of income, and in the average received by each citizen, disguise considerable changes in the relative share of each of the sectors of the economy. In 1963, the first year for which data on shares are available, agriculture contributed 53 per cent of GDP, industry 13 per cent and services 34 per cent. Seventeen years later, in 1980 when the economy was at its lowest point (see Table 6.3), the share of agriculture had increased to 72 per cent, and the shares of industry and services had fallen to 5 per cent and 23 per cent respectively. By now both industry and services have recovered somewhat, to 12 per cent and 37 per cent of total GDP; but their share of industry is no higher that it was 30 years before. The share of services is higher than it was in 1963, but much if not all of the increase is represented by military expenditures, which still consume over one-fifth of the government's Recurrent Budget (see Table 6.4).

INVESTMENT FOR THE FUTURE

Not surprisingly, as Uganda's GDP declined during the late 1970s – early 1980s, total investment declined along with it (see Table 6.5, last column). Actually, the decline in investment preceded the decline in GDP by several years, as foreign ethnic groups, particularly the East African Indians, ceased to maintain their assets in Uganda. Fearing nationalization in general, and expropriation in particular, private entrepreneurs avoided making any investment. From a normal value of approximately 14 per cent, investment as a percentage of GDP fell to half that value in 1975, and to even less than that for the succeeding six years. It was only in 1982 that investment increased again, but only to two-thirds of its former value. By 1987, gross

Table 6.3 Uganda: share of GDP by sector 1971–1991

Year	GDP (at factor cost, billions 1987 USh)	Agricultural product (at factor cost, billions 1987 USh)	Share of agriculture in DGP (%)	Industrial product (at factor cost, billions 1987 USh)	Share of industry in GDP (%)	Manufacturing product (at factor cost, billions 1987 USh)	Share of manufacturing in GDP (%)	Services (at factor cost, billions 1987 USh)	Share of services in GDP (%)
1971	97	55	57	12	12	8	8	30	31
1972	102	58	57	11	11	8	8	32	32
1973	117	71	61	11	9	8	7	34	29
1974	143	89	62	16	11	11	8	38	27
1975	208	150	72	17	8	13	6	41	20
1976	240	176	73	18	8	15	6	46	19
1977	495	366	74	35	7	29	6	94	19
1978	552	410	74	28	5	24	4	114	21
1979	851	558	66	35	4	31	4	258	30
1980	1,240	893	72	56	5	53	4	291	23
1981	2,670	1,560	58	180	7	50	3	930	35
1982	3,950	2,210	56	340	9	180	5	1,400	35
1983	5,950	3,550	60	450	8	220	4	1,950	33
1984	9,491	5,176	54	730	8	336	4	3,585	38
1985	24,743	15,028	61	1,629	7	773	3	8,086	33
1986	59,125	36,615	62	4,520	8	2,254	4	17,990	31
1987	211,385	131,417	62	16,588	8	7,683	4	63,380	30
1988	593,128	353,304	61	52,451	9	25,567	4	187,373	32
1989	1,112,000	677,044	61	95,919	9	43,044	4	339,400	31
1990	1,495,000	12,459	55	155,784	10	60,769	4	527,017	35
1991	2,104,000	1,082,000	51	249,499	12	85,541	4	774,349	37

Sources: 1971–1991: World Bank, World Tables 1991, 1993

Table 6.4 Uganda: central government expenditures, total and percentages by Ministry 1977–1990

Year	Agriculture, forestry, fishing	Mining, manufacturing, construction	Transport and communication	Education	Health	Defence	Other	Total expenditures (millions current USh)
1977	13.0	2.0	0.5	15.5	8.0	21	40	47.17
1978	10.5	2.6	0	14.4	8.2	20	44	59.53
1979	8.4	3.8	4.4	17.6	5.2	19	42	60.86
1980	7.0	1.7	1.3	15.0	5.1	25	45	76.81
1981	10.4	1.9	1.0	12.8	5.9	31	37	127.7
1982	5.7	2.0	3.2	12.5	4.3	16.6	56	416.7
1983	3.9	1.4	2.0	11.0	3.9	14.5	63	664.5
1984	3.2	2.1	2.9	8.4	2.5	16.7	64	1,151
1985	4.3	2.5	2.9	12.8	3.0	15.6	59	2,300
1986	4.6	3.4	6.5	15.0	2.4	26.0	42	4,593
1987	5.4	6.4	1.3	10.7	2.1	25.4	49	10,264
1988	3.2	5.4	0.8	13.8	1.8	24.2	51	36,564
1989	3.8	3.9	0.8	13.7	3.0	29.2	49	70,424
1990	2.2	6.5	1.2	12.1	2.8	30.6	45	126,992

Sources: 1977–986: World Bank, World Tables, 1991, 1993
1987–1990: Government of Uganda, Ministry of Finance, Financial Statement of Revenue and Expenditure, 1988/9 through 1991/2

investment had reached approximately 12 per cent of GDP, at which value it has more or less remained. Although only 50 per cent of GDP invested by its neighbour Kenya, Uganda's rate of investment is still equal to that of most of the African economies at the same level of GDP per capita. Given the great stress under which the economy has existed for the last generation, Uganda's current ability to invest in capital goods must be considered satisfactory.

The division of gross investment between that carried out in the public sector and that in the private sector is not known. It appears that the bulk of investment is made within the public sector, although, again, the distribution between government establishments and para-statals is not known. In the government's budget, relatively large amounts are allocated to restoring the infrastructure: roads, bridges, ports and airports, and communications all require extensive rehabilitation.

Where foreign debt, and its servicing, is concerned, Uganda is probably in a worse position than the other three countries in our sample. It may be that Uganda's outstanding level of debt, *vis-à-vis* its economic potential, is relatively low; but, although Uganda's total foreign debt had not exceeded 45 per cent of GNP before 1986 (see Table 6.7), in subsequent years it has risen to equal one-year's GDP (compare total external debt in Table 6.6 with GDP in US dollars in Table 6.1), higher than both Ghana's and Kenya's. A re-negotiation of the interest rates on Uganda's foreign obligations did lead to a fall between 1985 and 1986 of Uganda's servicing charges. The figures in the last two columns of Table 6.7 show that debt servicing both as a percentage of GDP and as a percentage of total export earnings fell by more than half between those two years. So far as the latter ratio is concerned, Uganda's servicing charges as a fraction of the total availability of foreign exchange through exports may now be lower than those of our other three countries.

Uganda's position is worse than the other three countries, however, in respect to its obligations to the IMF and the World Bank. The figures in Table 6.7, columns 3 and 4 reveal that, in 1986 at least, more than half of the total debt outstanding is owed to the IMF and the World Bank. Uganda must repay these obligations faithfully if it is to continue having a 'seal of approval'.

THE R&D INSTITUTIONS

As in the preceding three chapters, so in this chapter on Uganda's efforts to advance science and technology we shall begin with the individual institutions. Once we have described the individual institutions, we shall

Table 6.5 Uganda: government revenues, expenditures and investment 1969–1991

Year	Government current revenue (billions current USh)	Government current expenditure (billions current USh)	Government surplus (+) or deficit (−) (billions current USh)	Government capital payments (billions current USh)	Government consumption (billions of current USh)	Total gross domestic investment (billions of current USh)	Gross investment as % of GDP
1969	n.a.	n.a.	n.a.	n.a.	0.009	0.012	15.0
1970	n.a.	n.a.	n.a.	n.a.	n.a.	0.013	13.3
1971	0.015	n.a.	n.a.	n.a.	n.a.	0.016	15.2
1972	0.012	n.a.	−0.009	n.a.	n.a.	0.012	11.0
1973	0.012	n.a.	−0.009	n.a.	n.a.	0.011	8.2
1974	0.021	n.a.	−0.015	n.a.	n.a.	0.017	10.7
1975	0.025	0.027	−0.012	0.006	n.a.	0.017	7.6
1976	0.034	0.031	−0.013	0.008	n.a.	0.015	5.5
1977	0.058	0.039	−0.013	0.008	n.a.	0.030	5.5
1978	0.026	0.046	−0.002	0.014	n.a.	0.046	7.8
1979	0.040	0.049	−0.035	0.012	n.a.	0.056	6.4
1980	0.031	0.067	−0.039	0.012	n.a.	0.077	6.1
1981	0.277	0.106	−0.101	0.025	n.a.	0.150	6.0
1982	0.537	0.346	−0.146	0.076	n.a.	0.290	7.9
1983	0.938	0.573	−0.134	0.098	0.183	0.530	9.0
1984	1.70	1.017	−0.221	0.142	0.920	0.805	7.7
1985	3.23	1.95	−0.64	0.36	2.13	2.04	7.7
1986	5.0	3.35	−1.35	1.22	4.68	6.12	10.0
1987	22.3	8.0	−3.0	n.a.	14.4	25.9	11.8
1988	49.7	27.2	−4.9	n.a.	38.7	64.8	10.6
1989	86.5	58.4	−8.7	n.a.	72.4	119	10.3
1990	207	105.5	−19.0	2.1	100.8	178	11.4
1991	435	320	−113	111	172.4	268	12.4
1992		671	−236	252		n.a.	n.a.

Sources: 1987–1990: columns 1–4, Government of Uganda, *Background to the Budget 1990–1991*, Tables 12a and 12b, p. 167 (for the fiscal years 1986/7 through 1989/90)
1969–1990: remainder, World Bank, *World Tables, 1991, 1993*
1991, 1992: Government of Uganda, Ministry of Finance, *Financial Statement of Revenue and Expenditure 1991/2* (1991 approved estimate, 1992, estimate)

Table 6.6 Uganda: debt 1970–1991 (millions current US dollars outstanding at end of year)

Year	External debt total	Long term debt total	Short term debt total	Private sector debt, total (including non-guaranteed debt)	Public sector debt
1970	138	138	0	1.2	137
1971	172	172	0	1.4	171
1972	178	178	0	1.3	177
1973	177	177	0	1.2	176
1974	203	203	0	1.2	202
1975	208	208	0	1.1	207
1976	242	242	0	1.0	241
1977	333	299	34	1.7	331
1978	442	421	21	4.3	438
1979	570	540	30	4.7	565
1980	695	632	64	15.0	680
1981	729	697	32	13.9	715
1982	893	852	41	12.6	880
1983	1,012	982	30	9.9	1,002
1984	1,065	1,023	42	9.0	1,056
1985	1,225	1,181	44	10.7	1,214
1986	1,400	1,334	67	12.6	1,387
1987	1,916	1,850	66	18.5	1,897
1988	1,946	1,863	83	19.2	1,927
1989	2,231	2,123	107	19.5	2,211
1990	2,637	2,495	143	21.1	2,616
1991	2,830	2,655	175	21.0	2,809

Source: World Bank, *World Tables 1991, 1993*

aggregate their activities, using the common denominator of budget allocations. When we have an estimate of the amount of R&D carried out within Uganda, we shall move on to the university, within which scientific and technical education takes place. Combining university expenditures on the pursuit of science and technology with those in the R&D institutes yields a measure of the contribution of government. This will be augmented by small amounts to allow for scientific and technical activities carried out within productive firms, mainly those within the state sector, but also in the private sector.

The first institutes that we will consider are those devoted to advancing

Table 6.7 Uganda: debt servicing 1981–1986

Year	Total debt outstanding (millions current US dollars)	Official debt (millions current US dollars)	Debt to IMF (millions current US dollars)	Debt to World Bank (IBRD/IDA) (millions current US dollars)	Private debt (millions current US dollars)	Total debt as % of GDP	Total debt service as % of GDP	Total debt service as % of total exports
1981	772	600	186	61.2	172	30	2.3	21
1982	969	744	269	91.8	225	35	2.0	16
1983	1,083	896	354	123	187	37	2.6	21
1984	1,084	927	315	217	158	39	3.3	22
1985	1,176	1,039	282	318	137	45	2.4	17
1986	1,199	1,091	229	401	108	45	1.1	7.0

Sources: Strack and Schönherr, 1989. (There are discrepancies between these figures and those in Table 6.6, chiefly in the volume of private sector debt)

Table 6.8 Uganda: balance of payments 1970–1991

Year	Total exports of goods and services (millions current $US)	Total imports of goods and services (millions current $US)	Balance on current account (before official transfers) (millions current $US)	Exports of coffee (millions current $US)	Exports of tea (millions current $US)
1970	297	271	19	n.a.	n.a.
1971	284	365	−88	1.2	1.7
1972	292	269	13	0.8	1.0
1973	290	246	40	0.6	1.0
1974	308	331	−28	0.9	1.1
1975	252	321	−72	2.0	1.2
1976	336	295	−35	47	1.0
1977	556	485	66	73	1.5
1978	337	472	−143	75	1.5
1979	414	387	10	58	1.2
1980	331	450	−121	96	2.0
1981	274	392	−118	102	2.1
1982	382	524	−123	112	2.3
1983	384	543	−93	112	2.3
1984	406	517	−78	109	2.2
1985	399	514	−45	120	2.4
1986	398	569	−72	113	2.3
1987	365	694	−219	152	3.1
1988	314	760	−446	162	3.3
1989	275	766	−491	167	3.4
1990	224	739	−515	173	3.5
1991	198	695	−497	163	3.3

Source: Exports, imports, balance: World Bank, *World Tables 1991, 1993*
Coffee, tea: Government of Uganda, Ministry of Agriculture, Secretariat for Research

science and technology in agriculture. (The background is provided in the comprehensive study of Opio-Ogongo, 1992.) Administratively, these are not separate research institutes, as they are in the other three countries, but dependencies of the Ministry of Agriculture. (This Ministry is called the Ministry of Agriculture, Fisheries and Forest, and is an amalgamation of the three former separate ministries. Using shorthand, we shall call it the Ministry of Agriculture.) Within the Ministry of Agriculture, there is a Secretary for Research, under whom the various research divisions are located. The Research Secretary and the majority of the research activity are located at the campus of the Ministry of Agriculture on the outskirts of Entebbe. There the most important research activities are carried out, commencing with coffee.

Research on coffee represents the largest single allocation of funds and of personnel to a single commodity. Aided by funds from abroad, the programme employs approximately 20 persons, led by the Coffee Coordinator. The projects bear considerable resemblance to the projects carried out by the sister Coffee Research Foundation in Kenya: research into the coffee berry disease, into other viruses that afflict the coffee plant, and into alleviating problems arising during planting, cultivation, harvesting, processing, storage and shipment.

Of the other research programmes undertaken within the Ministry of Agriculture some are new programmes, some are extensions of existing programmes, but the majority have prospered in recent years with the influx of foreign assistance. Tables 6.9 and 6.10 illustrate the increases that have occurred. We see that during the years of Uganda's turmoil, expenditures on research in coffee and other crops remained minimal, covering no more than the salaries and the wages of the employees, as the low amounts allocated to Development items indicate. It was only after the initiation of the Structural Adjustment Programme, and the arrival of funds supporting research, that expenditures were able to increase. The bulk of the foreign donations have still to be expended, so expenditures can be expected to increase substantially in the next few years (raising the estimate for 1991/2). Since substantial funds are allocated to the scheme for replanting coffee trees that had outlived their useful life, or had been destroyed during the chaotic decade (see Tables 6.12 and 6.13) not all the expenditures can be counted as R&D. Nonetheless, if the research into coffee is effective, the new trees should be yielding larger crops, which will increase Uganda's output and exports.

Table 6.10 also gives an indication of the relation between requests for funds for research in agriculture and actual expenditures: the last two columns summarize the figures. Within these averages for the entire

Table 6.9 Uganda: public expenditures on agricultural R&D, as percentages of government revenues and GDP arising in agriculture 1981/2–1991/2

Year	Expenditures on agricultural R&D (millions current USh)	Government current revenue (millions current USh)	GDP arising in agriculture (millions current USh)	Expenditures on agricultural research as % of	
				Government current revenue	GDP arising in agriculture
1981/82	0.022	31	658	0.071	0.003
1982/83	0.039	277	930	0.014	0.004
1983/84	0.051	537	1,360	0.009	0.004
1984/85	0.083	938	1,935	0.009	0.004
1985/86	0.187	1,669	5,651	0.010	0.003
1986/87	0.702	3,228	13,751	0.020	0.005
1987/88	n.a.	5,000	47,669	n.a.	n.a.
1988/89	125	22,300	136,046	0.56	0.09
1989/90	321	49,700	260,744	0.65	0.12
1990/91	486[a]	86,500	n.a.	0.56	n.a.
1991/92	200[a]	207,000	n.a.	0.10	n.a.

Source: Government of Uganda, Background to the Budget 1991/2

Note: a signifies Approved Estimates

Table 6.10 Uganda: Ministry of Agriculture requests and expenditures for agricultural research 1968/9–1991/2 (thousands current USh)

Year	Recurrent expenditures			Development expenditures			Expenditures as % of requests	
	Requests of Ministry to Treasury	Approved estimates	Actual expenditures	Requests of Ministry to Treasury	Approved estimates	Actual expenditures	Recurrent	Development
1968/9	n.a.	n.a.	n.a.	n.a.	n.a.	0.05	n.a.	n.a.
1969/70	n.a.	n.a.	n.a.	n.a.	0.6	n.a.	n.a.	n.a.
1970/1	n.a.	n.a.	n.a.	n.a.	n.a.	0.11	n.a.	n.a.
1971/2	n.a.	n.a.	n.a.	n.a.	n.a.	0.11	n.a.	n.a.
1972/3	n.a.	n.a.	n.a.	n.a.	n.a.	0.11	n.a.	n.a.
1973/4	n.a.	n.a.	n.a.	n.a.	n.a.	n.a.	n.a.	n.a.
1974/5	n.a.	n.a.	n.a.	n.a.	n.a.	n.a.	n.a.	n.a.
1975/6	n.a.	n.a.	n.a.	n.a.	n.a.	n.a.	n.a.	n.a.
1976/7	n.a.	n.a.	n.a.	n.a.	n.a.	n.a.	n.a.	n.a.
1977/8	n.a.	n.a.	n.a.	n.a.	n.a.	0.27	n.a.	n.a.
1978/9	n.a.	n.a.	n.a.	n.a.	0.15	n.a.	n.a.	n.a.
1979/80	n.a.	n.a.	n.a.	0.18	n.a.	0.21	n.a.	n.a.
1980/1	n.a.	n.a.	n.a.	n.a.	0.33	n.a.	n.a.	n.a.
1981/2	n.a.	84	22	2.2	n.a.	n.a.	26	n.a.
1982/3	n.a.	124	39	n.a.	2.8	1.4	31	50
1983/4	n.a.	180	51	n.a.	5.7	n.a.	28	n.a.
1984/5	n.a.	307	83	14.6	n.a.	n.a.	27	n.a.
1985/6	n.a.	421	187	n.a.	n.a.	n.a.	44	n.a.
1986/7	n.a.	1,925	702	n.a.	n.a.	n.a.	37	n.a.
1987/8	n.a.	n.a.	n.a.	n.a.	5,456	484	n.a.	9
1988/9	n.a.	n.a.	125,000	n.a.	987	n.a.	n.a.	n.a.
1989/90	n.a.	n.a.	321,000	13,339	n.a.	n.a.	n.a.	n.a.
1990/1	n.a.	486,432	n.a.	n.a.	n.a.	n.a.	n.a.	n.a.
1991/2	200,386P	200,386P	n.a.	n.a.	n.a.	n.a.	n.a.	n.a.

Sources: 1968/9–1989/90: Government of Uganda, Draft Estimates of Revenue and Expenditure (recurrent and Capital). (After 1981/82, includes research on animal industries and fisheries)
1990/1, 1991/2 Government of Uganda, Ministry of Agriculture, Secretariat for Research

Notes: P signifies preliminary, superceded by the figure 612,000 in Table 6.12

Table 6.11 Uganda: budgets for R&D and reconstruction by Ministry and project 1990/1 (millions of current USh)

| Ministry | Project | Recurrent expenditures | Section 1 (short term, by Ugandan government) | Development (capital expenditures) | | | Total development expenditures |
| | | | | Long-term | | | |
				Ugandan government	Foreign donors	Sub-total	
Agriculture, livestock, fisheries	Agriculture, total	427	30	n.a.	n.a.	n.a.	n.a.
	Coffee	131	0	0	0	0	0
	Agricultural tools	n.a.	n.a.	107	452	559	n.a.
	Livestock	37	10	n.a.	n.a.	n.a.	n.a.
	Fisheries	22	0	n.a.	n.a.	n.a.	n.a.
	Agriculture, livestock, fisheries total	486	40	n.a.	n.a.	n.a.	n.a.
Industry and technology	Industry and technology total	199	31	0	0	0	31
Minerals, energy and water	Minerals, energy and water total	2,040	n.a.	0	0	0	n.a.
Commerce	Commerce, total	397	n.a.	n.a.	n.a.	n.a.	n.a.
Makerere University	Total	3,571	417	145	224	369	786
Total 1990/1	Total (less medicine)	6,693	488+	n.a.	n.a.	n.a.	n.a.

Source: Government of Uganda, Ministry of Finance, *Estimates for Recurrent and Development Expenditures for 1991/2*

Table 6.12 Uganda: budgets for R&D and reconstruction by Ministry and project 1991/2 (millions of current USh)

Ministry	Project		Approved estimates (millions of current USh)					
				Development (capital expenditures)				
			Section 1 (short term, by Ugandan government)	Section 2 (long-term)				Total development expenditures
		Recurrent expenditures		Ugandan government	Foreign donors	Sub-total		
Agriculture, livestock and fisheries	Agriculture, total	612	66	n.a.	n.a.	n.a.		n.a.
	Coffee	157	n.a.	29	3,600	3,629		3,629+
	Agricultural tools	n.a.	n.a.	18	641	659		659+
	Livestock, total	165	8	n.a.	n.a.	n.a.		n.a.
	Dairy	n.a.	n.a.	75	4,083	4,158		n.a.
	Fisheries, total	169	0	n.a.	n.a.	n.a.		n.a.
	Agriculture, livestock and fisheries total	947	474	3,831	30,587	34,418		34,492
Industry and technology	Science and technology	n.a.	n.a.	0	368	368		368+
	Workshop for small scale industry	n.a.	n.a.	81	155	236		236+
	Food technology and ceramics	n.a.	n.a.	76	0	76		76+
	Industry and technology total	313	31	381	3,550	3,931		3,962
Minerals, energy and water	Minerals, energy and water Total	2,695	472	1,770	24,616	26,386		26,858
	Potable water	n.a.	n.a.	470	10,410	10,880		10,880+
	Forest rehabilitation	n.a.	n.a.	67	3,753	3,820		3,820+
Commerce	Commerce, cooperative, marketing total	1,355	48	312	6,594	6,906		6,954
Makerere University	Total	6,286	321	286	0	286		607
Works, transport, communication	Total	n.a.	n.a.	2,549	24,768	27,317		27,317+
Total 1991/2	Total (less medicine, land, housing and urban development)	5,596+	946+	9,129	90,115	99,244		100,190+

Source: Government of Uganda, Ministry of Finance, *Estimates for Recurrent and Development Expenditures for 1991/2*

Table 6.13 Uganda: estimated expenditures on science and technology, total and relative to GDP and to government revenues 1990/1 and 1991/2

Fiscal year	Estimated public expenditures on S&T (millions current USh)	Total domestic revenues (millions current USh)	Expenditures on S&T by government, as % of total government revenues	Estimated total expenditures on S&T (millions current USh)[a]	GDP (millions current USh)	Total expenditures on S&T as % of GDP
1990/1	1,425+	141,000	1.0+	2,101+	1,400,000	0.15
1991/2	6,184	204,000	3.0	40,321	1,800,000	2.2

Source: see Tables 6.1, 6.4, 6.11 and 6.12. Expenditures on science and technology are assumed to consist of recurrent expenditures for the Ministry of Agriculture and Industry, and development expenditures for agriculture, industry and Makerere University. Public expenditures consist of all of Section 1 and the Ugandan government's portion of Section 2 of the accounts GDP estimates, reported for calendar years in Table 6.1, are for the fiscal years

Note: a: Total expenditures on science and technology include public expenditures, foreign donations, and private expenditures

Ministry there are considerable variations by project: the greatest variation occurs between the Coffee Research Group and the Appropriate Technology Group. Commencing with the requests of the research officers, one can follow the sums subsequently recommended by the Director of Research; the sums accepted and recommended by the Research Secretary of the Ministry; the sums accepted and recommended by the Minister; and finally the sums approved by the Economic Planning Board. The contrast between the figures for the two research groups is quite startling: the Coffee Research Group has received funds equalling approximately half the original requests of the research officers, whereas the Appropriate Technology Group has received only 5 per cent of the funds its research officers requested.

Other, domestically consumed, crops seem also to be discriminated against. We have called this lack of attention to important, non-exportable crops the 'Banana Syndrome', because R&D on bananas, such a vital food in Uganda, is so neglected. Why should there be a 'Banana Syndrome'?

The explanation lies almost entirely in the support that research on coffee has drawn from foreign donors, and the lack of support for locally-consumed crops or for appropriate technology. Of the reasons suggested by Ugandans involved in the research, the chief one is based on the *locus* of decisions on research fundings; decisions are made chiefly in the aid agencies in the developed countries and reflect the priorities of the agencies and the beliefs of their employees. With these bodies Ugandans have relatively little contact and even less influence.

R&D in industry is the responsibility of a new Industrial Research Institute, established in 1990 and located administratively within the Ministry of Industry. So new is this industrial research institute that it is only just acquiring facilities and staff. A capital grant from the German government is permitting the design and construction of research laboratories; when they are complete research will be undertaken. The research agenda has not yet been fully established, but it appears that some activities will be directed towards improving the production of textiles, Uganda's largest industry and employer, and the processing of primary commodities.

As of the present, no overall agency exists within the Ugandan government to which the coordination of its R&D activities is assigned. However, most R&D expenditures are made by the government ministries, so an aggregation of data on expenditures on advancing science and technology can be drawn from the government's budget figures. This is done in Tables 6.11 and 6.12, the first for the fiscal year 1990/1 and the second for 1991/2. The fact that all the data are drawn from a single source is appropriate, for it symbolizes the importance of central government in determining how resources are to be allocated amongst different activities. In the other three countries that we studied, some research institutes had a considerable amount of freedom, both in soliciting funds and in determining how those funds should be allocated; in Uganda, the equivalent research bodies have less independence and authority. The major decisions on which activities are to be stimulated, and which curbed, is made at the ministerial level, upon recommendations from the Economic Planning Board (EPB). It is the EPB which has taken upon itself the responsibility for determining the structure of Uganda's economy in the future, through its current expenditures on advancing science and technology, as well as in the present, through its allocation of recurrent funds.

THE SCIENTIFIC AND TECHNICAL FACULTIES OF THE UNIVERSITY

In Uganda there is one university, Makerere, which provides most of the scientific and technical training in the country at the advanced level, and which acts as a model for all of the lesser academic institutions. Like the universities that we visited in the other countries, Makerere has benefitted on balance from the interest in its activities displayed by foreign donors. The Medical Faculty, the Engineering Faculty and the Economic and Social Statistics Division have all received donations from abroad and are all prospering as a consequence. The same cannot be said for the scientific faculties, which have not received an equal amount of foreign support.

Particularly deprived is the Mathematics Department. With an 'Establishment' of 13, the Mathematics Faculty has been able to attract and retain only four mathematicians, of whom two are former graduate students who have not progressed beyond the level of the MSc. Two professional mathematicians, trained abroad, and two local ex-graduate students are a dreadfully inadequate body to teach a subject which is the basis for all of the scientific and technical fields. Denied the support of foreigners, even those mathematicians who remain active in teaching cannot devote more than a portion of their time to fulfilling their main obligation. Without the supplement of their salaries provided to their colleagues in the Engineering and other faculties, the mathematicians must seek part-time employment outside the university, in order to maintain their incomes at a respectable level. This leads to the commonly observed practice in the four countries we visited of government employees supplementing their inadequate salaries with outside jobs. In the case of mathematicians, their skills can be used in the much less intellectually challenging field of accountancy; and it is as accountants that they find part-time employment. From the point of view of the Ugandan economy, accountancy skills, which are in very short supply, may be usefully augmented; but the mathematical skills devoted to teaching are much reduced. Whatever the overall effect on the Ugandan economy, the necessity to supplement the professorial income with outside work reduces the attractiveness of teaching in the University and is responsible, at least in part, for the empty posts in the Faculty.

With estimates of the expenditures at Makerere University on those faculties advancing science and technology we can augment the previous statistics on Ugandan expenditures on furthering science and technology. This augmentation is made in Table 6.13, column 1 whose sums represent the total of public expenditures for this purpose. To these must be added foreign donations and the expenditures of the private sector. So far as foreign donations are concerned, the figures in Tables 6.11 and 6.12, column 4 reveal that they far outweigh the Ugandan government's in 1990/1, and in subsequent years (see also Table 6.15). So far as the private sector's expenditures on advancing science and technology are concerned, we must admit almost complete ignorance. What we can say is that they are very small, given the relative unimportance of the industrial sector within the Ugandan economy and the relatively minor role of the private sector in industry. In making our estimate of the contribution of the private sector to the advance of science and technology in Kenya, we increased the figures for the public sector's contribution by 10 per cent. In Uganda, where the

Table 6.14 Uganda: estimated expenditures on science and technology as a percentage of GDP, 1981/2–1991/2

Year	Expenditures on S&T (as % of GDP)
1981/2	0.003
1982/3	0.004
1983/4	0.004
1984/5	0.004
1985/6	0.003
1986/7	0.005
1987/8	n.a.
1988/9	0.09
1989/90	0.12
1990/1	0.15
1991/2	2.2

Sources: 1981/2–1989/90: Table 6.9: final column
1990/1–1991/2: Table 6.13, final column

private sector makes a relatively smaller contribution, we will adopt a figure of 5 per cent, as representing the increase in the contribution of the public sector. In Table 6.13, column 4 the public and private sectors' contributions for 1990/1 and 1991/2 are given, and in the last column of the table the total expenditures on advancing science and technology are compared to Uganda's total level of economic activity, as measured by GDP. For earlier years, we shall assume that the total expenditures on science and technology, as a fraction of GDP, are equal to the fractions of GDP arising in agriculture which were expended on agricultural research (Table 6.9, last column). The whole series, 1981/2–1991/2, is given in Table 6.14. Hazy as all these figures may be, they do indicate overall increases, both in absolute terms and as a percentage of GDP, in the most recent years. The experience of the Coffee Research Unit, and a few other major programmes (but not that of the Appropriate Technology Group), is borne out at the aggregate level.

SUMMARY

In summarizing Uganda's experience in advancing science and technology, we must recognize that to the extent advances have taken place it has been in very recent years. The turmoil to which Uganda was subjected meant that for over a decade little if any advance was made. Much of the capability for advance remained, in the form of permanent employees of the Ministry of Agriculture and of the technical departments of the university, but using an automotive analogy, the engine of research was just 'ticking over'. Fuel, in the form of donations from abroad, arrived only after the economy had stabilized and the structural adjustments been undertaken (see Table 6.15). To the extent that the adoption of the Structural Adjustment and Reconstruction programmes stimulated the issuance of loans and donations needed to stabilize the economy, it was a necessary condition for the renewal of the advance of science and technology. That the wherewithall for advance is available can be seen from the figures in Table 6.14, where the two jumps in financing science and technology, in 1988/9 and in 1991/2, are readily apparent.

With Uganda's recent history complete, we have finished our description of what we learned about expenditures on science and technology in the four Sub-Saharan African countries. These chapters have been descriptive; the analysis is contained in Part III where all the evidence is presented. The evidence will first be presented on a macro-economic scale, next on a 'meso-economic' scale and finally on a micro-economic scale. It is therefore to analyzing the overall advance in science and technology in these four countries that we proceed.

Table 6.15 Uganda: investment revenues and expenditures from domestic and foreign resources 1988/9–1991/2 (billions current USh)

Year	Revenues			Expenditures			Deficit expenditures less revenues	Foreign loans
	Domestic resources	Foreign grants	Total	Recurrent	Development	Total		
1988/9	47	11	59	56	31	87	29	n.a.
1989/90	81	37	119	108	105	213	94	n.a.
1990/1	141	66	207	209	111	320	111	85
1991/2	204	230	434	419	252	471	237	184

Source: Government of Uganda, Ministry of Finance, Financial Statement of Revenue and Expenditure, 1988/9–1991/2 (figures are approved estimates)

Part III

Effects of the pursuit of science and technology

7 Effects on the economy as a whole

INTRODUCTION

In this and the next two chapters we shall analyze the material collected in Ghana, Kenya, Tanzania and Uganda, in order to try to determine the effects of the adoption of Structural Adjustment Programmes on the countries' ability to pursue science and technology. We have defined science and technology in the conventional manner, as the output of three sets of organizations – educational institutions purveying scientific and technological knowledge, R&D laboratories, and productive enterprises. The prime function of the second of these three is to advance science and technology; the prime function of the first and third is not; but in carrying out their prime function – education and production respectively – they actively promote increases in science and technology.

The division of material in this and the next two chapters is based upon the degree of aggregation of activities: in this chapter we shall analyze material of large scale, covering the economy as a whole; Chapter 8 will be devoted to an analysis of material at the level of the sector or the industry, and Chapter 9 to material covering individual institutions. Our chapters thus proceed from the macro-economic, through the meso-economic, to the micro-economic.

In choosing to divide the material by degree of aggregation we are not being guided by theory, which usually focuses on one level alone and makes simplifying assumptions about the other two. Nor are we following the course of our investigation, which focused on one country at a time. Rather we are adopting the procedure of the botanist or the biologist, who begins with what the eye can see and then looks at smaller and smaller bits of organisms with visual aids. The economist's eye is trained to see the overall economy; his equivalent of the botanist's and biologist's visual aids are historical and statistical knowledge of specific economic activities.

In this chapter, our progress from the aggregate to the individual will advance no further than the subdivisions of all economic activity into that carried out within the public sector and that carried out within the private, and into that financed by the country itself and that financed by foreign donations. The division between public and private is more or less equivalent to activities carried out in the interests of the society as a whole and those carried out in the self-interest of the actors. To be sure, public servants do on occasion put their own interests first; and private citizens may put the public interest first; but the matter of primacy of interest will not concern us until Chapter 9. The distinction between what activities lie within the public sector and what within the private is never clear, so we shall have to consider this matter too. The division between local and foreign financing is clearer in nature.

Moving from degree of aggregation to the order of presentation, we shall follow, in all three analytical chapters, the same order: first we shall present our data, both the statistical compilations and the limitations to their accuracy. Secondly we shall draw whatever associations seem apparent, for the countries within our sample. Thirdly, we shall enlarge the sample to report whatever corroborating data there are for other Sub-Saharan countries, or, lacking comparable Sub-Saharan data, for other developing countries.

Having presented the data, we shall move to the fourth item on our list, namely attainment of the terms of Structural Adjustment Programmes. In this item we shall address such issues as the objectives to be achieved either within the span of the programme or over the longer run; and the conditions imposed upon the borrowing countries or commitments undertaken by the lenders. As an example, imagine that one condition imposed upon, and agreed to by, the developing country is that it increases the fraction of its GDP allocated to advancing science and technology to 1 per cent: we could then compare the actual allocation with this specification.

Such specificity, such a close association between, on the one hand, the activities that interest us and, on the other hand, the observations or objectives or commitments in the Structural Adjustment Programmes, is rather unlikely. More likely are either an inexact association between what interests us and what the lender and the recipient are committed to, or no association at all. We will not be surprised if what interests us is not mentioned in a Structural Adjustment Programme: lack of association can easily be explained in part because of the long-run focus of science and technology; in part by the difficulty in defining and measuring scientific and technological progress. In these cases, we will be able only to make explicit the lack of association.

Our order of presentation will terminate with a summary of whatever conclusions emerge from the analysis. To say that they will be conclusions on the effects of Structural Adjustment Programmes on the pursuit of science and technology at the macroeconomic level would be going too far: that exercise will be left to Part IV, where counterfactual cases will be formulated. After all, we cannot draw any conclusions about the effects of Structural Adjustment Programmes unless we can make some estimate of what would have happened had there been no such programmes, and the material presented here will give us no indication of that. This chapter, and the next two, present empirical material, not speculation.

OVERALL EXPENDITURES ON ADVANCING SCIENCE AND TECHNOLOGY

The first set of statistical estimates that we shall provide for our four countries are those of total expenditures on advancing science and technology. As will be seen subsequently, these have four components: the expenditures of educational institutions on science and technology; the expenditures of R&D institutes; the training and technical services carried out by productive firms, and (except for Ghana) foreign donations. The totals, by year for each country for the years for which we have made estimates, are presented in Table 7.1. The data are provided in both current values, and in constant values, at prices as of a common year, 1987.

The figures in Table 7.1 on yearly expenditures on advancing science and technology in the four countries, are very rough estimates: those for Ghana may be accurate for the period 1974–1987 (see Table 3.18), but later figures are based on the small sample of organizations reported in Tables 3.12–3.17, and include only some foreign donations; those for Kenya are shorter in sequence but reasonably accurate; those for Tanzania up to 1988 are on the low side, because of incomplete coverage; and those for Uganda have two different sources, being either blown up from expenditures on agricultural R&D (1981/2–1989/90) or taken from budget approvals (1990/1 and 1991/2). Since the figures are fragmentary, and the series interrupted, comparisons among them are hazardous. What seems apparent is that, within a single country, expenditures fluctuate widely year by year. In Kenya, Tanzania and Uganda there are upward trends over time, in Ghana there is not, but this may be a shortage in the statistics.

Table 7.2 relates each country's expenditures on advancing science and technology to its total expenditures on goods and services, as measured by GDP. Taking the results country by country, Ghana's percentages fluctuate widely: over the 14-year interval 1978/9–1991/2 the general trend appears to be downwards, from an average of 0.9 per cent over the first three years

Table 7.1 Estimates of total expenditures on advancing science and technology by Ghana, Kenya, Tanzania and Uganda in units of the national currency at current and constant prices 1978/9–1993/4

Year	Total expenditures at current prices				Total expenditures at constant prices of 1987			
	Ghana (millions of Cedis)[a]	Kenya (millions of KSh)	Tanzania (millions of TSh)	Uganda (millions of USh)	Ghana (billions of Cedis)	Kenya (billions of KSh)	Tanzania (billions of TSh)	Uganda (billions of USh)
1978/9	230	n.a.	97	n.a.	n.a.	n.a.	0.55	n.a.
1979/80	190	n.a.	85	n.a.	1.2	n.a.	0.43	n.a.
1980/1	400	n.a.	136	n.a.	6.3	n.a.	0.66	n.a.
1981/2	260	n.a.	145	0.04	2.4	n.a.	0.56	0.0027
1982/3	n.a.	n.a.	200	0.07	n.a.	n.a.	0.65	0.0033
1983/4	110	n.a.	437	0.09	0.35	n.a.	1.17	0.0031
1984/5	1,300	n.a.	499	0.14	3.1	n.a.	1.10	0.0028
1985/6	2,860	n.a.	756	0.30	5.7	n.a.	1.25	0.0024
1986/7	3,600	510	1,135	1.1	5.0	0.54	1.50	0.0037
1987/8	2,510	820	1,005+	n.a.	2.5	0.82	1.01+	n.a.
1988/9	4,200	1,100	3,700	205	3.1	1.01	2.69	0.079
1989/90	9,200	1,730	9,300	584	5.4	1.45	5.31	0.128
1990/1	7,600	2,650	10,300	2,100	3.4	2.02	5.00	0.357
1991/2	5,600	n.a.	14,200	40,300	2.1	n.a.	5.36	5.07
1992/3	n.a.	n.a.	5,905+	n.a.	n.a.	n.a.	1.86+	n.a.
1993/4	n.a.	n.a.	5,752+	n.a.	n.a.	n.a.	1.51+	n.a.

Sources: Tables 3.1, 4.1, 5.1, and 6.1 (GDP deflators); and 3.18, 4.18, 5.22 and 5.26, 6.13 and 6.14 (expenditures on science and technology)
For Ghana, calendar years listed as the later of the two fiscal years; e.g., calendar year 1991 listed as 1991/2

Notes: a: Ghana's totals exclude most foreign donations, in unknown amounts

to an average of 0.4 per cent over the last three. There may have been a recovery in the most recent two years, as foreign donations have flowed into the country at an increased rate, but it is doubtful that the percentages of the late 1970s have been attained.

Kenya's percentages show a steady increase from 1986/7–1990/1, but have probably fallen since then. The next column of Table 7.2 provides Tanzania's, which indicate two upward shifts, from roughly 0.3 per cent to roughly 0.6 per cent, in the year 1983/4, and again to an average of 2.4 per cent in the years 1989/90–1991/2. This quadrupling in the intensity with which resources are devoted to furthering science and technology coincides with the institution of reforms and the receipt of substantially greater foreign assistance.

Uganda's series displays an even greater shift, occurring between 1986/7 and 1988/9, five years later than Tanzania's, followed also by a second shift in 1991/2, the last year for which we have data. Both shifts were of an order of magnitude, from approximately 0.004 of a percentage point to one-tenth,

Table 7.2 Total expenditures on advancing science and technology by Ghana, Kenya, Tanzania and Uganda as percentages of GDP 1978/9–1991/2

Year	Ghana[a]	Kenya	Tanzania	Uganda
1978/79	1.1	n.a.	0.3	n.a.
1979/80	0.7	n.a.	0.2	n.a.
1980/81	0.9	n.a.	0.3	n.a.
1981/82	0.4	n.a.	0.3	0.003
1982/83	n.a.	n.a.	0.3	0.004
1983/84	0.0	n.a.	0.6	0.004
1984/85	0.5	n.a.	0.6	0.004
1985/86	0.8	n.a.	0.6	0.003
1986/87	0.6	0.4	0.7	0.005
1987/88	0.3	0.6	0.6	n.a.
1988/89	0.4	0.7	1.3	0.09
1989/90	0.7	1.0	2.5	0.12
1990/91	0.4	1.3	2.3	0.15
1991/92	0.2	n.a.	2.4	2.2

Sources: GDP, at current prices; Tables 3.1, 4.1, 5.1 and 6.1
Total expenditures on advancing science and technology; Table 7.1

Notes: a: Ghana's percentage in the latest years is biased downwards, because of incomplete coverage of foreign donations

and from one-tenth to 2.2, the last a figure as high as any encountered elsewhere in Africa. Later we shall decompose the data for these recent years, which will provide an explanation for the extraordinary surge in Uganda's expenditures on advancing science and technology.

The figures in Table 7.2 permit a comparison across countries, as do those in Table 7.3. In Table 7.3 the comparisons are of the volume of resources committed to advancing science and technology, in total and per capita. The common basis for measurement is current US dollars; the first four columns of Table 7.3 measure total expenditures, the second four columns expenditures per capita. Looking at the first four columns, the figures for the beginning of the span of 14 years shows Ghana as spending far more than any of the others, and Uganda far less. The end of the span of years shows Ghana in last, rather than first place, and the other three countries more or less equal. The decline of Ghana and the rise of Uganda were both precipitous, the former occurring around 1982/3 (for which year, unsurprisingly, there is no estimate), the latter in the very last year for which figures are available, 1991/2.

Allowing for differences in population between the four countries, as is done in the final columns of Table 7.3, yields similar conclusions: in the initial years Ghana allocated substantially more, per capita, to pursuing science and technology; in the last year Uganda more than caught up. In the intervening years Ghana's, Kenya's and Tanzania's expenditures were of the same order of magnitude, and Uganda's (during the period of turmoil) of two orders of magnitude less.

An additional conclusion can be drawn from the figures in the last four columns of Table 7.3, namely that annual expenditures per capita were and are extremely low. The highest figures were US$14 (Ghana in 1978/9 and 1980/1), but the median was between US$1.00 and US $2.00 per inhabitant per year. When we remember that total expenditures on advancing science and technology include both R&D and technical education, a median expenditure of one to two US dollars per year, per person, is woefully inadequate. How can science and technology progress in countries which devote such paltry amounts to their pursuit?

The above are the most tentative of conclusions, for we cannot ascribe much accuracy to the data, being as they are informed guesses rather than respectable statistics, and presented more for completeness of coverage – to provide a measure of the commitment to advancing science and technology – than for persuasion. However, as we shall see in Chapter 10, there are a few data from countries outside our sample of four which will enable us to put them in some perspective.

Table 7.3 Expenditures on advancing science and technology by Ghana, Kenya, Tanzania and Uganda total and per capita, in US dollars 1978/9–1991/2

Year	Total expenditures (millions of US dollars at current prices)				Expenditures per capita (US dollars at current prices)			
	Ghana	Kenya	Tanzania	Uganda	Ghana	Kenya	Tanzania	Uganda
1978/9	140	n.a.	13	n.a.	14	n.a.	0.74	n.a.
1979/80	70	n.a.	10	n.a.	6.7	n.a.	0.55	n.a.
1980/1	145	n.a.	17	n.a.	14	n.a.	0.90	n.a.
1981/2	70	n.a.	18	0.02	6.5	n.a.	0.93	0.002
1982/3	n.a.	n.a.	22	0.04	n.a.	n.a.	1.1	0.003
1983/4	28	n.a.	39	0.03	2.4	n.a.	1.9	0.002
1984/5	36	n.a.	33	0.03	3.0	n.a.	1.5	0.002
1985/6	53	n.a.	43	0.03	4.2	n.a.	1.9	0.002
1986/7	40	31	35	0.07	3.1	1.5	1.5	0.005
1987/8	16	50	16+	n.a.	1.2	2.3	0.67+	n.a.
1988/9	21	61	37	0.81	1.5	2.7	1.6	0.05
1989/90	34	84	65	1.5	2.4	3.6	2.7	0.09
1990/1	23	110	54	3.7	1.5	4.6	2.2	0.23
1991/2	15	n.a.	65	48	1.0	n.a.	2.6	2.9

Sources: Total Expenditures: Table 7.1
Exchange rates into US dollars; Tables 3.1, 4.1, 5.1 and 6.1
Populations: Tables 3.2, 4.2, 5.2 and 6.2

EXPENDITURES OF R&D INSTITUTES

It is by reducing the scope of our inquiry that we can better improve the accuracy of our data. The reduction is to locally financed expenditures by institutes whose primary function is R&D. We have observed that it is these expenditures that are reported by African governments in response to the questionnaires of international agencies like UNESCO (UNESCO, 1990). For R&D institutes, the coverage may be nearly complete, for they are relatively few in number and resident, almost all, in the public sector. As a consequence, their budgets may be collected and published as a regular part of governmental statistical programmes.

Our data on the expenditures of public R&D institutes are presented in Tables 7.4 and 7.5. For Uganda, the institutes have been all in the agricultural sector; for the other countries they have operated in other sectors as well. The raw data in the first four columns of Table 7.4 are not very revealing, but the data in the second four columns of the Table, and in Table 7.5, are. Let us examine government expenditures on the R&D institutes in terms of constant prices (of 1987). Those for Ghana approximately doubled, in 1986/7, from their previous rate; those for Kenya seem to have doubled also in 1990/1 (although there is only one year's observation to support this statement); those for Tanzania have fluctuated without any noticeable trend; and those for Uganda were restored to respectable amounts in 1989/90. For three countries out of the four, therefore, in recent years increased public support, in terms of increased funds, has been afforded to the R&D institutes.

Table 7.5, in which total public expenditures are noted, places these increases in support for R&D institutes in perspective. The first four columns of the table list total government expenditures, the second four columns the percentages of these totals expended on the R&D institutes. Examining the trends within countries, the percentages are upwards, generally from one plateau to a higher one, the ascensions occurring in 1982/3 for Ghana, 1990/1 for Kenya, 1986/7 for Tanzania and 1988/9 for Uganda. The rises amounted to an approximate doubling in the cases of the first three countries, and a multiplication of roughly twenty-fold in the last. Comparing the figures across countries, on their higher plateaux, the differences appear to vary with the absolute level of GDP: Kenya is consistent across the years, allocating the largest percentage of its current government expenditures to its R&D institutes, Ghana the second largest, and Tanzania the third, and Uganda the smallest. This is an unsurprising result, holding generally across countries of similar sizes at all levels of GDP.

Table 7.6 gives us our first opportunity to extend our analysis beyond

Table 7.4 Public expenditures on R&D institutes in Ghana, Kenya, Tanzania and Uganda (in units of the national currency, at current and constant prices) 1978/9–1991/2

	Public expenditures on R&D institutes at current prices				Public expenditures on R&D institutes, at constant prices of 1987			
Year	Ghana (millions of Cedis)	Kenya (millions of KSh)	Tanzania (millions of TSh)	Uganda (millions of USh)	Ghana (millions of Cedis)	Kenya (millions of KSh)	Tanzania (millions of TSh)	Uganda (millions of USh)
1978/9	14.7	n.a.	n.a.	n.a.	490	n.a.	n.a.	n.a.
1979/80	17.7	n.a.	n.a.	n.a.	430	n.a.	n.a.	n.a.
1980/1	19.1	n.a.	n.a.	n.a.	310	n.a.	n.a.	n.a.
1981/2	37.2	n.a.	n.a.	0.022	340	n.a.	n.a.	1.04
1982/3	53	n.a.	n.a.	0.039	370	n.a.	n.a.	1.34
1983/4	59	n.a.	40	0.051	300	n.a.	106	1.04
1984/5	123	n.a.	61	0.083	290	n.a.	134	0.65
1985/6	286	n.a.	76	0.187	560	n.a.	126	0.62
1986/7	760	253	155	0.702	1,070	266	204	0.70
1987/8	1,900	408	186	n.a.	1,900	408	186	n.a.
1988/9	1,400	512	200	125	1,050	471	148	27
1989/90	3,100	571	328	321	1,820	481	191	55
1990/1	2,500	782	328	486	1,120	595	158	55
1991/2	1,900+	n.a.	413	200	719+	n.a.	156	25

Sources: Expenditures of R&D institutes: Tables 3.15 (column 9); 4.16, 5.21, and 6.9
GDP deflator: Tables 3.1, 4.1, 5.1, and 6.1

Table 7.5 Total public current expenditures of Ghana, Kenya, Tanzania and Uganda, and the percentages claimed by public R&D institutes 1978/9–1991/2

Fiscal Year	Total government current expenditures (billions in constant prices of 1987)				Public expenditures of R&D institutes as % of total government current expenditure			
	Ghana (Cedis)	Kenya (KSh)	Tanzania (TSh)	Uganda (USh)	Ghana	Kenya	Tanzania	Uganda
1978/9	84.3	12.0	31.5	14.3	0.58	n.a.	n.a.	n.a.
1979/80	85.0	19.4	30.6	8.90	0.51	n.a.	n.a.	n.a.
1980/1	65.2	20.0	25.0	5.60	0.47	n.a.	n.a.	n.a.
1981/2	58.0	20.0	22.4	7.04	0.58	n.a.	n.a.	0.015
1982/3	35.0	25.0	23.0	16.4	1.09	n.a.	n.a	0.008
1983/4	32.9	23.7	23.3	19.8	0.91	n.a.	0.45	0.005
1984/5	54.0	23.9	25.7	20.7	0.54	n.a.	0.52	0.003
1985/6	79.2	24.9	26.8	15.4	0.72	n.a.	0.47	0.004
1986/7	102	26.5	27.5	11.6	1.04	1.01	0.74	0.006
1987/8	111	30.0	25.0	8.0	1.71	1.36	0.74	n.a.
1988/9	118	31.5	22.6	10.4	0.92	1.49	0.66	0.27
1989/90	68	36.3	23.4	12.8	2.68	1.32	0.82	0.43
1990/1	74	31.1	23.8	17.9	1.51	1.92	0.66	0.31
1991/2	72	n.a.	35.5	40.0	1.00+	n.a.	0.44	0.068

Sources: Total Government Current Expenditures: Tables 3.8, (1978/9–1988/9, government current expenditure; 1989/90–1991/2, government consumption), 4.8, 5.1, and 6.4, all converted to constant prices of 1987 by the GDP deflators in Tables 3.1, 4.1, 5.1 and 6.1
Total Public Expenditures of R&D Institutes: Table 7.4

the four countries of our Sub-Saharan sample. For a few other countries comparable data are available on expenditures of R&D institutes; these data are divided into a first category, those appropriate for countries which, at the time the data were collected, were also undergoing Structural Adjustment, and a second category of countries, for those which were not undergoing Structural Adjustment. The observations are few and scattered, both geographically and chronologically, but they do yield much the same variety of behaviour as do the four countries in our sample. Looking at public expenditures per capita, UNESCO's sample of countries has generally higher figures than ours, although the range from lowest to highest is about the same (US$0.2 per capita to 6.4, compared to 0.05 to 1.15).

Another, perhaps more revealing, way of comparing the different countries' expenditures on R&D is to place next to each other, in pairs, the local expenditure of one country undergoing Structural Adjustment and another, similar country, not undergoing Structural Adjustment. (This is the method of comparison used by Harrigan and Mosley, 1991, in their evaluation of the macro-economic effects of the World Bank's lending activities.) Of the four countries in our sample, we pair Ghana with Benin, Kenya with Nigeria, Tanzania with Gabon and Uganda with Burundi and Rwanda (taken together). If we make these pair-wise comparisons we find Ghana's own contributions to its R&D institutes are inferior to Benin's on grounds of both US dollars per capita and percentages of GDP, and Uganda's are inferior to the sum of Burundi's and Rwanda's on all three grounds represented in Table 7.6. Tanzania's contributions are only 10 per cent of those of Gabon in terms of US dollars per capita, but are greater in terms of percentage of GDP. Kenya's exceed Nigeria's on all three grounds. Thus, for two of the four countries in our own sample of countries undergoing Structural Adjustment, public expenditures on R&D are less, for one more, and for the final one intermediate, to expenditures of paired countries not undergoing Structural Adjustment. The comparisons seem to be so few and so diverse that we can draw no conclusions. Disappointed we must be at the paucity of results, but that is only a reflection of the paucity of data, in addition to those that we have collected. Perhaps there are other ways of presenting our aggregate data that will be more fruitful.

GOVERNMENT FINANCING OF ADVANCES IN SCIENCE AND TECHNOLOGY

R&D institutes are not the only public bodies advancing science and technology; educational bodies also fulfil that function. Let us now consider them as well. The data needed to determine whether or not government

Table 7.6 Comparison of expenditures, total and per capita, on R&D institutes in African countries; averages of various years 1982–1991

Category of country	Country	Years of expenditure[a]	Average annual public expenditure (millions of US dollars, at current prices)	Average annual public expenditure per capita (US dollars, at current prices)	Average annual public expenditure as % of GDP
Our sample	Ghana	1983–1991	6.4	0.47	0.13
	Kenya	1987–1991	24.7	1.15	0.31
	Tanzania	1986–1991	2.7	0.12	0.08
	Uganda	1988–1991	0.8	0.05	0.02
Other countries undergoing[b] structural adjustment	Madagascar	1988	n.a.	0.9	0.4
	Mauritius	1989	1.2	6.4	0.3
Countries not undergoing[b] structural adjustment	Benin	1989	n.a.	2.3	0.7
	Nigeria	1987	21.4	0.2	0.1
	Gabon	1986	n.a.	1.1	0.0
	Burundi and Rwanda	1989 and 1985	2.5	1.1	0.4

Sources: Ghana, Kenya, Tanzania and Uganda:Tables 7.4 (Expenditures); 3.1, 4.1, 5.1 and 6.1 (exchange rates); and 3.2, 4.2, 5.2 and 6.2 (populations) Others: UNESCO, *1990*, Tables 5.10, and Appendix p. A-12 (exchange rates *vs* US$).

Notes: a: the initial years for Ghana and Tanzania are those chosen by the World Bank as the dates Structural Adjustment reforms began (Gulhati, 1988); for Tanzania (for which the World Bank set a date of 1980) the initial year is the first for which statistics on expenditures are available; and for Uganda the initial year is that in which foreign donations began to appear in substantial amounts
b: as of the date when UNESCO's data were gathered

expenditures on advancing science and technology overall have changed, and if so, in which direction, have been retrieved from the individual country chapters, and collected in Table 7.7. The figures on expenditures on advancing science and technology are the sum of those spent by the governments on their own research institutes (but not those spent by the para-statals on theirs) plus those spent on scientific and technical education, primarily the budgets of the science and engineering faculties of the universities. These sums are then compared with total government expenditures and their ratios calculated.

Given the ten years for which we have data, the figures in the final four columns of Table 7.7 must be taken with some caution. Looking at the experience of Ghana, we find considerable fluctuations, between 0.8 and 5.8 per cent, for public expenditures on science and technology relative to the totals. Nonetheless Ghana's expenditures, on the average, exceed those of both Kenya and Tanzania, which are stable at approximately 2 per cent and 1.6 per cent respectively. Uganda's public expenditures on science and technology are now reaching these percentages, after years of neglect. Looking at all four countries we can conclude that the expenditures in the different countries are now of the same order of magnitude (roughly 2 per cent per year of total government expenditures), and that the constraints placed upon government expenditures by the conditions inherent in the Structural Adjustment Programmes do not seem to have led to any further restrictions on public funds allocated to the pursuit of science and technology.

FLOW OF FOREIGN FUNDS INTO SCIENCE AND TECHNOLOGY

Scattered data on capital (development) expenditures indicate that, to an increasing extent, the major portion of the funds allocated to increasing the capacity of R&D institutes is coming from abroad. The percentages of total 'development' expenditures of R&D institutes financed by foreign bodies varies substantially from country to country: Uganda having negligible percentages till the 1990s and the highest since then; Tanzania substantial percentages over the last several years; and Kenya moderate percentages. For Ghana, percentages cannot be calculated, since the data on foreign donations are almost never identified: our guess is that Ghana's receipts are of the order of Kenya's (up to 1991), but less proportionately, than Tanzania's and Uganda's (see Table 7.9).

Moving on to total expenditures on advancing science and technology, we encounter percentages of foreign donations of substantial size, country by country. The figures are presented in Table 7.8; they reveal that Kenya and Tanzania received foreign donations sufficient to increase their

Table 7.7 Comparison of public expenditures on the advance of science and technology with total government expenditures for Ghana, Kenya, Tanzania and Uganda 1982/3–1991/2 (millions of units of the national currency, at constant prices of 1987)

Year	Expenditures on R&D institutes				Expenditures on technical education in schools, colleges and universities				Total public expenditures on science and technology				Expenditures on science and technology as % of total government expenditures			
	Ghana	Kenya	Tanzania	Uganda	Ghana	Kenya	Tanzania	Uganda	Ghana	Kenya	Tanzania	Uganda	Ghana	Kenya	Tanzania	Uganda
1982/3	370	n.a.	n.a.	1.34	n.a.	n.a.	n.a.	1.0	n.a.	n.a.	n.a.	3.3	n.a.	n.a.	n.a.	0.017
1983/4	300	n.a.	106	1.04	50	n.a.	794	2.1	350	n.a.	900	3.1	0.8	n.a.	1.8	0.013
1984/5	290	n.a.	134	0.65	2,810	n.a.	688	2.1	3,100	n.a.	822	2.8	4.8	n.a.	1.4	0.012
1985/6	560	n.a.	126	0.62	5,140	n.a.	825	1.8	5,700	n.a.	951	2.4	5.8	n.a.	1.7	0.012
1986/7	1,070	266	204	0.70	3,930	97	899	3.0	5,000	368	1,103	3.7	4.2	1.5	1.7	0.025
1987/8	1,900	408	186	n.a.	600	139	915	n.a.	2,500	547	1,101	n.a.	2.0	1.9	1.4	n.a.
1988/9	1,050	471	148	27	2,050	194	835	52	3,100	665	983	79	2.1	2.3	1.2	0.27
1989/90	1,800	481	191	55	3,600	156	1,268	73	5,400	637	1,454	128	n.a.	2.2	1.8	0.20
1990/1	1,120	595	158	55	2,300	131	184	302	3,420	726	972	3,572	n.a.	1.7	n.a.	0.40
1991/2	720+	n.a.	156	25	1,380	n.a.	1,550	5,045	2,100+	n.a.	1,706	5,070	n.a.	n.a.	n.a.	1.2

Sources: Expenditures of R&D Institutes: Table 7.4
Expenditures on Technical Education; Tables 3.19 (total, less public expenditures of CSIR); 4.17 (universities only); 5.19; and 7.1 (for Uganda, total less R&D Institutes for 1982/3–1989/90; Tables 6.11 and 6.12 for 1990/1 and 1991/2)
Total Government Expenditures (current plus development): Tables 3.8, 4.8, 5.5 (Government Consumption plus Total Investment), and 6.4 (all converted to constant prices of 1987 by GDP deflators)

expenditures on advancing science and technology by one-quarter to one-third prior to adopting Structural Adjustment Programmes, but subsequent to their adoption the increases have been by two-thirds to four-fifths. In the case of Uganda, the figures are even higher, but Uganda's figures include foreign loans destined for public budget support, especially Maherere University, as well as donations.

If we neglect variations between the three countries and take only the most recent two years for each country, we could strike an average figure for foreign donations, as a percentage of total expenditures on furthering science and technology. On this basis, approximately 70 per cent of scientific and technological activities seem to be financed from abroad.

SUMMARY OF THE STATISTICAL EVIDENCE

In this chapter we have assembled for the four countries, Ghana, Kenya, Tanzania and Uganda, the figures that are available on expenditures designed to advance their science and technology. In addition, again to the extent that they are available, we have identified the sources of the funds expended, separating local from foreign. We have not discussed the uses to which these resources have been put, that being the subject of the next two chapters; but we have examined the overall changes in both expenditures and finances over time, in order to determine their trends. We have also tried to relate these changes to concurrent changes in macroeconomic variables.

The main finding is that expenditures on advancing science and technology have increased somewhat, from abysmally low levels (of the order of a US dollar or two per head of the population), since the adoption of Structural Adjustment Programmes. The modest increases (to approximately twice the previous figures) are apparent whatever the basis against which they are calculated: in absolute amounts, as a fraction of total expenditures of the governments, and as a fraction of the assistance these countries receive from abroad.

When we break down total expenditures into those provided by the national governments and those from abroad we find that increases have come about chiefly from foreign donations (and loans). The governments of the countries have, at best, just been able to maintain their contributions; the institutions engaged in R&D and in technical education have not been able to dislodge other claimants for the limited amounts of money that the governments can expend. Foreign assistance has compensated for the shortage of local funds to a certain extent, and of this foreign assistance, an increasing share appears to have been allocated to advancing science and

Table 7.8 Foreign donations for science and technology to Ghana, Kenya, Tanzania and Uganda as a percentage of total expenditures on science and technology 1981/2–1991/2 (millions of units of national currency, at constant prices of 1987)

Year	Government expenditures				Foreign donations				Foreign loans and grants as % of total expenditures			
	Ghana	Kenya	Tanzania	Uganda	Ghana	Kenya	Tanzania	Uganda	Ghana	Kenya	Tanzania	Uganda
1981/2	n.a.	n.a.	n.a.	n.a.	n.a.	n.a.	n.a.	n.a.	n.a.	n.a.	n.a.	n.a.
1982/3	n.a.	n.a.	n.a.	3.3	n.a.	n.a.	n.a.	n.a.	n.a.	n.a.	n.a.	n.a.
1983/4	123	n.a.	900	3.1	n.a.	n.a.	270	n.a.	n.a.	n.a.	25	n.a.
1984/5	3,100	n.a.	822	2.8	n.a.	n.a.	278	n.a.	n.a.	n.a.	25	n.a.
1985/6	5,700	n.a.	951	2.4	n.a.	n.a.	299	n.a.	n.a.	n.a.	24	n.a.
1986/7	5,000	368	1,103	3.7	n.a.	172	397	n.a.	n.a.	32	26	n.a.
1987/8	2,500	547	1,101	n.a.	n.a.	273	n.a.	n.a.	n.a.	33	n.a.	n.a.
1988/9	3,100	665	983	27	n.a.	345	1,707	52	n.a.	34	64	66
1989/90	5,400	637	1,459	55	n.a.	813	3,851	73	n.a.	55	72	57
1990/1	3,420	726	972	55	n.a.	1,294	4,028	302	n.a.	64	81	85
1991/2	2,100+	n.a.	1,706	25	n.a.	n.a.	3,654	4,9457	n.a.	n.a.	68	98

Sources: Government Expenditures: Table 7.7, columns 9–11 for Ghana, Kenya and Tanzania, Table 7.4 for Uganda
Total Expenditures: Table 7.1, columns 5–8
Foreign Donations: by difference (for Uganda, foreign donations and loans)

Table 7.9 Foreign loans and grants to R&D institutes as a percentage of total capital expenditures to Ghana, Kenya, Tanzania and Uganda, various years 1981–1992 (billions of units of the national currency, at current prices)

Year	Local financing of science and technology capital expenditures				Foreign financing of science and technology capital expenditures				Foreign financing as % of total financing of capital expenditures			
	Ghana	Kenya	Tanzania[a]	Uganda	Ghana	Kenya	Tanzania	Uganda	Ghana	Kenya	Tanzania	Uganda
1982/3	n.a.	n.a.	0.2	n.a.	n.a.	n.a.	n.a.	n.a.	n.a.	n.a.	n.a.	n.a.
1983/4	n.a.	n.a.	0.3	n.a.	n.a.	n.a.	0.1	n.a.	n.a.	n.a.	25	n.a.
1984/5	n.a.	n.a.	0.4	n.a.	n.a.	n.a.	0.1	n.a.	n.a.	n.a.	20	n.a.
1985/6	n.a.	n.a.	0.6	n.a.	n.a.	n.a.	0.2	n.a.	n.a.	n.a.	25	n.a.
1986/7	n.a.	0.4	0.8	n.a.	n.a.	1.0	0.3	n.a.	n.a.	71	27	n.a.
1987/8	n.a.	2.0	1.0	n.a.	n.a.	0.1	0.0+	n.a.	n.a.	5	n.a.	n.a.
1988/9	n.a.	0.9	1.3	n.a.	n.a.	0.2	0.1+	n.a.	n.a.	18	n.a.	n.a.
1989/90	n.a.	3.4	3.5	n.a.	n.a.	0.3	4.3+	n.a.	n.a.	8	55+	n.a.
1990/1	n.a.	0.5	2.0	1.2	n.a.	0.1	9.6+	1.2	n.a.	20	82+	46
1991/2	n.a.	n.a.	4.5	5.9	n.a.	n.a.	8.1	3.7	n.a.	n.a.	64+	86

Sources: Local Financing: Tables 4.13 and 4.15 (R&D Institutes and all universities); 5.22; 6.11 and 6.12; and 7.8; all converted to US dollars at the official exchange rate (Tables 3.1, 4.1, 5.1 and 6.1)

Note: [a] Local financing of both recurrent and capital expenditures

technology. It is as if foreign donors recognize the importance in the long run of advancing science and technology and admit the difficulty faced by African governments in reallocating their own resources to this desirable end. But it does seem that if science and technology are to flourish financially, they will flourish only through the contributions of outsiders.

What we could not resolve was the issue of the effect of adopting Structural Adjustment. A comparison between those countries 'adjusting' and those not (Table 7.6) was not revealing, chiefly through a lack of comparable data. To our knowledge, no one else has collected data on expenditures on science and technology for other countries over an extended interval. We did not have the resources to examine, ourselves, expenditures in Sub-Saharan African countries not subject to the constraints imposed by the foreign lenders, and others have not yet attempted the task. It is quite possible that the funds available to advance science and technology in these, non-conforming, countries have increased too; perhaps via the same device, namely increased donations by foreign bodies. We do not know the answer: our guess would be that foreigners have not been so generous to those Sub-Saharan African countries which do not have the 'seal of approval' awarded to those which conform to the conditions imposed by the Bank and the Fund.

But we should not leave the issue unresolved; we have one tactic that we can employ – that of the counterfactual. We can try to estimate what would have happened in the countries we studied, in Ghana, Kenya, Tanzania and Uganda, had Structural Adjustment Programmes not been adopted.

A COUNTERFACTUAL EXPERIMENT

To carry out a counterfactual experiment, one needs two items, a set of basic assumptions and a model within which to represent the alternatives. The alternatives are, of course, the adoption of a Structural Adjustment Programme and the non-adoption of a Structural Adjustment Programme. We shall call the first alternative Case I and the second Case II.

The crucial assumption in the experiment is over the amount of foreign assistance granted in the absence of a 'seal of approval'. It appears, given the data in Tables 7.1 and 7.8, that it is via an increase in foreign assistance that expenditures on science and technology have increased; the issue is whether or not the foreign assistance would have been forthcoming if the countries had not accepted the conditions imposed by the IMF/Bank. We shall make the most extreme assumption, that less foreign assistance would have been available to finance advances in science and technology; to pick an illustrative figure, we will say less by half.

So far as the total contributions to the advance of science and technology by the national government are concerned, we shall assume that these are unaltered in Case II from Case I. Our reason for assuming no difference in total expenditures in the two cases is that the claims of those engaged in carrying out scientific and technological activities would have been greater had foreign assistance not been available; but that these greater claims would have been matched by greater claims by all other public bodies, resulting in a standstill. When all interest groups increase their claims upon public funds the result is usually no change in their relative receipts (Wildavsky, 1979; Olson, 1982). We shall make an additional assumption, though, based upon our observations of the nature of the budget allocation decisions in the four countries that we studied; namely that all the funds assigned to 'Development' in the budgets of the public R&D institutes would have been transferred to the 'Current' expenditure account; in other words, that what would have otherwise been expended on capital investment would be expended instead in maintaining wages and salaries. Since some of the funds made available by foreign donors were actually used to subsidize salaries of scientists and engineers, in the absence of these subsidies the scientists' and engineers' salaries would have had to be maintained by injections of local funds. The net effect, therefore, would be to reduce capital expenditures in R&D activities by the amount of foreign donations: in Case II, compared to Case I, therefore *capital* expenditures are assumed to be 60 per cent lower than in Case I, 50 per cent lower because of reduced foreign assistance and 10 per cent lower because of reduced local government expenditure.

The only effect that we are trying to capture at this point is the reduction in total expenditures on advancing science and technology; other effects will be captured in subsequent chapters. How can this effect be captured in the model that we have already, in the penultimate section of Chapter 2, chosen to serve as the guide to our inquiry? There are two possible means, both of which we shall use. The first is in the volume of resources devoted to the pursuit of science and technology; the second in the efficiency with which R&D is carried out.

Taking the first phenomenon, we have already assumed that in Case II, as compared to Case I, the total amount of resources allocated to furthering science and technology is reduced by the amount of foreign assistance denied. Reducing foreign assistance by half would reduce total expenditures on science and technology by roughly 35 per cent. In terms of Fung and Ishikawa's model, the reduction in funds allocated to R&D in Case II *vis-à-vis* the allocation in Case I, is equivalent to a reallocation of approximately 1 per cent of the total resources of the country from R&D to the production of the goods, labelled Y, which do not profit from R&D. In other words, there is a reallocation from future production of goods (via investment in R&D in which the country has a future) to present production of goods in which the country does not have a future. We would expect there to be more current output of good Y in Case II than in Case I, and less future output of good X, the good which does benefit from the affiliation of R&D.

Taking the second phenomenon, the efficiency with which R&D is carried out, the model includes this phenomenon as a parameter, δ (delta), whose value is exogenous to the system of equations. How might this parameter differ in value between Cases I and II? The answer lies in the reallocation of resources that we have not yet taken into account, namely that from capital expenditures to current expenditures. We recall that this reallocation is assumed to take place as local governments compensate scientists and engineers for the supplements to their salaries that would otherwise, in Case I, have been contributed by foreign donors. Let us assume that the reduction in capital investment in R&D reduces the efficiency with which R&D is carried out by 10 per cent: in the model this is reflected by a reduction in the value of the efficiency parameter, δ, of 10 per cent.

With these two changes from Case I – a shift of total resources of 1 per cent from R&D to the production of good Y, and a reduction in the value of δ by 10 per cent – the conditions for Case II are set. What is the outcome, in terms of the difference in behaviour of the model in Case II as against its behaviour in Case I? Assuming an intermediate value for the other parameter of the system (β, the elasticity of substitution of intermediate goods), the outcome can be visualized as in Figure 7.1. Expenditures of the country's scarce resources on R&D fall; production of good X, the good which benefits from R&D, remains the same; and the production of good Y rises. For the economy as a whole, income is unaltered; but, compared to Case I, total output increases, by the amount of the extra output of good Y.

This is the result in the short run. In the long run, as indicated by the (upper) trajectory for Case II, and the parallel but swifter trajectory for Case I, the economy advances more slowly. The reasons are twofold: less R&D is being carried out; and what is being carried out is carried out less efficiently. In Figure 7.1 these two consequences are shown by the trajectory for Case I lying closer to the horizontal axis – the axis along which the output of the good with the higher potential is measured – and for successive outputs of good X (labelled X_1, X_2, X_3, etc.) being obtained more speedily (i.e. X, being obtained in half the time in Case I as in Case II).

Summarizing the deductions from Fung and Ishikawa's model for our

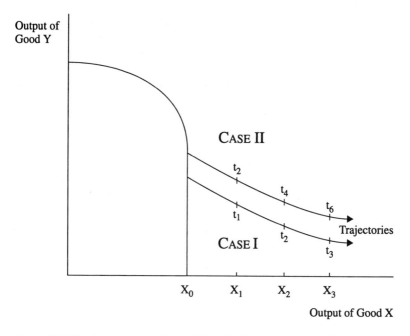

Figure 7.1 Visual comparison of actual Case I with counterfactual Case II

two cases, we conclude that the counterfactual case, Case II, is more attractive to the economy in the short run, through higher total output (via more good Y); but is less attractive in the long run, through lower output of the other, more desirable good X (via less R&D directed towards improving its production). The future is traded-off for the present.

This is not the only counterfactual case that we will construct, for it addresses only the macroeconomic issues discussed in this chapter. Still to be addressed are the meso- and micro-economic issues: these will occupy us in the next two chapters. Before we turn to these chapters we might well recall two assumptions that underlie Fung and Ishikawa's own theory:

1 that the economy's resources are fully employed; and
2 that there is no cost, nor any time taken, in shifting resources from one activity to another.

The relevance of these two assumptions for our Cases I and II are that, faithfully following Fung and Ishikawa, we have assumed that those resources not employed in R&D (in Case I) are, in Case II, shifted, immediately and without cost, to the production of good Y. One of the questions we shall address in the next chapters is: are scientific and technological personnel in Ghana, Kenya, Tanzania and Uganda perfectly mobile? If so, can they be expected to be productive in these activities for which their background and training have not prepared them? Moreover, the equally important question of potential for R&D, raised in the theoretical chapter, will have to be addressed also. In terms of the variables appearing in Figure 7.1, this means addressing the practical question: what goods actually belong in category X? What in category Y?

8 Effects among the sectors of the economy

INTRODUCTION

In this chapter we shall attempt to determine the effects of the adoption of Structural Adjustment Programmes on the allocation of resources between the sectors of the economy. This analysis will focus on the 'meso-economics', signifying not macro-economics, nor micro-economics, but what lies in between. When examining activities more aggregated than those encompassed in the single organization, and less aggregated than those in the overall economy, we can be guided by theory, and by what has appeared to others and to ourselves during our enquiry. Let us start with the issues raised by theory.

The theory developed in Chapter 2 suggests that important issues for a developing country are:

1 the volume of resources the nation devotes to advancing science and technology;
2 the extent to which these resources are made available in the early years of the country's economic development;
3 the allocation of these resources assigned to improving the production of those commodities with the greatest potential to increase income;
4 the efficiency with which scientists, engineers, technicians and other complementary workers are employed; and
5 the degree to which the 'intermediate' capital goods can be substituted one for another in producing those goods with the highest potential.

In addition, examination of the assumptions underlying the theory suggests that we also try to determine whether or not resources are perfectly mobile, and always fully employed.

The first two of these issues – the overall volume of resources devoted to advancing science and technology and the timing of the application of these resources – were addressed in the previous chapter; and the fourth and fifth issues – the efficiency with which scientists, engineers and others are employed, and the substitutability of capital goods – will be addressed in Chapter 9. What remain for this chapter are the third, fourth and fifth issues – those of the direction of R&D, the mobility of resources and the intensity of their employment. In addition, there is another issue absent in the theory but deserving attention, one to which the IMF/World Bank attach great emphasis, that of the assignment of activities to the public, or to the private, sector of the economy.

Although we have introduced them separately, all four issues to be addressed in this chapter – the mobility of resources, their full or less than full employment, the activities to which the specialized resources necessary in advancing science and technology are assigned, and in which branch of the economy, public or private, those activities are to be carried out – are interrelated. Although we can identify them separately, we will not be able to consider them in a piece-meal fashion, for our data do not permit it, nor does our understanding of the interrelationships warrant it. We shall be led by the information we have been able to accumulate; all these data enable us to do is to draw implications. We can only hope that at the end of our analysis the four issues will be a little less unclear than they are at the beginning.

ECONOMIC ACTIVITY BY SECTOR

In presenting our data on the 'meso-economy', we will focus on two items, the overall figures on economic activity and the figures measuring the advance of science and technology, both by sector of activity. These data appear in Table 8.1, which contains figures on economic activity, and Table 8.2, which contains figures on R&D. For our purposes the 'meso-economy' consists of three sectors: agriculture, industry and services: the contributions of each of these three sectors to the GDPs of Ghana, Kenya, Tanzania and Uganda over recent years appear in Table 8.1. We notice considerable differences in the shares between countries, with Ghana and Kenya deriving larger fractions of total GDP from industry than Tanzania and Uganda. Within each country, over their recent histories, Ghana's and Uganda's agricultural shares have been falling, and Tanzania's rising, with compensating movements in industry's shares. To the extent that one of the objectives of Structural Adjustment Programmes is to reallocate resources between sectors, chiefly from services to industry to agriculture, this objective has not yet been wholly achieved.

Table 8.1 Shares of total GDP by sector in Ghana, Kenya, Tanzania and Uganda, various years 1980–1992

Year	Share of agriculture (%)				Share of industry (%)				Share of services (%)			
	Ghana	Kenya	Tanzania	Uganda	Ghana	Kenya	Tanzania	Uganda	Ghana	Kenya	Tanzania	Uganda
1980	58	33	55	72	12	20	12	5	31	47	31	23
1981	51	33	56	58	9	20	11	7	40	47	31	35
1982	57	33	57	56	6	20	11	9	38	47	31	35
1983	60	34	59	60	7	19	9	8	34	47	31	33
1984	54	34	60	54	12	19	9	8	37	47	31	33
1985	52	32	62	61	13	19	9	7	39	49	30	38
1986	49	33	62	62	13	19	9	8	38	48	29	33
1987	47	32	63	62	14	19	8	8	39	49	29	31
1988	46	32	61	61	14	19	7	9	40	49	33	30
1989	46	31	62	61	14	20	5	9	40	49	32	32
1990	43	27	60	55	14	20	6	10	43	52	35	31
1991	42	27	61	51	15	20	5	12	43	53	34	35
1992	n.a.	n.a.	n.a.	n.a.	n.a.	n.a.	n.a.	n.a.	n.a.	n.a.	n.a.	n.a.

Source: Tables 3.3, 4.3, 5.3 and 6.3

Table 8.2 Shares of total expenditures by R&D institutes by sector in Ghana, Kenya, Tanzania and Uganda, various years 1980–1992

Year	Share in agriculture (%)				Share in industry (%)				Share in services (%)			
	Ghana[a]	Kenya[b]	Tanzania[c]	Uganda[d]	Ghana[a]	Kenya[b]	Tanzania[c]	Uganda[d]	Ghana[a]	Kenya[b]	Tanzania[c]	Uganda[d]
1980	n.a.	n.a.	n.a.	100–	n.a.	n.a.	n.a.	0	n.a.	n.a.	0+	0+
1981	98	n.a.	n.a.	100–	1	n.a.	n.a.	0	1	n.a.	0+	0+
1982	96	n.a.	n.a.	100–	1	n.a.	n.a.	0	3	n.a.	0+	0+
1983	94	n.a.	78–	100–	2	n.a.	22	0	4	n.a.	0+	0+
1984	86	n.a.	59–	100–	2	n.a.	41	0	12	n.a.	0+	0+
1985	82	n.a.	49–	100–	1	n.a.	51	0	16	n.a.	0+	0+
1986	92	51	43–	100–	8	9	57	0	7	40	0+	0+
1987	92	67	54–	100–	1	6	46	0	2	27	0+	0+
1988	97	72	71–	100–	2	6	29	0	2	22	0+	0+
1989	n.a.	75	65–	100–	2	5	35	0	n.a.	21	0+	0+
1990	93	87	70–	100–	5+	7	30	0	5	17	0+	0+
1991	n.a.	n.a.	63–	52	n.a.	n.a.	37	11	n.a.	n.a.	0+	37
1992	n.a.	n.a.	66–	88	n.a.	n.a.	34	11	n.a.	n.a.	0+	2

Source: Tables 3.15; 4.11 and 4.16; 5.21; and 5.22, columns 1 and 5; and 6.10, 6.11 and 6.12

Notes: a: in Ghana, the sectoral allocations of R&D institutes were as follows: agriculture, the Food Research Institute (FRI) and the Cocoa Research Industry of Ghana (CRIG); industry, the Industrial Research Institute (IRI), and the Technology Consultancy Centre TCC; and services, the Scientific Instrumentation Centre (SIC)

b: in Kenya, the sectoral allocation of R&D institutes was as follows: agriculture, the Coffee Research Foundation, the Kenya Agricultural Research Institute (KARI), the Kenya Forestry Research Institute (KEFRI), and the Kenya Marine and Fisheries Research Institute (KEMFRI); industry, the Kenya Industrial Research and Development Institute (KIRDI), and the National Council for Science and Technology NCST Trypanosomiasis Research Institute (KETRI), and services, the Kenya Medical Research Institute (KEMRI), the Kenya

c: in Tanzania, the sectoral allocations were as follows: industry, Tanzania Industrial Research Organization (TIRDO) and Tanzania Engineering and Manufacturing Design Organization (TEMDO); services, none; and the balance (of total expenditures of R&D institutes, Table 5.), allocated to agriculture

d: in Uganda, the sectoral allocations were as follows: agriculture, Recurrent and Development estimates of the Ministry of Agriculture; industry, Recurrent and Development estimates for the Ministry of Industry; and services, Development Estimates for Maherere University

+–: signifies more than, and less than

When we turn to the contributions of R&D – where contributions are measured by expenditures – the data in Table 8.2 do reveal changes in the shares *within* countries. To be sure, the data are fragmentary and relate almost entirely to public and semi-public R&D institutes, but these carry out almost all R&D in Sub-Saharan African countries. Taking the four countries of our sample alphabetically, in Ghana, the figures are reasonably accurate although not exhaustive; they indicate that the bulk of expenditures are devoted to the agricultural sector, and within the agricultural sector, to cocoa (see Table 3.13). The industrial and service sectors have received small sums, and these have fluctuated widely from year to year, depending chiefly upon the timing of receipts of foreign assistance.

Kenya's experience is somewhat different;although this is more apparent than real, since alone of the four countries the statistics of expenditures on R&D in services include those in medical research. Nonetheless, over the five years for which we have figures we still observe a rapidly increasing share being allocated to agricultural R&D, and declining shares in both the other sectors.

The statistics on the allocation of funds to R&D by sector in Tanzania are the weakest of the four countries. Industry's share arises through expenditures of the two industrial R&D institutes, which are recorded; but the share of services, although very small, cannot be estimated. Agriculture's share is the larger, but the data on agricultural expenditures on R&D (with the exception of TPRI's) are aggregated in the Ministry's accounts. We have resolved the statistical difficulty by assuming that all expenditures of R&D institutes not allocated to industry are allocated to agriculture. No trend over the period 1980–1992 is observable; agricultural and services' R&D are allocated between half and two-thirds of the total; industry's R&D between one-third and a half, but with considerable fluctuations between years. Allowing for allocations to services (medical research and the Tanzanian Institute of Standards) would reduce agriculture's share to well below half.

Last of all is Uganda, whose tendency towards concentrating all R&D in agriculture seems, in the last two years at least, to have been reversed. Two separate events have led to the reversal: large foreign grants to Maherere University in 1990/1 (for renewal and expansion of the sciences and social sciences), and the initiation of public R&D in industry in 1991/2, also with assistance from abroad. But the bulk of the foreign assistance that Uganda does receive for R&D is still directed towards agriculture, whose total expenditures have also risen substantially in the two most recent years. The conclusion throughout is that the agricultural sector receives the vast majority of funds for R&D, and industry very little.

That the shares, by sector, of expenditures on R&D by public institutes should fluctuate year-by-year is not surprising; that these should be relatively stable indicates a close correlation with the shares of economic activity overall, an association we shall comment upon in the next chapter. But if we were to consider not expenditures on R&D by public research institutes (the basis of the figures in Table 8.2) but the larger category of total expenditures on R&D, we would probably find a reallocation from industry to agriculture. We cannot back up this statement by statistics, but our impression is that expenditures in the other components filling the larger category – expenditures on research in the universities; and on R&D, training and technical services by producing firms, both public and private – have increased in the agricultural sector while remaining on balance more or less unchanged in the industrial. The latter impression – that there has been no *net* change of expenditures in the industrial sector – is the result of R&D in the universities increasing and R&D of productive firms decreasing. This impression is quite strong for the two more industrialized countries, Ghana and Kenya, and appears to be similar for Tanzania; it is only Uganda, where there has previously been no attempt to advance science and technology in industry, that the impression is the reverse.

MOBILITY BETWEEN SECTORS

The two issues to be considered in this section are the mobility and employment of labour. We recall that the assumptions underlying Fung and Ishikawa's model of a growing economy, as well as almost all mathematical models of economic growth, are that workers move effortlessly and speedily between sectors of the economy in response to inducements, and that all workers are fully employed. The economies represented are perfectly flexible and responsive.

Since the same assumptions underlie those economic models espoused by the IMF and World Bank, models to which we will refer in the penultimate chapter, we would find it wise to ask if the economies of Ghana, Kenya, Tanzania and Uganda, particularly their scientific and technological portions, exhibit perfect flexibility and responsiveness.

For employment overall, there are some data to which we can refer. These data do not cover unemployment, for which statistics from countries like those of Sub-Saharan Africa are either unavailable or unreliable, but rather employment in different activities in the urban or modern sector. Table 8.3 provides a few easily obtainable figures on employment in manufacturing industry. What we can observe is that employment in manufacturing industry is highly unstable in Ghana, less so in Kenya and

Tanzania. The differences between Ghana, on the one hand, and Kenya and Tanzania on the other, are probably the result of two factors: overall fluctuations in economic activity and the proportion of industry in private hands. Ghana, with severe economic fluctuations and with a high proportion of total industrial employment in the private sector, suffers wide variations; Kenya with a relatively stable growth rate, and Tanzania, with a high degree of concentration of the public sector (in which output, rather than employment, swings), suffer less. What can we infer from these figures? We would like to ask: is it likely that the fluctuations in employment in manufacturing arose either by chance, or through transitional unemployment, or through both? Since there is no precise answer to such questions, we ask rather: are we content with statistical or transitory explanations for the phenomenon we observe? We think that the answer is no: it strains belief to attribute fluctuations of the magnitude observed in Ghana, and perhaps Kenya and Tanzania, to chance or transition. That manufacturing employment in Ghana should rise by 91.5 per cent between 1982 and 1983, or fall by 45 per cent between 1987 and 1988 in a country whose workforce is fully employed, is implausible. Unfortunately, the statistics on employment in manufacturing industry summarized in Table 8.3 cease at just the time that most interests us, namely when import liberalization programmes were beginning to be instituted. We have no official data on employment in manufacturing since then, but the anecdotal evidence cited in the country chapters indicates that employment in manufacturing may have fallen, except in Uganda. As of the time of writing, the assumption of full employment is not tenable.

Yet, we may be pushing this argument too far, for we have not come across any claims that employment is full in Sub-Saharan economies. Rather we have come across statements in the development of theory such as 'We shall assume full employment of resources' (without any discussion of its alternative 'We shall assume that a substantial portion of the total resources are unemployed'). Nonetheless, the impression that we received from our inquiry, an impression not inconsistent with employment statistics from three of the four countries, leads us to prefer the antithetic assumption.

We must also ask if one portion of total employment, that portion representing employment in scientific and technological activities, is full, and if those workers are mobile. To answer the questions about this specific group we have to rely upon our scattered observations of employment, and of shifting employment, in scientific and technological institutions. This is difficult to do, because when one visits an institution one encounters the employed and the stable. The unemployed, the mobile, are absent. Scattered surveys of turnover in the institutions, however, indicate that

Table 8.3 Fluctuations in manufacturing employment, and in its components in Ghana, Kenya, and Tanzania 1980–1991

	Employment by activity (1987 = 100)			Annual change in index of manufacturing employment (% of previous year's figures)		
Year	Ghana	Kenya	Tanzania	Ghana	Kenya	Tanzania
1980	n.a.	82.4	90.5	n.a.	n.a.	n.a.
1981	n.a.	88.2	93.5	n.a.	+7.0	+3.3
1982	28.5	86.8	90.2	n.a.	−1.6	−3.4
1983	64.0	93.7	84.0	+91.5	+1.0	+3.0
1984	58.4	90.1	87.8	+6.9	+2.5	−5.5
1985	64.0	93.7	84.0	+13.0	+4.0	−4.3
1986	67.7	97.1	98.2	+5.8	+3.6	+16.9
1987	100.0	100.0	100.0	+32.8	+3.0	+1.8
1988	55.0	100.0	101.7	−45.0	0	+1.7
1989	n.a.	105.2	n.a.	n.a.	+5.2	n.a.
1990	n.a.	110.6	n.a.	n.a.	+5.2	n.a.
1991	n.a.	n.a.	n.a.	n.a.	n.a.	n.a.

Source: ILO, *Yearbook of Labour Statistics*, 1992

scientists and engineers, particularly the younger ones, are quite mobile within their professions, not only between institutions within their country, but abroad. In Ghana and Tanzania, departures were as often to foreign countries, chiefly African countries with higher wage scales, as they were to competing Ghanaian or Tanzanian institutions.

Of greater frequency than changes from one full-time job to another are entry into additional, part-time occupations, in order to supplement incomes. The individual remains 'fully employed' in his/her institution, in the sense that his/her status is unaltered, but an appreciable amount of time is devoted to the second career. The second career may be closely allied to the first – e.g. a mathematician working as a consultant in accountancy – or it may be quite different – e.g. a chemist growing tomatoes for market – but it seems to be becoming increasingly common, as wages and salaries in scientific and technical institutions fall in real terms. What foreign donors' subsidies to workers in favoured organizations achieve is to permit them to devote themselves full-time to their normal duties. The subsidization of salaries of scientists and engineers and administrators will not show up in statistics on employment, but it will presumably have a beneficial effect on productivity in R&D, teaching and training.

Although there does appear to be close to perfect mobility of scientists and engineers institutionally and geographically, there may not be perfect mobility professionally. By this, we mean that they do not shift readily from one field to another. Agricultural scientists do not change to industrial scientists, nor do industrial scientists to agricultural. Some progression does seem to take place from the pure sciences to the applied, but not in the opposite direction. To redirect the country's scientific and technological effort from one field to another would be difficult and time-consuming where personnel are concerned. If confronted with radical changes in occupations, narrowly defined, the population of scientists and engineers would be anything but mobile.

TRANSFER OF RESOURCES AND INSTITUTIONS FROM THE PUBLIC TO THE PRIVATE SECTOR

One of the major structural changes sought by the IMF/World Bank relates to the proportion of all economic activity carried out in the public sector: the aim is that this proportion be substantially reduced. We must ask: is this change taking place in the realm of science and technology? What appear to be the consequences? In the last two chapters we shall also ask if the changes seem desirable; or, if not, how should the policies of the international bodies be altered so as to bring about better results. But the issues to be addressed now are what are the likely effects of a shift in scientific and technological activities from the public to the private sector; and what are the likely effects on the pursuit of science and technology of a shift in *other* activities from the public to the private sector. Both the narrower and the broader issues are of consequence.

So far as the first, narrow type of shift – from R&D carried out by institutions within the public sector to R&D carried out by similar institutions in the private sector – is concerned, we can conclude quickly that no such shift has taken, or is likely to take place. Government financed, government administered R&D institutes do not lend themselves to privatization. To stagnation perhaps, to dissolution possibly, but once established within the public sector, public organizations promoting science and technology remain there. The reason is obvious: the benefits accruing to the nation from the dissemination of general advances in science and technology are so diffuse and pervasive that they cannot be fully appropriated by any private firm. They are of the nature of a public good, from which potential users cannot be excluded and rents cannot be collected.

So far as the second, broader type of shift – a transfer of the resources allocated to R&D from public sector to private sector, as a consequence of the larger exercise in privatization – is concerned, we can come to no quick conclusion. Nonetheless, that such a shift is already happening, is apparent; that it is of considerable importance for the pursuit of science and technology in Sub-Saharan Africa is, to us at least, also apparent.

Let us approach this issue of reassignment of resources from public to private sector by means of an example from one of the four countries in our sample, namely Ghana. The IMF/World Bank are putting emphasis on this shift, with one prime target being the Ghana's Cocoa Marketing Board: fulfilment of the condition will only be met when its activities have been transferred to private citizens or firms. Our question is what will then happen to the pursuit of science and technology in cocoa? Previously a para-statal firm, the Cocoa Marketing Board had been granted by the legislature a monopoly in the export of cocoa, enabling it to appropriate all the revenues from the sale of the commodity. Each year a stated percentage of these revenues was allocated by the Finance Ministry to R&D in cocoa; this allocation is the chief source of finance for the Cocoa Research Institute of Ghana. The funds available for R&D in cocoa provided a relatively stable base for Recurrent expenditures, (wages and salaries of the Institute's employees), and an unstable base for Development expenditures (other expenses) which vary with export revenues. With these funds the Institute maintained a relatively steady and sizeable programme of R&D.

Not only was the Institute's programme relatively soundly financed, it was also substantial in terms of its size, and outstanding in terms of its accomplishments. Year after year the Institute's expenditures have accounted for those of approximately half of the total of Ghana's public R&D institutes (compare Tables 3.13 and 3.15); year after year, since its foundation in the 1920s, it has offered a model of how R&D in Ghana should be conducted and how, through its extension programme, results should be disseminated.

With privatization, the Cocoa Marketing Board will no longer monopolize exports: private firms will sell the commodity abroad and draw the revenues. There will be no mechanism by which R&D can be automatically financed. Even if a levy is set, each firm, acting in its self-interest, will have an incentive to avoid payment; it will prefer to be a 'free-rider'.

What is likely to happen? Most likely is that the Ghanaian Government will take over the funding of R&D in cocoa, but on a reduced scale, in line with its other, competing commitments for public R&D. If one assumes that R&D in cocoa continues to receive half the financial support of all public R&D institutes, and that total funds available for R&D are reduced by half (the other half being the former levy on the Cocoa Marketing Board's revenues, now unavailable), all public R&D, including that in cocoa, will only proceed with half its former funds. The likely outcome would be a collapse of R&D not only in cocoa, but also in most other areas.

In our final chapter on policy we shall consider other sources of finance for R&D, but, anticipating our deliberations, we can state here that none seems to have the same potential for raising revenue as the conventional levy on the sales of the public monopoly. Our conclusion here is that the privatization of the Cocoa Marketing Board will deal a serious, perhaps a death blow, to the financing of R&D in cocoa; and, by extension, and because of the importance of cocoa in Ghana's overall scheme of R&D, to many other institutes engaged in the pursuit of science and technology.

Our example comes from Ghana; is Ghana unique in the vulnerability of its programmes of R&D to the structural adjustment of its public sector? The answer is clearly No: we could equally well have chosen Kenya's Coffee Marketing Board, whose revenues provide the financial resources for the Coffee Research Foundation, or Kenya's Tea Marketing Board, or Tanzania's Coffee Marketing Board, or Tea Marketing Board, or Sisal Marketing Board. The conditions defining privatization are uniform across Structural Adjustment loans; the consequences for the financing of R&D in the major export crops are likely to be uniform too.

SUMMARY

In this chapter we have addressed those issues that bear chiefly upon the sectors of the economy, rather than upon the economy as a whole or upon its individual agents. In order, these issues were the changes, by sector, in economic activity brought about by the adoption of Structural Adjustment Programmes, the parallel changes in R&D, the transferability of resources within scientific and technological activities, and the provision of these resources. Our impressions, supported imperfectly by what statistical evidence is available, are that overall sectoral shifts have been minor in Ghana and Kenya, have resulted in a reallocation away from industry in Tanzania, and a reallocation towards (the recovery of) industry in Uganda.

More marked, and of more consequence for the future, have been shifts in the sectoral allocation of funds for advancing science and technology. Based on the measure of expenditures by public R&D institutes, there has been a reallocation of funds during the periods of Structural Adjustment into agriculture, substantial in the case of Kenya and less so in the cases of Ghana and Tanzania. Only Uganda has been able to buck the trend, thanks to foreign assistance. Expanding the measure to allow for private expenditures is not possible statistically, but our observations within the four countries reinforce the negative portion of the above conclusion, namely that there has been a marked loss of resources from the industrial sector. The impression is strongest in the two countries with the largest industrial sectors – Ghana and Kenya – whose private and para-statal firms, now open to competition from abroad, have practically ceased their formal attempts to advance science and technology.

The third issue we addressed was that of the intensity of use of labour, and of its mobility, within sectors. On the basis of a few statistics, and some argument, we concluded that full employment does not reign in our sample of Sub-Saharan African countries, and that the skilled labour employed in advancing science and technology is not mobile *across* sectors. These conclusions, of both theoretical and practical importance, are tentative, given the lack of empirical evidence for their support (or rejection), and controversial, penetrating to the heart of the ideas buttressing programmes of Structural Adjustment.

The final issue raised in this chapter was that of the probable disappearance of monies financing R&D, in those commodities currently exported by public monopolies, in the event of privatization. Transferring to diversified private ownership bodies like the Cocoa Marketing Board of Ghana or the Coffee Marketing Boards of Kenya and Tanzania is a prime aim of the IMF/World Bank; such transference will choke off that flow of funds which supports their R&D. With governments of these countries unable to replenish the flow out of their general revenues, and unlikely to tap alternative sources, the financing of R&D in exportable commodities is therefore increasingly in the hands of foreign agencies.

9   Effects within organizations

INTRODUCTION

In our attempt to evaluate the effects of Structural Adjustment Programmes on the pursuit of science and technology we now descend to the individual organization, particularly those organizations whose primary duty is that pursuit. How have the R&D institutes, the productive firms, the universities been affected?

In these questions we shall draw chiefly upon our inquiries into specific organizations, in each country at least one agricultural research institute, one industrial research institute, one group attempting to develop appropriate technologies, and one university. The country samples are small, but so are the universes of scientific and technological organizations, so that our data are probably representative of the whole.

Theory suggests that the distinction between those goods with greater future potential and those with lesser is very important, particularly where the assignment of resources for R&D is concerned. We approached this issue in the last chapter, where we considered the sectors of the economy within which goods are produced; but we recognize that the issue is not so broad as to enable it to be resolved merely by offsetting one sector against another. It is not that agricultural goods have higher potential than industrial, nor that industrial have a higher potential than agricultural: the distinction is not so simple. In the long run, some agricultural goods face deteriorating terms of trade. Commodities like coffee, whose income and price elasticities of demand are low and whose total supply seems destined to increase substantially, have poor potential; but there are other agricultural commodities which do not meet these conditions. We must narrow our focus to the individual commodity, to the individual organization, if we are to address this issue adequately. In this chapter therefore, we will adopt the microscopic approach.

Theory also suggests that we should be aware of the efficiency with which resources devoted to advancing science and technology are utilized, and of the elasticity of substitution of resources devoted to producing goods with future potential. We have said little about these matters in the two previous chapters;it is now time to address them more fully. Finally, the theory which we, and those who promote Structural Adjustment, use is based upon assumptions that there are single decision-makers, making decisions with objectives clearly stated, with perfect knowledge of how these objectives can best be secured, and with the ability fully to implement these decisions. Such assumptions may be unrealistic, for there may be more than several decision-makers, each with conflicting objectives, inadequate knowledge, and limited power. The assumptions of perfect knowledge and single motives should be checked against reality in our sample of Sub-Saharan African countries; if they are not fulfilled some allowance should be made, both in principle and in practice.

Theory is not the only source of questions to be asked in a study such as ours, but those posed are sufficient in number and scope to cover our area of micro-economic analysis. We shall address them in the order listed above, starting with the very difficult matter of discriminating between different commodities according to their economic potential.

DISTINGUISHING BETWEEN GOODS OF GREATER AND LESSER ECONOMIC POTENTIAL FOR SUB-SAHARAN AFRICAN COUNTRIES

Theory is of itself little help when it comes to distinguishing between goods of greater and lesser economic potential: all it does is suggest certain phenomena that will tend to determine the outcome. Two such phenomena have already been mentioned – elasticities of demand and supply. A third should be mentioned, for it has interesting ramifications: it is in whose interest the distinction is made. This is a matter all too often left vague, but we had better state our preference, which is that the choice should be in the interests of the countries of Sub-Saharan Africa. We do not believe in over-arching harmony in international economic relations. We do not believe that what is best for, say, the consumer in a developed country, is also best for the producer in the developing country. Sometimes their interests run in parallel, but at least as often they will be in conflict. What may be best for the consumer in a developed country may even be worst for the producer in the developing country. What may be best for the producer in the developed country may even be worst for the producer, or the consumer, or both, in the developing country. We believe that the world does not, in its economic relationships, offer opportunities for Pareto improvements, in which a reallocation of resources makes at least one person better off, without making anyone else worse off. Nor does it resemble, and never will it resemble, a Walrasian economy. The Walrasian economy may have splendid properties (although Pareto improvements are not one of them), but the accurate representation of the reality of Sub-Saharan Africa, internally and *vis-à-vis* the rest of the world, is not one of them.

Our criterion for judgement will be the interest of Ghana, Kenya, Tanzania, and Uganda. And if the interest of the country is not congruent with the interests of all its citizens, our criterion will be the interest of those directly involved, since it is their activities that we have observed and their interests that we can identify. There is danger that we will be too parochial, that we will neglect the interests of all citizens. The presumption of those urging Structural Adjustment is that the sacrifices made by the persons who must 'adjust' today are more than compensated for by the benefits that will accrue to the rest of the population, perhaps even to those 'adjusting', in the future. We do not believe in the generality of this argument: our belief is that some sacrifices are never compensated for, and others inadequately. As a consequence, we argue that each sacrifice should be considered individually, and the balance totted up.

So, elasticities of demand and supply, interests of local producers and consumers: these are two considerations in distinguishing between goods with greater potential and goods with lesser. What else matters in making the distinction? The third factor we shall try to include is the extent to which advances in science and technology will promote still further the attractiveness of goods with potential. In other words, we shall try to determine the extent to which the production of goods responds favourably to additional R&D: we shall attempt to determine for what attractive products R&D is most effective.

Given the brevity of our inquiry we will not be able to consider more than a few products within the above framework; after all we have spent no more time on this entire project than is often spent on a single project appraisal. Nonetheless, we believe that distinguishing between products of differing potential is an important exercise, worth carrying out. Perhaps it can serve as a model for further application. The ingredients for the exercise are five-fold: commencing with the choice of a particular commodity, one makes an estimate of the productive potential of the country; a guess as to how this potential will be improved if R&D is directed towards it; a similar guess as to how the potential of other competing countries will improve over the same time horizon; an estimate of changes in the terms of trade, again over the same horizon; and an identification of special interest groups that will tend to encourage or thwart the commodity's development.

As illustrations of the exercise let us take four general types of commodities, two primary commodities (one an exportable and the other produced for domestic consumption), and two manufactures (one competing with more highly processed imports, the other with technologically more sophisticated imports). Summaries of the elements of the exercises are tabulated in Table 9.1: taking the first (traditional exportable primary commodities with intense foreign competition and unfavourable supply and demand elasticities) as an example, the results of the exercise appear in the cells in the first row of the table. Coffee, tea, cocoa and sisal are typical commodities, in which various Sub-Saharan African countries have a comparative advantage. Provided that they reduce their costs steadily, through advancing science and technology in growing, harvesting, processing, transporting etc., they should remain competitive suppliers in world markets (columns 4 and 5 of row 1). It is the factors determining shifts in the terms of trade over the long run, (columns 6–8) that militate against the prospects for these commodities, at least as far as the exporting countries are concerned. For these commodities the price elasticity of demand is low, as is the income elasticity, whereas the supply elasticities are high, the worst possible combination for the sellers (and, symmetrically, the best for the buyers, which are the developed countries). Since the producers of these primary commodities are, individually, encouraged or even compelled to expand production, collectively their output can be expected to increase, exaggerating the unfavourable aspects of the elasticities. Consequently (in the last column) we deduce that the prospects for this type of deteriorating-terms-of trade commodities are not encouraging. Hence R&D should not be concentrated in these, but rather in more favourable product types e.g. in types two, three and four in Table 9.1. (We shall have more to say in our final chapter on policy, about the preferred direction of R&D, and the factors that make it difficult to redirect R&D away from the traditional, exportable primary commodities.)

The exercise carried out in Table 9.1 was superficial: in practice a considerable amount of time and energy should be invested in deciding the best direction for R&D. Those resources which yield advances in science and technology are so scarce, and the effects over the long run of effecting R&D so profound, that the choice of direction should be made with as much care as possible, and by the developing country. It is all too easy to allocate scarce resources in the future as they have been in the past, or as international agencies and foreign donors urge that they should be; but neither

Table 9.1 Evaluation of the prospects for different types of products

Product type	Examples	Current production potential	R&D's contribution to productive potential		Future terms of trade			Factors influencing potential		Conclusion
			in Sub-Saharan country	Elsewhere	Demand elasticity	Supply elasticity	Trend over long term	Positive	Negative	
Traditional exportable primary commodity	Coffee, tea, cocoa, sisal	Excellent	Moderate	Moderate to substantial	Low	High	Deteriorating	Consuming countries encourage R&D	Opposition by consuming countries to further processing. World over-supply at current prices	Unfavourable
Traditional, locally consumed primary commodity	Bananas, plantains, peanuts, soya beans, cotton	Excellent	Moderate to substantial with sufficient R&D	Moderate to substantial	Medium	High	Stable	Large local (domestic) demand	Opposition by competing exporters, (bananas by Lomé countries) and by distributors in developed countries (bananas in EC). Opposition by competing producers in developed countries (peanuts, USA)	Exports: unfavourable, domestic markets: favourable
Locally processed, perishable consumer goods	Soap (manufacture) flour (milling) cooking oils (refining)	Good	Moderate, only if R&D directed towards appropriate technology	Moderate to substantial	Medium	High	Stable	Large potential, domestically	Consumers prefer more highly processed (imported) goods	Potentially favourable, domestically
Simple, traditional capital goods	Agricultural mechanical	Fair	Substantial, only if R&D directed correctly	Moderate to substantial	Medium	High	Stable	Large potential domestically	Severe competition from imports	Potentially favourable, domestically

Source: See text

of these criteria ensures that the allocation will be the best for the developing country. They must take their future in their own hands, and plan for the future systematically.

THE MAINTENANCE OF FIRMS' CAPITAL EQUIPMENT

Lest we give the impression that local governments and firms always choose the best allocation of scarce resources to advance science and technology, and foreign donors never, we shall single out one activity internal to productive organizations in which the latter appear to have made the better choice: this is the activity which leads to the maintenance of the productivity of capital, both physical and human. In singling out maintenance and training we shall first examine their roles in the activities of Sub-Saharan African firms, public and private; and then report on our and others' observations of the current contributions made by foreign donors.

Our evidence on the roles of maintenance and training is drawn chiefly from two countries, Ghana and Tanzania. The Ghanaian source is Lall *et al.* (1994); the Tanzanian is Mjema and Kundi (1993), on maintenance, and our own interviews with Tanzanian educators and foreign consultants (on training). So far as maintenance in Ghana is concerned, Lall and his colleagues investigated both the maintenance of product quality and of equipment. Of 30 firms in four industries (textiles and garments, food processing, wood working and metal working), 18 had no employee assigned to quality control and 14 no one to equipment maintenance (*ibid.*: Table 6.2). None of the 14 firms without equipment maintenance personnel fell into Lall's category of 'technologically competent' firms (*ibid.*: Table 4.3; 11 firms for which data were reported in his Table 6.2); the 11 'technologically competent' firms all assigned a higher percentage of their total employees to quality control and equipment maintenance than the others.

In Tanzania the situation regarding maintenance is quite similar. Mjema and Kundi's sample of firms was larger, comprising over 50 firms, although their inquiry was limited to the maintenance of equipment. Of the 50 firms answering the questionnaire, exactly half replied that they kept no records of maintenance; of the half who reported (two very large, 23 medium-and small-sized firms) 90 per cent repaired equipment when it broke down, 50 per cent carried out some preventative maintenance (regular oil changes, lubrication, etc.), but only 10 per cent of the respondents had a system of predictive maintenance. In those cases where a machine fell out of service because of a failed part, the tendency was to order a replacement only after the failure occurred. The larger firms employed qualified engineers within a maintenance department, but 40 per cent of the respondents relied upon technicians or artisans. Finally, asked reasons for the existence of problems in maintaining equipment the two most frequent answers were a lack of spares (75 per cent of respondents) and of skilled personnel (70 per cent).

So far as the maintenance or augmentation of human capital is concerned, Lall and his associates found that one factor leading to technological competence in the firms they surveyed was the deliberate investment in creating skills and information (*ibid.*: 85). More highly educated entrepreneurs and production managers were found in the more competent firms (*ibid.*: 86), as were higher proportions of scientists, engineers and technicians in their workforce (*ibid.*). They found it difficult to judge the effects of external training on firm efficiency, although the extent to which external training is practised by Ghanian firms seemed very low by world standards. Internal training, chiefly through the traditional method of apprenticeships, but also, on the parts of affiliates of foreign firms and local firms managed by foreigners, through on-the-job training schemes, is common (*ibid.*: 111 and Table 5.6); although some firms in the wood and metal working industries appear to employ apprentices as ordinary workers at low wages. In summary, it is only the larger and more progressive firms that approach maintenance and training systematically and devote any efforts to their conduct.

As to the contributions that foreign agencies make to maintaining the productivity of physical and human capital in Sub-Saharan Africa, our impression is that they are proportionately more substantial and more effective than those of local firms and governments, but substantially less so than similar contributions in the rapidly growing countries of Asia and Latin America. The main vehicle for the contributions in this applied area of science and technology is the industrial consulting firm, hired by the foreign donor to help restore the facilities and improve the performance of large firms (public and private but more often public) engaged in manufacturing and the provision of services (but more often services). Examples of the recipient African institutions are railways, highways, ports and harbours, post and communications, hospitals, schools and universities and public administration. The foreign consulting firms arrive knowing that maintenance is one of the integral functions of any enterprise and aware that Sub-Saharan African firms are ill-equipped, both intellectually and professionally, to carry out the function. (In Swahili there are no words for 'maintenance', 'reliability', 'availability'.) They therefore expect to devote a good portion of their consulting to establishing systems of maintenance, training managers and operators, obtaining implementation, and persuading all involved, at all levels of authority, of the necessity for undertaking the task. Given their terms of reference the consultants are required to work on improving activities within the firm to which they are attached; but their employers, the foreign donors, may also finance ancillary, outside projects, such as the publicizing of recommendations and the provision of courses (e.g. the introductory courses on maintenance laid on by TEMDO in Tanzania).

We do not know how effective these foreign-inspired efforts to promote the adoption of programmes of maintenance of physical and human capital are, but we can conclude that, even if they are extraordinarily effective within their own terms of reference, they, and their local counterparts, are a tiny fraction of what is needed. One comparison will illustrate this conclusion: maintenance can only be performed by technical personnel, who are so very scarce in Sub-Saharan African countries. Tanzania has an enrolment of approximately four thousand students in its technical colleges; South Korea, albeit with half again as many inhabitants, has nearly one hundred times as many. The deficiency in technical training is of an order of magnitude higher even than in R&D, to which so much of our, and others', attention has been directed.

THE EFFECTIVENESS OF R&D EFFORTS

Yet we return to R&D, for it is to R&D that most of our data apply. The selection of products-with-potential, towards which R&D should be directed, may be a necessary condition for its contribution being as large as possible, but it is not alone sufficient. Whatever scarce resources are allocated to R&D should be applied efficiently. What does our research reveal about the effluency with which the countries in our sample conduct their R&D, in the course of Structural Adjustment?

Questions concerning efficiency are notoriously difficult to answer when R&D is carried out in developed countries; in developing countries answers are even more difficult, but also even more important, to obtain. It is the importance of the answers that leads us to attempt them, even if the confidence that we can place on them is meagre. We shall focus on three matters, for which we gathered some evidence: two of these three have to do with the sources and uses of funds for R&D; the third with the allocation, within a single organization, of effort among competing activities.

Let us consider first the sources of finance for advancing science and technology. In Ghana, Kenya, Tanzania and Uganda private firms and individuals have little money to spare for such problematic activities as R&D, with such uncertain returns. The author of one study, for Kenya during a relatively prosperous period (see Chapter 4), estimated that private agents carried out no more than 10 per cent of the country's total R&D, a paltry fraction.

Domestic finance for R&D stems from the government, either directly through the budget or indirectly through levies on the revenues of para-statal firms. The former public source is generally the larger in total, the latter generally the more closely related to need. The greater volume of public funds devoted to R&D has been documented in the previous chapter: the Ghanaian government spends approximately as much public money on R&D institutes as do the para-statal bodies; the Kenyan government spends approximately twice as much; and the Tanzanian and Ugandan governments account for almost all domestic R&D expenditures.

The close tuning of para-statal contributions to needs is illustrated by our data on Ghana's R&D institutes' requests for and authorizations of funds. Table 9.2 provides the data; juxtaposed are requests and authorizations for one para-statal research organization and four public R&D institutes. The results are clear; the para-statal organization, financed indirectly by levies on sales of the para-statal's crop, had approved, on the average, 86 per cent of all its requests, whereas the public institutes, financed directly from the government's budget, had approved, again on the average, 71 per cent of their requests for recurrent funds and 56 per cent for development funds.

Moreover, the data in Table 8.2 reveal that there was less fluctuation year by year in the para-statal's percentages, particularly where Development items were concerned. This observation deserves some comment, since it seems to be general across Sub-Saharan African countries and since it has implications for the efficiency with which resources are applied in R&D. To conduct R&D effectively it is necessary to plan activities so that objectives are agreed upon, and matched with resources, and so that the resources are available in the types and at the times that they are required. To plan coherently one needs, at a minimum, stability, in the senses both of a relatively assured and steady source of finance and of a core of experienced personnel. If the income of an R&D institute is insecure, and if it fluctuates widely from year to year, coherent planning is not possible. Goals cannot be set with any likelihood of their being attained, resources cannot be procured in synchrony with the plan, and standards of performance cannot be established, let alone attained. In such an uncertain environment, a systematic allocation of resources, so vital for an activity with such a long gestation period as R&D, becomes impossible and what resources as are applied are used inefficiently.

Let us consider another matter covered by the statistics above. Commonly, in Sub-Saharan African research institutes, the major (usually almost the

Table 9.2 Ghana: approvals as a percentage of requests for expenditures for para-statal and public R&D institutes 1981–1991

	Recurrent items		Development items	
Year	Para-statal institute (CRIG)	4 public research institutes[a]	Para-statal institute (CRIG)	4 public institutes[a]
1981	80	67	79	0
1982	80	52	80	21
1983	80	59	78	15
1984	80	79	n.a.	165
1985	80	95	80	154
1986	91	56	91	70
1987	91	103	91	12
1988	91	62	91	40
1989	90	72	91	43
1990	91	74	91	49
1991	91	67	91	28
Average[b]	86	71	86	56

Sources: Tables 3.9–3.12

Note: a: The Industrial Research Institute (IRI), Scientific Instrumentation Centre (SIC), Food Research Institute (FRI) and Technology Transfer Centre (TTC)

b: Simple arithmetic averages of the four public institutes, and simple arithmetic averages over the 11 years

sole) use on which recurrent items are expended is wages and salaries of the employees of the institutes. The figures for Ghana over the period 1974–1981 are typical: in the eight-year interval wages and salaries consumed from 88 to 98 per cent of the *total* expenditures (95 per cent on the average) of all the country's public R&D institutes (see Table 3.16). In the other three countries in our sample, much the same phenomenon was observed for recent years. To be sure, these figures exclude foreign loans and gifts, most of which are for development items, but the conclusion is that almost all local funds are devoted to paying the wages and salaries of the institutes' personnel. Negligible sums are left for buying books, subscribing to scholarly journals, ordering supplies of reagents and other working materials, constructing laboratories and field stations, and procuring laboratory equipment (corroborating evidence is provided by Gaillard, 1991: 68–75). Even those pieces of capital equipment that the institutes do procure, usually with funds from foreign donors, cannot be properly maintained and repaired; the institutes themselves may not employ capable technicians

('. . . Africa seems to be in the worst position since over half [51 per cent] of the institutions on this continent do not have the technical staff required to ensure that their scientific equipment will work well . . .' *ibid.*: 70) or may not have been allocated the foreign exchange necessary to secure spare parts and/or hire technicians from abroad ('more than two-thirds of the scientists [68 per cent] had to wait 5 months or more to have their equipment repaired by a foreign technician, and more than one-fourth had to wait 10 months or longer,' *ibid.*: 72). With almost all their funds consumed in paying wages and salaries, the R&D institutes can tick over; but, isolated, uninformed and impecunious, they cannot fulfil their potential.

There is even some evidence that the allowances for Recurrent items are not even sufficient to keep some institutes ticking over. In such cases, it is those employees *not* entrenched in the resident bureaucracy who tend to be released, agricultural extension workers in Ghana and Kenya having been one such vulnerable group (Duncan and Howell, 1992). One can hardly imagine an act more likely to delay the dissemination of results of R&D in agriculture, and hence more likely to reduce R&D's efficiency, than cutting extension staff. To the extents that meeting the conditions on Structural Adjustment loans requires a reduction in government expenditures, that a reduction in government expenditures leads to a reduction in funds for public R&D, and that a reduction in funds for public R&D bears most heavily on 'development' items and on extension services, the outcome will be a reduction on the effectiveness with which the remaining R&D is carried out.

The above argument rests on the assumption that scholarly books and journals, laboratory supplies, scientific equipment, extension staffs, etc. cannot be replaced by more scientists. To be sure, it does appear that there is an abundant supply of university-trained scientists in Sub-Saharan Africa, and that employment in a public R&D institute is a career to which most aspire; but the question does arise as to whether or not scientists, maintained in employment with domestic funds, can substitute for the other factors of production requiring scarcer resources. Putting the question in the marginal terms familiar to economists, would an extra scientist contribute more or less to the output of an R&D institute than (the last) 50 scholarly books or (the last) five research journals or the last three extension workers? We suspect that the answer, given the conditions prevalent today in Sub-Saharan Africa, is that the marginal scientist would contribute less to R&D output than the alternative uses of expenditure.

A COUNTERFACTUAL EXPERIMENT

Having addressed the issues of the choice of product towards which R&D should be directed, the efficiency with which R&D is carried out, and the extent to which there is substitutability in R&D between more abundant and less abundant factors of production, we shall now try to combine these within a single frame of analysis. The frame we shall use is that of Fung and Ishikawa, described in Chapter 2 and applied already in Chapter 7.

We have argued in this chapter that the consequences of the adoption of Structural Adjustment Programmes are leading to R&D being directed increasingly towards products that have unfavourable prospects for the Sub-Saharan countries and, perhaps, to its being performed with lower efficiency (because of domestic constraints on its financing, the constraints being felt most acutely on non-wage and salary components of expenditures and, within the wage-and-salary component, on bureaucratically isolated staff). Let us now use Fung and Ishikawa's model to illustrate these consequences.

Within the model, the consequences of Structural Adjustment are represented by three specifications: first, R&D is directed towards good Y (for which the country's potential is unfavourable), rather than good X; secondly, the efficiency with which resources are employed in R&D is lower; and thirdly, the substitutability of inputs in production (of R&D, and consequently of R&D's output, intermediate goods) is reduced. In order to illustrate these alterations, we shall construct Case III, and compare its implications to those of Case I, which are the most attractive for a Sub-Saharan African country. The differences in assumptions are as follows:

1 in Case III, R&D is allocated to advancing science and technology in good Y (the good with unfavourable prospects for Sub-Saharan Africa) whereas in Case I R&D is allocated to good X (with favourable prospects);
2 more R&D is carried out in Case III than in Case I (foreign grants more than compensating, in Case III, for any reduction in local expenditure);
3 the efficiency with which R&D is carried out (measured by the parameter δ) is lower in Case III than Case I; and
4 the substitutability of factors of production in R&D, and subsequently in intermediate goods (measured by the parameter β) is lower in Case III than Case I.

For both cases we shall consider the long run, over which R&D comes to fruition and the terms of trade for good Y, *vis-à-vis* good X, steadily deteriorate.

Four figures are necessary to display fully the comparison of Cases I and III. The first compares the possible production patterns, the second and third, trading postures, and the fourth consumption patterns. Common to both Cases I and III are identical volumes of domestic consumption of good Y (the good with unfavourable prospects: we could think of it as coffee); and identical relative prices of goods X and Y (i.e. identical terms of trade), based upon assumptions that the country is 'small' (i.e. does not, by its own behaviour, influence world market prices) and 'open' (i.e. that domestic prices are set by world market prices). Over time, the world market and domestic price of Y falls relative to the price of X.

Looking first at Figure 9.1, we represent the initial production pattern (at t (o) the 'o' standing for the present), common to both cases, by the heavy solid curve $(X, Y)^c$, this curve representing the locus of all possible pairs of outputs of X and Y, given current (c) technology and resources.

Future production patterns will differ, depending upon the direction of R&D, as well as the portion of the country's total resources allocated to it, the efficiency with which they are applied, and the substitutability of scarce inputs one for another. So far as the direction of R&D is concerned, we are assuming that it is towards good X (the good with favourable prospects) in

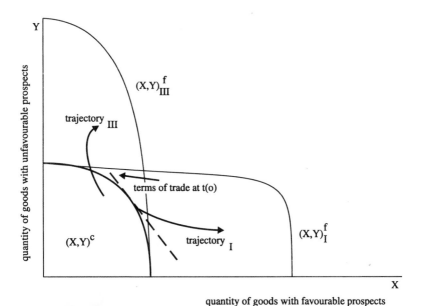

Figure 9.1 Production possibility curves for the present and future under Cases I and III

Case I and towards good Y (the good with unfavourable prospects) in Case III; so far as the volume of resources devoted to R&D is concerned, we are assuming no difference between the two cases; and so far as both efficiency of R&D and substitutability of scarce inputs are concerned, we are assuming that they are higher in Case I than III.

Given these assumptions, the production possibility schedules (drawn in light solid lines in Figure 9.1) at some future date will be $(X, Y)_I^f$ and $(X, Y)_{III}^f$, the superscript 'f' standing for some distant future date, and the subscripts indicating the cases. In Case I, over time, the production possibility curve has swung out to the right, pivoting on its intersection with the vertical axis, indicating the growing productivity of the country's resources in producing good X, consequent upon its advancing technology. In Case III, in a similar manner, the production possibility curve moves upward, pivoting on its original intersection with the horizontal axis. Over time, as a comparison of the two curves $(X, Y)_I^f$ and $(X, Y,)_{III}^f$ show, the productive potentials of the country become more and more different: in Case I it is an ever-increasingly efficient producer of X, in Case III of Y.

Let us turn to Figures 9.2 and 9.3, in order to compare the different effects of increasing efficiencies of production on the country's international trade. Remember that the terms of trade are identical for both cases, and have deteriorated over time for good Y, *vis-à-vis* good X. The original terms of trade are 1:1 (as drawn in Figure 9.1), which was represented graphically by a (dashed) line of 45 degrees: let us represent the terms of trade in the distant future as a (dashed) line of 60 degrees. (At time zero, one unit of Y commands the same price in world markets as one unit of X: hence terms of trade 1:1. In the distant future, because of the deterioration in the terms of trade, the price of a unit of Y will be, say, only half that of a unit of X: hence terms of trade 1:2. Terms of trade of 1:2 are represented in Figures 9.2 and 9.3 by (dashed) lines of slope 2, or of angle 60 degrees.)

The slopes of the relative price (the dashed) lines are significant, for they represent the country's future possibilities for trade. Assuming that the country is to be in balance of payments equilibrium (i.e. value of total imports equal to value of total exports), the country can, in Case I (see Figure 9.2), trade anywhere along the (dashed) line passing through $p(X,Y)_I^f$, and, in Case III (see Figure 9.3), anywhere along the (dashed) line passing through $p(XY)_{III}^f$. (The reason is that the relative price or terms-of-trade lines are the loci of points of equal total value of outputs of X and Y. Between any two points along the relative price lines the increment in value of the good whose quantity is increasing is equal, but opposite in sign, to the increment in value of the good whose quantity is decreasing.

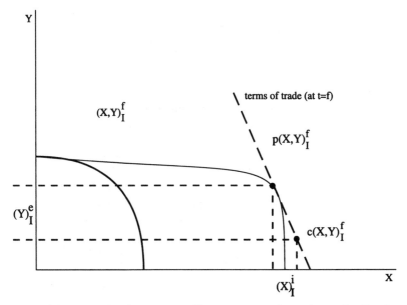

Figure 9.2 Terms of trade, exports and imports at some future date under Case I

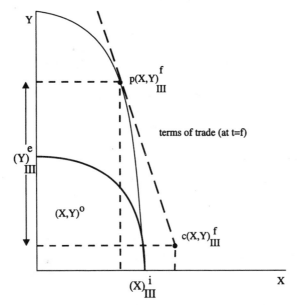

Figure 9.3 Terms of trade, exports and imports at some future date under Case III

For example, in Figure 9.2, the value of the additional quantity of good X between the points $p(X, Y)^f_I$ and $c(X, Y)^f_I$ is equal, but opposite in sign, to the value of the reduction in quantity of good Y. The country can, by exchanging Y for X (or conversely X for Y) move from point $p(X, Y)^f_I$ to $c(X, Y)^f_I$ (or conversely from $c(X, Y)^f_I$ to $p(X, Y)^f_I$ and remain in balance of payments equilibrium. Let us imagine that the country, in Case I, produces at point $p(X, Y)^f_I$. The letter 'p' stands for production, and, assuming that production is efficient, $p(X, Y)^f_I$ will lie along the production possibility curve $(X, Y)^f_I$. Let us also assume that the country wishes to export an amount of Y equal to Y^e_I ('e' for export). At world market prices, the country can exchange this amount of Y for an amount of X equal to X^i_I ('i' for import). Therefore by giving up, to foreigners, the amount of Y equal to Y^e_I the country can acquire for its own citizens an extra amount of X equal to X^i_I. Any point along the (dashed) relative price line is a point of potential consumption; the point $c(X, Y)^f_I$ ('c' for consumption, the use to which all goods are assumed to be put) is selected to represent the country's actual choice. The country produces goods at point $p(X, Y)^f_I$, consumes at point $c(X, Y)^f_I$, exports $Y(X, Y)^e_I$, imports X^i_I, and is in balance of payments equilibrium.

The outcome for the country in Case III is determined analogously, and portrayed in Figure 9.3. Total exports Y^e_{III} and imports X^i_{III} are considerably larger in volume than they are in Case I, a result to be expected since, in Case III, the country is specializing in the production of the good that had unfavourable prospects (a good like coffee); but, because both cases operate under identical terms of trade, the ratios $X^i_I \div Y^e_I$ and $X^i_{III} \div Y^e_{III}$ are equal (to $1 \div 2$).

We have yet to explain how the production points $p(X, Y)^f_I$ and $p(X, Y)^f_{III}$ and consumption points $c(XY)^f_I$ and $c(X, Y)^f_{III}$ were selected, and how the final outcomes compare. The production points were selected so as to maximize the value of total national output, given the country's technological potential, resources and relative prices (i.e. terms of trade). Graphically they are the points of tangency between the production possibility curves, $(X, Y)^f_I$ and $(X, Y)^f_{III}$, and the (common) relative price line.

The consumption points are selected so as to maximize satisfaction from total consumption of X and Y, according to the community's relative preferences for the two goods. In both cases, the quantity of good Y preferred is equal, at $c(Y)^f_I$ and $c(Y)^f_{III}$ in Figure 9.4. (Thinking of it as a good like coffee, domestic demand can be assumed, as a first approximation, to be independent of the price it commands in world markets.) As a result of this assumption there is no ground to prefer the outcome in Case I or Case III, or vice versa, so far as consumption of good Y is concerned.

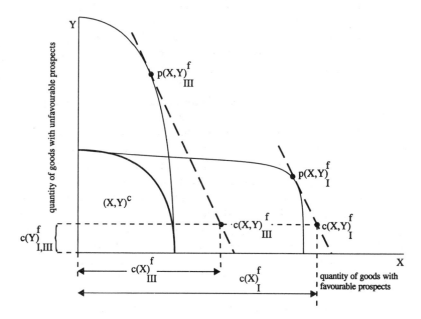

Figure 9.4 Total consumption at some future date under Cases I and III

It is in the consumption of good X (the good which had favourable prospects and towards which R&D was directed in Case I, but not in Case III) that the difference between the two cases arises: having directed its R&D towards the good with favourable prospects the country can consume more of it in the future ($c(X)_I^f$ exceeds $c(X)_{III}^f$ in Figure 9.4). The outcome is unambiguously superior in Case I: consumption of the same amount of good Y, and a greater amount of good X. Focusing R&D on the good with improving terms of trade has been the contributor to the happy outcome.

SUMMARY

In this chapter on the effects of Structural Adjustment within organizations, we have focused on those organizations whose chief function is the pursuit of science and technology. The major issues confronting these organizations are, in our judgement: first, towards which products/processes should they direct their efforts? and secondly, how should they improve their efficiency? We argued that the direction of R&D should be towards those products/processes with the most favourable prospects for the future, where favour will be determined not only by movements in the terms of trade, but also by comparative advantage in production and distribution, its efficiency in conducting R&D, and ability to disseminate the results. The data we collected and analyzed suggested means by which organizational efficiency could be improved: by maintaining, year by year, relatively stable funding and by re-allocating internally some of the funds from wages and salaries to the non-wage and salary components (supplies, reference material, equipment, maintenance, etc.). Dissemination of results could be more effective if employment of core staffs, rather than extension workers, was curtailed.

Where the proper direction of R&D efforts was concerned, we argued that the choice should be made deliberately, with several factors in mind – trends in terms of trade for individual commodities; potential for improvements of production methods through R&D, both in the country under consideration and elsewhere; support for, or opposition to, the expansion of production and export, etc. Such deliberations should be done systematically and with the long-run interest of the developing country in mind. We shall consider this matter further in Chapter 11, where we will see, unfortunately, that proper choices are extremely difficult to make, both bureaucratically and politically.

Although we did not attempt to make any such choices ourselves, we did illustrate, via a counterfactual experiment, the consequences of right and wrong choices ('right' and 'wrong' from the point of view of the developing country). Case I illustrated the right choice of direction of advance of science and technology, Case III the wrong. Comparison of the two cases revealed quite different patterns of production (specialization on the production of the good without favourable prospects in Case III as against production of the good with favourable prospects in Case I), quite different volumes of international trade (large exports of the good with unfavourable prospects in Case III as against small and diminishing exports of the same good in Case I), and a lower level of consumption (equivalent to a lower standard of living) in Case III than in Case I. To be sure, this was only an illustration; but we know of no better way of making explicit the effects, over the long-run, of choosing the right rather than the wrong realms in which to advance science and technology.

Part IV

Conclusions and recommendations

10 Conclusions

INTRODUCTION

Our objective in this study has been to try to determine the effects of the IMF/World Bank's Structural Adjustment Programmes on the pursuit of science and technology in four Sub-Saharan African countries. Given the near-ubiquity of such programmes in this part of the world, our findings may well have a relevance that transcends Ghana, Kenya, Tanzania and Uganda: we rather hope not, for the findings, which we will summarize in the next section, are not optimistic for the countries in our sample.

After the summary, we shall return to the findings one by one, in order to supply the evidence in support of each. Would that the evidence were more persuasive; but science and technology are complex subjects, defying precise measurement, and even in the best of circumstances evidence can be interpreted differently by different individuals. At the outset we should confess that our evidence, the bulk of which we collected ourselves, is sufficient in our minds to support our conclusions; but may not be sufficient in the minds of those already committed to the rectitude of the IMF/World Bank's programmes. To convert those with opposing beliefs would require the incontrovertible evidence that we cannot provide.

After supplying the evidence to the effects of Structural Adjustment Programmes on the pursuit of science and technology in the following chapter, we shall draw the implications, both for the countries we studied and for the international financial institutions and the development assistance bodies. Chapter 11 will be concerned with policy, i.e. with how the pursuit of science and technology can be accelerated and how its potential benefits can be appropriated by the developing countries.

A SUMMARY OF THE CONCLUSIONS

We will state our conclusions baldly as five propositions:

1 under Structural Adjustment Programmes, domestic expenditures on advancing science and technology fluctuate from year to year, with a slight upward trend;
2 total expenditures, counting both local and foreign, are likely to rise at a considerably higher rate;
3 within the total, different areas of endeavour have considerably varying fortunes;
4 which areas prosper, and which do not, are increasingly determined by foreigners; and (most contentiously)
5 the choice of areas to be pursued is currently based upon the benefits of such choice for the developed countries, to the detriment of the developing countries.

We shall now expand upon these five propositions, presenting for each, in turn, embellishments and summaries of evidence.

FLUCTUATIONS IN LOCAL GOVERNMENT EXPENDITURES ON THE PURSUIT OF SCIENCE AND TECHNOLOGY

Of the five propositions, the first is the most difficult to explain. In principle, since almost all Sub-Saharan African countries run substantial deficits in their government budgets. The IMF and World Bank, feeling strongly that these deficits should be eliminated, require efforts towards elimination, as one of the standard conditions for the awarding of loans. In attempting to fulfil this condition, the borrowing country generally finds it easier to reduce government expenditures than to increase government revenues. And of government expenditures, the least difficult to reduce is investment. Investment takes many forms, one of which is in advancing science and technology. Therefore, in principle expenditures on science and technology should be among those most likely to be curtailed.

The argument is plausible, but of our five propositions, it turns out that it is the one for which the evidence is contradictory. The reason seems not to be that pursuing science and technology is given higher priority than some current activities, but rather that some of the countries find it impossible, or undesirable, to reduce government expenditures at all. Moreover, the loans and grants that are made to the country adopting a Structural Adjustment Programme may reduce the immediate pressure on its budget, enabling it to expand government expenditures in the year of their receipt.

There is evidence, both in our sample of four countries, and in the larger universe of Sub-Saharan African countries undergoing structural adjustment (see World Bank, 1990; and Harrigan and Mosley, 1991) that government expenditures, and even the budget deficit, may, in the first years of a Structural Adjustment Programme, rise rather than fall. In all our four countries it seems as if that is what has happened.

In Table 10.3 (based on the data in Tables 10.1 and 10.2), we summarize the experience of the four countries under the conditions of budgetary restraint urged from outside; the first column in the table gives the period over which Structural Adjustment is taking place, from the year it was initiated to the present. The second column reports average rates of change in total government expenditures, in terms of constant prices, over the years following the adoption of the Structural Adjustment Programme. All are positive. Enumerating our countries, Ghana's expenditures changed on the average, 22 per cent each year; Kenya's 9 per cent; Tanzania's 4 per cent; and Uganda's 61 per cent.

The chief reason for Ghana's budgetary expansion lies in the reduction in the government's obligation to service overseas debt: this is in turn a consequence of the reduction in the total, achieved in the debt renegotiations that took place after the design of the Structural Adjustment Programme was agreed upon. With less of the Ghanaian government's revenues going abroad, more could be used at home. The other countries' debts, not yet having been renegotiated, place ever-increasing demands upon their budgets; however in Uganda's case (see Table 6.7), funds are flowing into the country at an increasing rate, in order to finance its recovery programme.

From local government expenditures we move to that portion allocated to advancing science and technology. Of our various measures of the advance, it is only for inputs that we have data consistent across countries; and of these, it is only for monetary inputs to government R&D institutes that the data are sufficiently accurate to give us confidence in the figures. We have estimated the fluctuations in public funds expended by the R&D institutes in the four countries, since undertaking Structural Adjustment. The averages of these fluctuations in expenditures by public R&D institutes are presented in the third column of Table 10.3, where they can be compared with those in the second column. The comparisons indicate that the averages across countries are positively correlated; if total government expenditures change, so do expenditures on R&D, and by greater percentages for Ghana, Kenya and Tanzania. The elasticity of expenditure on R&D is greater than unity for these three countries; for Uganda the elasticity, with respect to increases in total government expenditures, is less than unity.

Would that we had a measure of the *output* of public R&D. Since we do

Table 10.1 Government expenditures, Ghana, Kenya, Tanzania and Uganda 1982/3–1991/2 (billions of units of national currency, at constant prices of 1987)

Year	Ghana (1)	Ghana (2)	Spliced series	Kenya	Tanzania	Uganda
1982/3	42.9	n.a.	42.9	31.6	65.8	20.0
1983/4	38.6	n.a.	38.6	29.9	50.3	23.2
1984/5	64.0	n.a.	64.0	27.9	60.5	23.6
1985/6	97.8	n.a.	97.8	29.7	62.2	18.3
1986/7	119	122	119	30.9	72.4	15.7
1987/8	137	135	137	37.5	79.3	13.2
1988/9	147	138	147	37.2	84.5	15.4
1989/90	n.a.	132	132	44.4	84.0	18.1
1990/1	n.a.	132	132	41.6	84.2	21.5
1991/2	n.a.	144	144	40.7	85.4	25.2

Sources: Ghana: (1) 1982/3–1988/9; Table 3.8 (total government expenditures, current plus capital, at 1987 prices).
(2) 1986/7–1991/2; Table 3.8 (government consumption plus government gross investment, at current prices; converted by GDP deflator)
Kenya: Table 4.8 (total government expenditures, current plus capital, converted by GDP deflator)
Tanzania: 1982/3–1991/2; Table 5.5 (government consumption plus total gross domestic investment, at current prices, converted by GDP deflator)
Uganda: Table 6.4 (1982/3–1986/7 and 1990/1–1991/2, government current expenditure plus capital payments; 1987/8–1989/90, government current expenditures plus 20% of total gross domestic investment: all converted by GDP deflator)

Table 10.2 Annual fluctuations in government expenditures and in public financing of R&D institutes, Ghana, Kenya, Tanzania and Uganda 1982/3–1991/2 (at constant prices of 1987)

Year	Annual change in government expenditures (as % of the previous year's figure)				Annual change in R&D institutes' public funding (as % of the previous year's figure)			
	Ghana	Kenya	Tanzania	Uganda	Ghana	Kenya	Tanzania	Uganda
1982/3	n.a.	n.a.	n.a.	n.a.	+8.8	n.a.	n.a.	+28.9
1983/4	-10.0	-5.4	-23.5	+16.0	-18.9	n.a.	n.a.	+22.4
1984/5	+68.3	-6.7	+19.7	+1.7	-3.3	n.a.	+25.3	-37.5
1985/6	+52.7	+6.5	+2.8	-21.8	+93.0	n.a.	-6.0	-4.6
1986/7	+21.6	+4.0	+16.4	-14.2	+91.0	n.a.	+61.9	+12.9
1987/8	+15.1	+21.3	+9.5	-15.9	+77.5	+53.3	-8.8	n.a.
1988/9	+7.3	-0.8	+5.6	+16.7	-47.0	+15.4	-20.4	n.a.
1989/90	-10.2	+19.3	-0.6	+17.5	+71.3	+2.1	+24.4	+104.0
1990/1	0	-6.3	+0.2	+18.8	-38.3	+23.7	-17.3	0
1991/2	+9.2	-2.2	+1.4	+15.9	-34.5	n.a.	-1.3	-54.5

Sources: Government Expenditures: Table 10.1
Public Finance of R&D Institutes: Table 7.4

Table 10.3 Averages of fluctuations in government expenditures and in local funds available to public R&D institutes during periods of structural adjustment, Ghana, Kenya, Tanzania and Uganda, various years to 1991/2

Country	Period of structural adjustment	Trend in real government expenditures (average annual rate of change, %)	Trend in government funds allocated to public R&D institutes (average annual rate of change, %)
Ghana	1983/4–1991/2	+21.6%	+52.8%
Kenya	1987/8–1991/2	+8.8%	+23.6%
Tanzania	1986/7–1991/2	+3.6%	+20.8%
Uganda	1988/9–1991/2	+16.8%	+16.5%

Sources: Column 1: Table 7.6
Column 2: Table 10.2

not, all we can do is draw the implications from some of the data we collected and some of the observations we made. The data are those on that fraction of the total monies received by public R&D institutes allocated to wages and salaries of employees. For Ghana, we have earlier figures for all public R&D institutes; for the other countries observations from only those institutes we studied ourselves. The trends in the fractions of public R&D institutes expended on wages and salaries, during the years in which the Structural Adjustment Programmes have been in force, suggest an increasing portion of the R&D institutes' revenues from public funds has been spent on wages and salaries.

We believe that the same result holds for the R&D institutes in the para-statal sector of the countries' economies. Here the evidence is drawn from just two para-statal firms in two countries, but our impressions of the experience in other para-statal firms in the same two countries, and in the other two countries, is consistent with the result. So what is the implication of an increasing portion of the R&D institutes' local funds being expended on wages and salaries? By subtraction, the portion going to other items must be falling. To what purposes are funds put, that do not go to wages and salaries? The answer is to such items as laboratory equipment and supplies; to books, journals and reports describing accomplishments elsewhere; to study and attendance at conferences abroad; and to the other impedimenta of R&D. It is difficult to imagine R&D being carried out successfully when these functions are not performed. How can a scientist pursue science without equipment, without supplies, without knowledge of what other scientists accomplished? All an institute can do, if its funds are consumed in paying its staff, is to maintain its establishment. In terms of progress, it is stationary; its scientific engine is merely ticking over.

Such seems to be the experience of the R&D institutes in Ghana, Kenya, Tanzania and Uganda; but it must also be asked if an increasing portion of their local funds need to be devoted to the wages and salaries of a stable number of employees. Why not reduce the number of scientists and technicians employed in the institutes, or pay the same number less, allocating the amount saved on wages and salaries to the other items? The answers seem to be two-fold, the first being contemporaneous, the second being political. The temporal answer is that foreign donations are currently so generous that they cover much of the non-wage expenditures of the institutes.

The political answer is the one common to so much of government activities in all countries, regardless of their stage of development, namely that it is very difficult to reduce public employment. Public sector employees are among the best organized groups in the country, adept at recognizing and promoting their own interests. Moreover, they are the very ones who administer reductions in their own employment, and can use the institutions of government to resist the proposals. It comes as no surprise that the civil servants in the countries we studied have succeeded in maintaining their numbers undiminished, or have even succeeded in increasing them. Politicians, keen to reward their supporters, and under great pressure from an expanding population to provide more jobs, reinforce the tendency to expansion of public employment. The same reason does not seem to hold where the level of individual wages and salaries is concerned. In all the countries in our sample, the real wage of scientists and technicians has fallen, not risen, over the period we covered, in line with the general fall in real government wages and salaries. The same or, more frequently, an increased number of employees has, each one, received less from their own employment.

We should like to be able to draw some conclusion on the effects of the adoption of Structural Adjustment Programmes on the pursuit of science and technology in the private sector. Our impression, consistent throughout the four countries of our sample, is that private firms have curtailed their already meagre expenditures on R&D, but the evidence is scanty and based chiefly upon the collapse of private R&D in Kenya. When we expand our focus beyond R&D to the mundane but very important activities of technical training, technical servicing, engineering and business consulting etc., even our impressions of changes in the amounts carried out by private firms become vague. Newspaper reports speak of retrenchment, of sacking, of bankruptcies, particularly by industrial firms; although they do not speak in equal terms of the establishment of new firms. But to the extent that most of the advances in science and technology occur in larger industrial firms, and that the firms that have been retrenching are the larger firms (and newly established firms are smaller in size) we would expect that the pace of advance in the private sector has slowed. Possible changes in the speed of advance of science and technology in the private sector would be an interesting topic for further research; to be sure, there have recently been many studies of industrial activity in the four countries in our sample, particularly in Ghana but, with one exception (see Lall *et al.* 1994), these studies have concentrated more on the establishment and growth, or decline, of private firms, not on the technology they employ and the improvements they secure in that technology.

INCREASES IN TOTAL EXPENDITURES ON THE PURSUIT OF SCIENCE AND TECHNOLOGY

The second of our conclusions is that total expenditures on the pursuit of science and technology in Ghana, Kenya, Tanzania and Uganda have increased substantially since these countries embarked upon Structural Adjustment Programmes. The increase has come about chiefly as a result of the substantial increase in the receipt of foreign donations.

The chain of reasoning is as follows: it commences with the need on the part of Sub-Saharan countries to borrow abroad to stabilize their economies. Given their poor performance over the early years of the 1980s, they find that banks and other institutions in the private sector of the developed countries are unwilling to increase their lending, and so they turn for funds to the international financial institutions, primarily the IMF and World Bank. These latter impose conditions upon the loans, to most of which the borrowers agree. Their agreement indicates to all other potential lenders, both government and private, that the recipients are determined to act according to principles of fiscal prudence and economic rectitude, which action will assure that loans will be repaid. Given this commitment on agreements sealed by the IMF and World Bank, the assistance agencies of the developed countries look more favourably upon the agreeable developing countries' requests for help. To their assistance agencies, faced with appeals from more than a hundred poor countries, it is very convenient to be able to separate appeals from countries that have the IMF and World Bank's 'seal of approval' from those that do not, giving more favourable treatment to the former. For the individual developing country which has just accepted the bulk of the conditions attached to the IMF/World Bank's loans, the probability of receiving additional assistance, from the developed countries, has increased markedly, and is applied for with greater vigour and confidence. So additional funds flow in.

Moreover, since the assistance agencies in the developed countries are very aware of the fragility of Sub-Saharan African economies and of the difficulty faced in conforming to the conditions attached to the IMF/World Bank's loans, they are reluctant to grant funds in the form of (additional) loans, requiring regular servicing and ultimate repayment. They therefore make their contributions available primarily in the form of grants. In choosing the sorts of projects which should be supported by grants, assistance agencies are drawn to those whose pay-off is incalculable, or distant in the future, or both. Projects designed to advance science and technology are of this sort. So foreign funds flow in to those local institutions engaged in advancing science and technology.

In order to record this inflow of foreign funds in support of advancing science and technology we should have had accurate data by donor, by recipient, and by project; but such detailed data are only available for Kenya and Tanzania for a few recent years. The number of donating countries and organizations is large, as is the number of recipients in each

Table 10.4 National and total expenditures on the advance of science and technology, as percentages of GDP, Ghana, Kenya, Tanzania and Uganda 1982/3–1991/2

Year	National expenditures on S&T, as % of GDP				Total expenditures (national plus foreign) on S&T, as % of GDP			
	Ghana	Kenya	Tanzania	Uganda	Ghana	Kenya	Tanzania	Uganda
1982/3	n.a.	n.a.	0.3	0.004	n.a.	n.a.	0.3	0.004
1983/4	0.0	n.a.	0.6	0.004	0.0	n.a.	0.6	0.004
1984/5	0.5	n.a.	0.6	0.004	0.5	n.a.	0.6	0.004
1985/6	0.8	n.a.	0.6	0.003	0.8	n.a.	0.6	0.003
1986/7	0.6	0.3	0.7	0.005	0.6	0.4	0.7	0.005
1987/8	0.3	0.4	0.6	n.a.	0.3	0.6	0.6	n.a.
1988/9	0.4	0.5	0.5	0.03	0.4	0.7	1.3	0.09
1989/90	0.7	0.4	0.7	0.05	0.7	1.0	2.5	0.12
1990/1	0.4	0.5	0.4	0.13	0.4	1.3	2.3	0.15
1991/2	0.2	n.a.	0.8	1.8	0.2	n.a.	2.4	2.2

Sources: National expenditures: Table 7.7, columns 9-12, divided by GDP (Tables 3.1, 4.1, 5.1 and 6.1)
Total expenditures: Table 7.2

country; the number of projects receiving, or failing to receive foreign funds is greater still by an order of magnitude. In some countries, Kenya for example, directors of public R&D institutes have been able to approach foreign donors directly; in others, Uganda for example, appeals have been negotiated by the Ministry of Finance. Sometimes foreign donations are identified by the recipient separately, other times they are lumped into total receipts; sometimes donations are recorded at the time of commitment; others at the time of receipt; still others at the time of expenditure. For these reasons, our accounting is faulty; since we compiled most of our data from two different sources – the internal records of a sample of the scientific and technological organizations and published accounts in the national budgets – the data are not even internally consistent. Some expenditures have been omitted from reports submitted to government by public R&D institutes and the universities: expenditures in the form of e.g. supplements to the salaries of scientists and engineers in favoured activities. As a consequence, there is bias, almost certainly towards an understatement of foreign donations actually spent in Ghana, Kenya and Tanzania in early years and in Ghana in recent years.

There is a third source of data in foreign donations that is not subject to such criticism, namely the compilations made by UNDP in Kenya and Tanzania (UNDP, 1991, 1992, 1993). By means of an exhaustive inquiry into the grants of donors, rather than receipts of beneficiaries, UNDP has obtained an accurate account of the volume of inflows. It is these figures that we shall rely upon in what follows. (For Ghana and Uganda our data should be read with caution.) Nonetheless, for all they do reveal that total expenditures of public R&D institutes and of university science and engineering departments have increased since the countries have committed themselves to Structural Adjustment Programmes.

The data on foreign donations, together with those on local expenditures and the totals of the two, are depicted in Figures 10.1–10.4 (the annual percentages are compiled in Table 10.4). The first, Figure 10.1 for Ghana, displays only the last of the three statistical series, total expenditures on the pursuit of science and technology, since neither foreign donors nor Ghanaian recipients provide sufficient data on donations for us to be able to separate them from local financing. It is almost certain that foreign donations have increased in the recent years, so the plot in Figure 10.1 is almost certainly biased downwards, particular in the most recent years. Whether the actual upturn since the mid-1980s has been enough to restore Ghana's expenditures on science and technology to the levels of the late 1970s, when they were of the order of 1 per cent of GDP, is a moot point.

For Kenya the data are more comprehensive, and more reliable. Figure

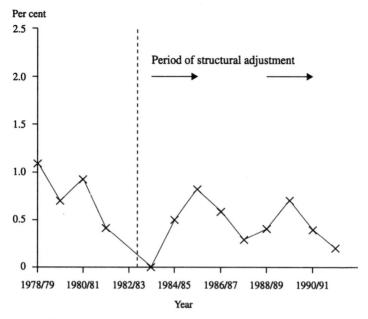

Figure 10.1 Ghana: Expenditures on advancing science and technology, as a percentage of GDP, 1978/9 – 1991/2

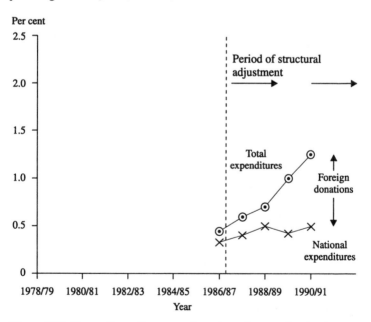

Figure 10.2 Kenya: Expenditures on advancing science and technology, as a percentage of GDP, 1986/7 – 1990/1

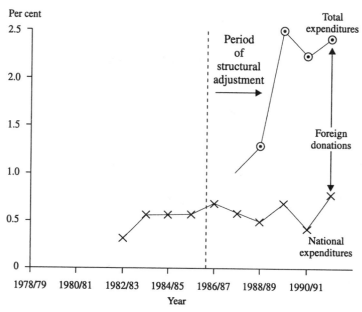

Figure 10.3 Tanzania: Expenditures on advancing science and technology, as a percentage of GDP, 1982/3 – 1991/2

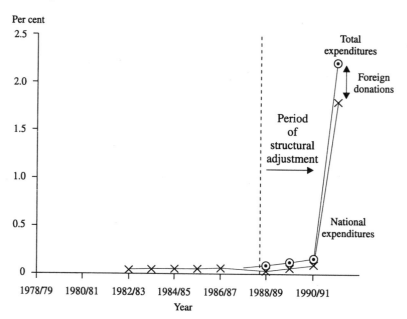

Figure 10.4 Uganda: Expenditures on advancing science and technology, as a percentage of GDP, 1982/3 – 1991/2

10.2 displays all three statistical series, local expenditures on science and technology, foreign donations (the difference between the two plots) and the sum of the two. The second and third series have discontinuities at 1989, the year when UNDP's compilations start; the previous years' figures must be considered slight underestimates. Given that the number of yearly observations is few, at five, and that the first three may be understated, our conclusion – that total expenditures on pursuing science and technology in Kenya have increased since the undertaking of Structural Adjustment programmes – must be tentative in nature.

No such qualification need be placed on the conclusion governing total expenditures on advancing science and technology in Tanzania and Uganda. Figures 10.3 and 10.4 show vividly how foreign donations have raised expenditures to new heights. Again discontinuities in the series appear, in the case of Tanzania because foreign donations were not fully acknowledged before 1989, in the case of Uganda because foreign donations did not arrive on a large scale until the country had been pacified in 1988.

THE EFFECTS UPON DIFFERENT AREAS OF SCIENCE AND TECHNOLOGY HAVE BEEN WIDELY DIFFERENT

The third conclusion is that the effects of the undertaking of Structural Adjustment programmes in Ghana, Kenya, Tanzania and Uganda have been extremely varied over different areas of science and technology. By different areas of science and technology we mean in different fields of scientific endeavour, in different sectors of the economy, and by different actors. (There are other ways of categorizing the differences: one involving different areas or types of products, will be considered in the next section of this chapter.)

The differences arising in different fields of scientific endeavour appear in the universities. In all but one, the engineering faculty has been particularly favoured, and the scientific faculties less favoured. But differences arise even within faculties, although these differences do not seem to be systematic across countries: in one, it may be the electronic and electrical engineering departments that prosper, in another the civil engineering, in still another the mechanical engineering.

Within the scientific faculties lesser favoured, the departments of Mathematics stand out as the least favoured of all. In all four countries, Mathematics is the Cinderella of the scientific disciplines. Posts for which finance is provided are fewer in number than posts established; posts for which suitably qualified candidates apply are fewer in number than posts financed; and posts filled are as often as not occupied by graduate students, rather than professional mathematicians. The evidence to support our conclusion that engineering is generally favoured over science, and science in its physical aspects over science in its metaphysical, is derived from Faculty and Departmental budgetary data. The funds which the different academic areas receive, in proportion to the funds they need (as measured by the requests of their advocates) were obtained for the chief university in each of the four countries in our sample. Approvals as a percentage of requests provide a relatively clear measure of the deprivation of Mathematics departments, for their ratios are universally lower than the ratios of the Faculties which they serve.

It is not difficult to explain the relative preference for supporting faculties devoted to applying, rather than advancing, science; but it is difficult to explain the lack of support for one branch of science – Mathematics – rather than for others – Chemistry, or Physics, or Biology. All are requisites in the education of scientists and engineers; all are part of the scientific base of a nation. If one searches for explanations, one could conceivably argue that Chemistry, or Physics, or Biology are more nearly applicable to industrial or agricultural activities; although this pragmatic argument does not carry over to the services sector of the economy, in which Mathematics is the unifying discipline. Our easy answers to the lack of support for Mathematics are that the discipline is more abstract and that mathematicians are more reserved. The other sciences deal with physical phenomena, whereas Mathematics deals with abstractions; the other scientists promote their disciplines, both in their own universities and, via their presence on advisory bodies, to foreign assistance agencies, whereas mathematicians tend to reserve their energies for the practice of their art. But whatever the answers, the pursuit of that portion of science and technology dependent upon Mathematics is suffering in those countries undergoing Structural Adjustment.

The second of the ways by which we express variability of effect of Structural Adjustment Programmes on the pursuit of science and technology is by looking at different sectors of the economy. The effect of the adoption of Structural Adjustment Programmes in our four countries seems to have resulted in an overall shift of direction: from industry and commerce, on the one hand, to agriculture and public administration, on the other.

Before discussing this strange finding we shall present what evidence we have at our disposal. The first evidence may not at first appear to be evidence at all: it is drawn from the list of conditions imposed upon the borrowers by the IMF and World Bank. For our four countries, the most nearly complete list is that governing for Ghana (see Chapter 3); for the Sub-Saharan African countries the most nearly complete list is that compiled by the World Bank and entered in the data bank covering structural adjustment programmes (World Bank, 1990). If we assign conditions to one of our four sectoral categories – agriculture, industry, services and public administration – we find that agriculture and public administration have the greater number of conditions attached to the conduct of their activities, and industry and services the lesser number. What significance do we attach to these proportions? (Notice that it is not the content of the conditions themselves that concerns us, only the sector of the economy on which they bear.) The significance we attach stems from the likely effects, so far as advancing science and technology are concerned, of directing attention to an activity. The thesis is that the more attention an activity gets, be it from government, from foreign bodies, from local businessmen, from the press and other media, etc., the more likely is that activity to be performed more efficiently. As an example, if local civil servants and foreign advisors direct their attention towards the formulation of the government's annual budget, this activity will be assumed to be carried out more skilfully than in the past. It is a short step from there to the thesis that directing attention to the budgeting process has generated an advance in the science of public administration. In summary, directing attention towards any activity is likely to yield improvements in that activity's performance. Attention provides information; attention stimulates the use of that information so as to obtain improvement; improvement is the consequence of advances in science and technology. Therefore if more attention is directed towards one sector of an economy, we would expect that sector's state of the art to progress; i.e. we would expect that the science and technology applicable to that sector would be likely to advance more rapidly. If less attention were directed towards another sector, we would expect its science and technology to advance less rapidly. More attention, more progress: less attention, less progress.

If this thesis is valid, our information indicates that science and technology in the four countries of our sample are advancing more rapidly in the sectors of agriculture and public administration, and less rapidly in the sectors of industry and the remaining services, as a consequence of the acceptance of the conditions underlying the structural adjustment programmes.

Is there any corroborating evidence for our conclusion that science and technology in different areas of activity have fared quite differently? Some there is from budgetary data on the generation of the national product in the various sectors of the economy (Table 8.1) and on the expenditures of the public research institutes (Table 8.2). Table 8.2 is constructed by grouping public research institutes according to the sector to which their accomplishments chiefly relate. Thus the agricultural research institutes are assigned to the agricultural sector, and the industrial to the industrial sector. There are very few public research institutes specifically devoted to advancing science and technology in the other two sectors – services and public administration – so those sectors have few entries. The research institutes whose assignment is questionable are those devoted to intermediate or appropriate technology, of which we studied one each in Tanzania, Ghana and Uganda, and two in Kenya, and those devoted to the creation and promulgation of standards of measurement, of which we studied one in Ghana. Since most of the technologies investigated in the appropriate technology institutes are applied to the manufacture of products utilized in both the agricultural and industrial sectors – e.g. transport vehicles, stoves, hand tools – the nature of the product does not offer any criterion for categorizing activities. What we have done is to assign the intermediate technology standards organizations to that sector from which they draw their income. Thus the Appropriate Technology Group in Uganda, which receives its funds from the Ministry of Agriculture, is assigned to the agricultural sector; the Technology Consultancy Centre in Ghana, which derives its income from consultancies, is assigned to the services sector; the Centre for Agricultural and Mechanical Technology (CAMARTEC) in Tanzania to the Agricultural Ministry. The Scientific Instrumentation Centre in Ghana and the Appropriate Technology Group at Kenyatta University in Kenya are assigned to the sector of public administration.

The shares of GDP, by sector, and of expenditures by R&D institutes, again by sector, are compared in Table 10.5.

Would that there were consistency in the comparison between the two sets of figures in Table 10.5, but there is not. As it is, the figures suggest that the agricultural sector is universally and consistently well-favoured, and that services are not. In three of our four countries, the industrial sector receives a smaller share of the total funds devoted to furthering science and technology, than of value added in the sector; the exception is Tanzania, where the share of industrial R&D in total R&D has always exceeded the share of value-added. In Uganda, an explanation is immediately at hand for the different outcome since the establishment of a Structural Adjustment Progamme; there was no R&D institute devoted to industry in Uganda until 1991, and so the mere establishment of one, with its initial injection of funds, results in a sudden increase in R&D's share.

The Tanzanian case aside, the other countries display a similar pattern; the direction of advance in science and technology appears to be mainly towards agriculture. Industry and services receive less. There do appear to be substantial differences in the extent to which R&D in the different sectors is treated.

Table 10.5 Comparison of shares of GDP and of expenditures by R&D institutes among agriculture, industry and services for Ghana, Kenya, Tanzania and Uganda 1980–1992

| | Agriculture | | | | | | | | Industry | | | | | | | | Services | | | | | | | |
| | Ghana | | Kenya | | Tanzania | | Uganda | | Ghana | | Kenya | | Tanzania | | Uganda | | Ghana | | Kenya | | Tanzania | | Uganda | |
Year	GDP	R&D	GDP	R&D	GDP	R&D	GDP	R&D	GDP	R&D	GDP	R&D	GDP	R&D	GDP	R&D	GDP	R&D	GDP	R&D	GDP	R&D	GDP	R&D
1980	68	n.a.	33	n.a.	55	n.a.	72	100–	12	n.a.	20	n.a.	12	n.a.	5	0	31	n.a.	47	n.a.	31	0+	23	0+
1981	51	98	33	n.a.	56	n.a.	58	100–	9	1	20	n.a.	11	n.a.	7	0	40	1	47	n.a.	31	0+	35	0+
1982	57	96	33	n.a.	57	n.a.	56	100–	6	1	20	n.a.	11	n.a.	9	0	38	3	47	n.a.	31	0+	35	0+
1983	60	94	34	n.a.	59	78–	60	100–	7	2	19	n.a.	9	22	8	0	34	4	47	n.a.	31	0+	33	0+
1984	54	86	34	n.a.	60	59–	54	100–	12	2	19	n.a.	9	41	8	0	37	12	47	n.a.	31	0+	38	0+
1985	52	82	32	n.a.	62	49–	61	100–	13	2	19	n.a.	9	51	7	0	39	16	49	n.a.	38	0+	33	0+
1986	49	92	33	51	62	43–	62	100–	13	1	19	9	9	57	8	0	39	7	48	40	29	0+	31	0+
1987	47	92	32	67	63	54–	62	100–	14	8	19	9	8	46	8	0	39	2	49	27	29	0+	30	0+
1988	46	97	32	72	61	71–	61	100–	14	1	19	6	7	29	9	0	40	2	49	22	33	0+	32	0+
1989	46	n.a.	31	75	62	65–	61	100–	14	2	20	5	5	35	9	0	40	n.a.	49	21	32	9+	31	0+
1990	43	93	27	87	60	70–	55	100–	14	2	20	7	6	30	10	0	43	5	52	17	35	0+	35	0+
1991	42	n.a.	27	n.a.	61	63–	51	52	15	5+	20	n.a.	5	37	12	11	43	n.a.	53	n.a.	34	0+	37	37
1992	n.a.	n.a.	n.a.	n.a.	n.a.	66–	n.a.	88	n.a.	n.a.	n.a.	n.a.	n.a.	34	n.a.	11	n.a.	n.a.	n.a.	n.a.	n.a.	0+	n.a.	2
Average since structural adjustment	49	91	30	75	62	62	57	88–	13	3	20	6	7	38	10	4	39	7	50	22	33	0+	33	7+
	(1983–1991)		(1987–1991)		(1986–1991)		(1988–1991)		(1983–1991)		(1987–1991)		(1986–1991)		(1988–1991)		(1983–1991)		(1987–1991)		(1986–1991)		(1988–1991)	

Sources: Tables 8.1 and 8.2

Notes: Structural adjustment begins in Ghana 1983, in Kenya 1987, in Tanzania 1986 and in Uganda 1988

The third and final way by which we can express the variations that have arisen in the favour which different areas of science and technology receive is via different treatment of different actors. What we observed is that certain groups of individuals engaged in advancing science and technology in Ghana, Kenya, Tanzania and Uganda have been relatively favoured within the regime of Structural Adjustment and others have not. The differences appear to reflect status: both the status of the organization that provides their employment, and the status that is derived from their own educational attainments. Taking the latter first, those individuals favoured appear to be generally well-educated persons occupying positions at high levels, engaged in intellectual endeavour, either academic, scientific or administrative. The unfavoured appear to be the less well-educated, occupying mundane positions at lower levels, and engaged in practical endeavour. The first group includes scientists in R&D organizations, academics and public administrators; the second engineers and technicians in productive firms (both para-statals and privately owned firms in industry and services), farmers, school teachers, and low-level civil servants, For this statement we cannot provide any statistical evidence, since our quantitative data do not cover the sorts of establishments within which the second groups work. Perhaps we, too, are guilty of holding the same presumptions, namely, that science and technology are advanced by extraordinary individuals placed in elevated positions, and not by ordinary individuals carrying out ordinary activities. In defence of our lack of empirical evidence, we could argue that ordinary persons are more difficult to study, particularly if their contributions to scientific and technological advance are only a minor part of their role, or an occasional output of their activity. Even in modern firms in developed countries the contribution in advancing science and technology of non-scientists is little studied and seldom understood; it should come as no surprise that the same deficiency holds in developing countries too.

Considering organizations advancing science and technology, their status is crucial under regimes of Structural Adjustment. Research institutes within the public sector and universities are generally immune to 'reform' (agricultural research in Tanzania is an exception to this generalization), but the developmental activities of the para-statal organizations are extremely vulnerable, since the para-statal firms are targeted for privatization. Whether the activities take place within R&D laboratories or productive entities like factories and technical facilities, these activities can be terminated, or greatly reduced in scope, in the course of a transfer of ownership. In the cases of the commodity distributing and marketing organizations (like Ghana's Cocoa Marketing Board) the transfer of ownership is often, under the prescriptions of the Structural Adjustment programme, from one owner (the state) to many, many owners engaged in quite different activities (e.g. in the case of the Cocoa Marketing Board to peasant cultivators, processors, brokers, transport firms, exporters, etc.). Thus the transfer is not only from public to private hands, but also from one pair of hands under, in principle, single direction, to numerous hands responding to many interests. In such a multiplicity of ownership where lies the source of funds? of direction? of planning? necessary to undertake advancing science and technology.

THE AREAS OF SCIENCE AND TECHNOLOGIES MOST VIGOROUSLY PURSUED ARE INCREASINGLY DETERMINED BY FOREIGNERS

In countries as poor as those we studied, particularly at times when their economies are under such strain, it is not at all unexpected that their provision for the future is minimal; they are stretched to the limit providing for the present. Where the pursuit of science and technology, the epitome of investment for the future, is concerned, the resources must come mainly from abroad. Come they do, as we have observed.

Yet the foreign donations for advancing science and technology do not come without strings. This too is not at all unexpected. Foreign donors wish to be assured that the recipients are committed to the projects they, the foreign donors, support. As guarantee of local participation in the joint endeavour they usually require that the local government make a substantial contribution. Generally, this is interpreted by foreign donors as a contribution exceeding what the local government would have allocated to the project in the absence of the donation. So the favoured project receives both the foreigner's contribution and an augmented local contribution: it is doubly favoured.

One then asks what happens to the funding of projects that fail to secure foreign assistance; the answer is that they are likely to receive even fewer local funds. The reason that the unfavoured projects receive less funds from local government is that the local supplier of funds, be it a Ministry or a para-statal firm, has a fixed overall budget, authorized by the Finance Ministry. This budget is, itself, seldom augmented to allow for 'counterpart funds'; rather the 'counterpart funds' are offset by an equal reduction in the funds allocated to other activities within the same Ministry or firm. In this manner, projects designed locally but not preferred by the foreign donors receive relatively less than they otherwise would.

Illustrations of the way in which foreigners influence the direction of advances in science and technology are seen in the *Masterplans* that are being formulated in Sub-Saharan African countries. The objectives of these *Masterplans* are to make explicit those lines of endeavour on which the country should concentrate, and those from which it should back off. Tanzania's Agricultural Masterplan (Tanzania, Ministry of Agriculture, Livestock and Cooperatives, 1991), for example, assigns first priority in R&D to coffee, cotton, tea, rice, animal health, soil and water management, and 'farm systems' research, in that order. Only these activities would command *more* resources. Items of second priority – the list comprises maize, roots and tubers, phaseolus beans, grain legumes, and vegetable and oil seeds – would be rationalized but would not command more resources; and activities of third and last priority would receive little support (*ibid.*: x), and that in diminishing amounts.

Setting priorities, planning and allocating resources to their attainments and adhering vigilantly and strictly to subsequent programmes, are highly desirable actions: the questions that arise in the case of the *Masterplans* are: on what bases are the priorities set? and who does the setting?

According to the Tanzanian Agricultural Masterplan the criterion for setting priorities is to promote the most economic use of resources within the context of the country's national R&D objectives. 'This implied a concentration on research projects which are likely to provide important socio-economic returns within the shortest time, i.e. programs with clear targets and identifiable concepts' (*ibid.*: xi). 'Due to the importance of agricultural export earnings for financing national development, research on export commodities was given special attention' (*ibid.*: xi, xii). In light of this criterion (increasing foreign earnings from agricultural exports) the ordering of the first three items of highest priority – coffee, then cotton, then tea – naturally followed.

The second question is who set those priorities? Who decided that export crops should receive the major share of scarce resources for R&D? Who determined the direction in which agricultural science and technology should advance? For the answer to these questions we must turn to the composition of the committees that formulated the Agricultural Masterplan, and infer from their composition who exerted influence.

The origins of the Tanzanian Agricultural Masterplan are laid out in the *Masterplan* itself (*ibid.*: ix–xi; 1–5; the full title is the National Agriculture and Livestock Research Masterplan, abbreviated NALRM). The stimulus and initial finance came from the World Bank: as part of Tanzania's Economic Recovery Programme (of 1986) the Bank and the Tanzanian government established the National Agriculture and Livestock Research

Project, whose long-range objectives were to consolidate the organizational structure and management of the country's agricultural research programmes. From mid-1988 to December 1990 committees were formed, personnel from the Ministry of Agriculture, from the research institutes and from abroad appointed, and working papers produced. Commencing in December 1990 a 'Task Force' absorbed the previous material and formulated the *Masterplan*. The core group within the Task Force was comprised of two coordinators (one Tanzanian, the other foreign), seven staff from the Ministry of Agriculture, one from Sokoine Agricultural University, and four (additional) foreign consultants (recruited by the International Service for National Agricultural Research, ISNAR). The plan, when it emerged in March 1991, was published by ISNAR in the Hague. Simultaneously, the Tanzanian government freed agricultural producer prices and commanded the various crop marketing boards to act as commercial, profit-making entities, in competition with private operators.

Were Tanzania's the only Masterplan in existence, one could infer that the initiative lay partly with the local government, but the near ubiquity of *Masterplans* suggests that it is the ubiquitous agencies, i.e. the international organizations like the World Bank and ISNAR, that press for their promulgation. Moreover, the identity of the criterion governing the direction of R&D – so as to increase foreign exchange earnings from expanded exports of traditional commodities – suggests that there is a uniformity of belief in the efficiency of such a prescription, again an attribute of a single, or a group of cooperating, agencies.

The very similarity of the type of commodity filling the category given highest priority – coffee, tea, cocoa, cotton, sisal, i.e. relatively homogeneous tropical and sub-tropical crops traditionally imported by the developed countries – also points to a single sponsor, motivated by a pervading belief in the desirability of concentrating on the production of coffee, tea, etc. The general argument supporting concentration on traditional exports – an argument frequently cited but seldom backed with systematic comparisons – is that it is in these commodities that developing countries, like Tanzania, have a comparative advantage. (But Tanzania may also have a comparative advantage in the production of maize, roots and tubers, beans, grain legumes and vegetable and oil seeds, i.e. those crops of medium priority, into whose R&D considerably less attention is to be directed.)

It seems to be more than coincidental that the commodities granted highest priority should not be produced in the countries sponsoring *Masterplans*, and those granted lesser priority should be produced in competition with the countries whose agencies are sponsoring *Masterplans*. Moreover, it is these agencies, representing the developed counties, which provide most of the funds which are used to further R&D in the traditional export crops: in Tanzania R&D in coffee is financed by the European Union, while it is Germany and the Netherlands which financed the *Masterplan*; R&D in cotton and tea are also funded by the UK, which also contributed to the formulation of the *Masterplan* (*ibid.*: 13, 18–20). Not only do developed countries support R&D into those commodities which they import but also they tend to ensure that these are the very commodities towards which most R&D – that financed by themselves and that financed by others including the producing country – will be directed. 'To meet the funding requirements for NALRM implementation, Government will have to make all efforts to mobilize donor funding. In principle, such funding should be geared in the future exclusively to NALRM implementation' (*ibid.*: xii).

Do we have any additional support for the principle that which areas prosper, and which do not, are increasingly determined by foreigners? The answer is that support is found in the manner by which funds in R&D are generated. Consider the procedures by which foreign donations are decided upon. In some cases, the potential donor conceives of a worthy project, usually because some official or advisor within the foreign assistance agency recommends it; in other cases, the initiative comes from the local R&D organization, whose Director or, less frequently, Project Leader, establishes contact with a person of equivalent rank in the developed country, who in turn introduces him to the relevant official in the assistance agency. In a few instances other channels are followed: Ministers of one country or the other may take up the cause of a project and promote it; or outsiders (the media, domestic or foreign; advisors to governments, particularly those in the organizations intermediate between the operating ministries and the R&D institutes; and officials in the World Bank and in the regional development banks) may intervene on the project's behalf.

But there is a difference between who takes the initiative in promoting a project and who has the choice in providing the wherewithal. In our opinion the choice lies effectively with the foreign donor. The reason follows from the conditional logic of support. For countries as poor as those of Sub-Saharan Africa, R&D and scientific education are activities that cannot be afforded alone; they also require foreign support, in amounts sufficient to finance buildings, equipment, supplies, and all the 'back-up' of any sophisticated endeavour. Foreign support is not something that the poor countries can command; it is provided only if those who are in a position to provide the support are willing to do so. Since they have far more claims on their foreign assistance that they can provide, the foreign agencies and countries are forced to make choices: this project deserves support, that does not. Faced with competing claims for scarce donations, foreign assistance agencies decide upon the allocation, a decision which cannot be abdicated.

This shift in the locus of decisions, decisions concerning the future direction of the economies, from the local authorities to foreign assistance bodies is likely to be of lasting duration, because of the scarcity of local resources which can be devoted to the pursuit of science and technology. It may well be years, or even decades, before the Sub-Saharan African countries have sufficient resources to be able to finance scientific education and R&D unaided. It may be years, or even decades, before the locus of decision-making returns to the countries in which the primary effects are felt.

THE CHOICE OF THE AREAS OF SCIENCE AND TECHNOLOGY TO BE PURSUED IS BASED PRIMARILY UPON THE EFFECTS OF SUCH CHOICE ON THE DEVELOPED COUNTRIES

We now move on to our fifth and final presumption, which is a consequence of the shift in the locus of decision-making. In one sense, the fifth principle – that decisions about the direction in which science and technology should progress are likely to be made on the basis of their potential effects on the developed countries – is unobjectionable. The argument is as follows: the countries in our sample, as representatives of Sub-Saharan Africa, are desperately short of foreign earnings, with which to finance their growth. The only sure way in which earnings of foreign exchange can increase is through an increase in the capability of these countries to provide goods and services desired abroad. The main foreign markets for these goods and services have always been, and almost certainly will remain, in the developed countries, primarily Western Europe, but also North American and North-east Asia.

Economies exist to satisfy needs: the relative importance of different needs are reflected in the prices that the goods satisfying those needs command in world markets. Guided by these prices, the efficient economy will direct its production of goods and services so as to maximize the value of its output. The smaller and the poorer the country, the more it must submit to the imperative imposed by world market prices. The Sub-Saharan African countries must therefore increase their provision of the goods and services demanded in the developed countries, at the prices these goods command. Since the current provision is inadequate, resources must be shifted into activities which will yield the necessary increases. If these new resources, as well as those currently allocated to providing the goods and services foreigners demand, are to be applied successfully, attention will have to be directed towards the efficiency with which they are applied: such attention will involve the entire economy, from producers to managers to civil servants to scientists and engineers. The last have the vital roles of better understanding the production of goods and services already provided to foreigners and of discovering new goods and services with which to tempt them. So, science and technology in Sub-Saharan Africa should be (re)directed towards helping to generate increased export earnings from the developed countries. Who better can judge what goods and services will appeal to the developed countries than intelligent people within their own assistance agencies?

Such is the sense in which R&D should be directed towards exports currently in demand in the developed countries. In another sense, however, such a thesis is objectionable, in that it presumes that the purpose of the Sub-Saharan economies is to serve people in the developed countries; or, to put it less provocatively, that the Sub-Saharan economies will best serve their own members by conforming to the existing pattern of world trade.

In the world of perfect competition, both at home and abroad, and of self-seeking individuals, such a presumption may be valid; but in an imperfect world, all that can be said for such a thesis is that it may be true, or it may not. In the imperfect and dynamic world, objectives are not necessarily compatible; to move toward one goal today may mean departing farther from another goal tomorrow. In this context, moving towards the goal of maximizing current export earnings may mean moving away from the competing goal of employment maximization, or the goal of self-sufficiency, or the goal of raising the growth rate, or the goal of raising the standard of living of the poorest in the community, or any of several other admirable objectives. Believing in national self-determination, we argue that the choice of objective, and of the means to be employed in attaining that objective, should reside in the country itself; it should not reside abroad. In the cases of the four countries in our sample, the decisions which shape the future structure and performance of the economy should be made in Ghana, in Kenya, in Tanzania and in Uganda, and not in Washington DC or one of the Western European capitals.

CHANGES IN DECISION-MAKING FOR SCIENCE AND TECHNOLOGY

But all we do in this chapter is argue that such decisions are, increasingly, not being made in Ghana, in Kenya, in Tanzania, or in Uganda: how they might be, and what changes in policy would be required to effect the change will be the subject of our final chapter. What we wish to do in the remaining part of this chapter is determine the implications of the shift in decision-making from within the local countries to foreign bodies. To us, these implications seem to be four in number, and can be abbreviated as a change in the aim of development, an increase in vulnerability, a shift in the subject of attention, and an elevation in intent. We shall now address these four in turn.

Change in the aim of development

The first implication of the shift in decision-making on the future direction of science and technology is the change in the aim of economic development of the Sub-Saharan African countries. In brief, the shift is from domestic expansion to export promotion. Export promotion is clearly understood; it involves focusing on world markets, discovering those products most in demand, mobilizing domestic resources so as to concentrate on the production of products in which the country has a comparative advantage, and devoting scientific and technical resources to their improvement. Domestic expansion is less clearly understood, being a term not in common use, and yet expressing better the objective of the Sub-Saharan African countries themselves. The term can be taken to mean increasing the provision of employment and output in the monetized section of the economy, and increasing consumption overall.

Between export promotion and domestic expansion there is an obvious clash, in the short run at least. There is a cost, both in time and in lost output, in shifting resources from those activities involved in domestic expansion to those involved in export promotion, chiefly, from manufactures and government to traditional export crops. How long the 'short run' is and how great the loss in output will be no one knows; those favouring domestic expansion argue that it is very long and that the loss in output is very large; those favouring Structural Adjustment argue that the time is short and the lost output more than compensated for by the additional foreign goods purchased by the increased export earnings. Our belief, as has been obvious, is the former.

Regardless of the nature of the costs and benefits of shifting resources from domestic expansion to export promotion, and of their balance, the point that we wish to make is that there has been a change in the aim of development, from the former to the latter. This coincides with a change in the group of individuals who select the objective, namely from the leaders of the Sub-Saharan African countries to those foreigners who formulate and administer the programmes of foreign assistance. (Note: we deliberately use the word 'objective' to represent what others might call 'means', believing that an economy-wide process like export promotion, so all-embracing, affects the entire structure and behaviour of the society, and so is better encompassed in a transcendental term.) This change is not a sly and subtle shift in the locus of decision; it is open and articulated, in bold and assured language. Those who articulate it do so in the belief that export promotion is in the best interest of the developing countries; this is not denied. It may even be in the best interest of the developing countries; the point is that it is not *their* choice.

Looking into the future, we can conceive of a change in the perception of the development community, from a belief in the efficacy of export promotion to one in the efficacy of, say, 'going it alone': there have been, after all, several such changes in perception since the end of World War II. The developing countries, after having altered their economies from an expansion to an export mode, would then find themselves under great pressure to change their aim yet again. Fashions in development do alter, and it is the developing countries who bear the costs of alteration.

Increase in vulnerability

The decisions that foreigners make regarding the direction to be taken by science and technology are based primarily upon the principle of comparative advantage. The principle states that a country should invest in those activities which can potentially be carried out at a cost relatively lower than those of other countries. Also in principle, but not in fact, all activities should be governed by comparative advantage; in practice certain activities – the production of temperate foodstuffs, of textiles, the processing of tropical foodstuffs, and some others – are excluded from the menu of activities appropriate for developing countries. They are reserved for producers in the European Union, the USA and Japan.

Therefore it is from a smaller menu of activities that individuals, deciding what activities in the developing countries to stimulate, choose. Essentially the choice descends on those commodities consumed but not produced in the developed countries, the rationale being that consumption creates the demand that makes profitable the production of these commodities, and that production is not attractive in the developed countries and so can be profitable in the developing countries.

What commodities fit into this reduced menu? They are chiefly 'primary commodities', meaning products extracted from, or beneath, the soil of the developing countries. In the case of the four countries in our sample, the meaning of 'primary commodities' is beverages – cocoa, coffee and tea – and to a lesser extent fibres – sisal, cotton and wood. Focusing on these, the officials of the development agencies, acting with a proxy from the leaders of developed countries, direct resources towards primary commodity production. Scientific inquiries are undertaken to increase the production and lower the cost of producing cocoa, coffee, etc., and education is directed towards the training of people who will devote their careers accordingly.

The likely outcome, over the relatively long time it takes to shift resources further into the production of primary commodities, is that their output does rise, and that average costs of production do fall. From the point of view of the single developing country whose resources are channelled in this direction, the result is all to the good: more output is produced and conveyed to the markets of the world. But from the collective point of view of *all* developing countries producing this primary commodity, the result can be disastrous. First, the total volume of the primary commodity placed on world markets rises substantially, at a rate far faster than the rate at which consumption in the developed countries rises. Given that the nature of the demand for primary commodities is price inelastic, the fall in the world market price is greater, proportionately, than the increase in output; the total value of the commodity marketed falls.

Secondly, the developing country has reallocated some of its scarce resources into, rather than out of, an activity that is yielding fewer returns as time passes. The cost of reallocation may be high, and is 'sunk', i.e. unrecoverable. Moreover, any subsequent re-reallocation, back out of the production of the primary commodity, may again be high, and unrecoverable.

Finally, the developing country is left, after the initial reallocation, with a monoculture. It has a very large portion of its total scarce resources, of scientific and technological resources in our case, devoted to the production of one, or at best a few, commodities alone. It is vulnerable to events arising in the developed countries, events over which it has no control. Imagine what would be the effect upon the country producing, say, coffee, if tastes in the developed country shifted out of coffee into another beverage, say cola. Imagine what would happen if coffee were discovered, or even rumoured, to have deleterious effects on health!

How does it happen that it is the production of primary commodities that is so encouraged by foreign donors? Some of the answers have been given already – the restricted menu of possibilities, the need not to offend powerful groups of competing producers in the developed countries, the universal aim of export promotion, and the reliance upon the criterion of comparative advantage – but there is one remaining answer, involving the fallacy of composition. An aid official, assigned the duty of determining in what commodity *his* country (usually the developing country to whose aid programme he is assigned) should invest, looks solely at the possible effects on *his* country, under the presumption that it is *his* country only that increases its output. But he does not make allowance for the simultaneous concentration of another aid official in another developed country on what commodity *his* country should invest in, and another official, and another, and another. Assume they all settle on a single commodity, each on the presumption that it is *his* country alone whose output should increase. The increase is therefore much greater, being a multiple of that of each single country.

This general problem of what is the correct decision for a single country, (in the absence of other countries also adopting the same decision), being the wrong decision, when many countries adopt the decision, is quite apparent in three countries in our sample. If, encouraged by one foreign donor, Kenya devotes more of its scientific and technological resources to raising the output of coffee, and no other country does so, that may be fine for Kenya, and not disadvantageous for Tanzania and Uganda. But if, independently, encouraged by two other foreign donors, Tanzania and Uganda also devote more of their scientific and technological resources to raising the output of coffee, the combined rise is much greater, and the fall in price swifter and further. Looked at from the point of view of each single country, its dependence upon a single commodity, coffee in this case, has grown, and its vulnerability increased.

Not only is the above argument, based upon the fallacy of composition, one that is relevant for the developing countries (although generally unappreciated), but it is an argument that is also relevant for the developed countries (and very much appreciated). The comparable commodity for the developed countries is not coffee, but, say, iron and steel. Iron and steel have much the same characteristics as coffee; they are demanded by non-producing countries – in the case of iron and steel, the developing countries – their demand is price-inelastic, resources committed to their production cannot be easily shifted to alternative commodities, and scientific and technological resources devoted to improving their production are effective in increasing output and lowering average costs. Yet the developed countries know better than to concentrate their scarce resources on iron and steel. They do just the opposite: they restrict output of iron and steel, and devote their scientific and technological resources to better uses (meaning chiefly a greater variety of commodities, each with a growing market characterized by elastic price and income demands). No monoculture for the developed countries! No risk of their being vulnerable to deteriorating export earnings! No obeisance to the doctrine of comparative advantage for them!

Shift in the subject of allocation

That foreign donors have directed their attention to export crops – forming what we might call a 'Kaffee Klatch' – is indicative of a general switch in focus from the particular to the general and from the private to the public domain. It is this second aspect of the switch – from focusing on the private sector to focusing on the public – that we now wish to address. Underlying this switch seem to be two quite different presumptions. Both have to do with adaptability, but one presumes that the private sector is very adaptable and can be left to itself to adapt to the structural changes imposed; whereas the other presumes that the public sector is rigid and needs considerable assistance and supervision. Let us take liberalization as our example of a structural change, and look specifically at the policy of reducing, or possibly even eliminating, controls on the import of manufactured goods. The presumptions are that local firms under private ownership will be perfectly capable of adapting to the new, liberal regime; and that the various government ministries and state firms that operated under the previous restricted regimes will not be. They, the public sector organizations, will therefore need considerable attention.

To us, this shift in attention was most vividly evident in the areas of production categorized as agriculture. The presumptions seem to be that private producers of agricultural and other products of the soil can adapt quickly and easily to a change in their external conditions, but that the para-statal agencies involved in collecting, transporting, marketing, and improving their activities cannot. So public agencies are urged to disband, and foreign assistance is given to the government to help secure compliance. In the course of the disbanding, the task of advancing science and technology may be forgotten.

Incidentally, we are not claiming that public bodies are adaptable, in the sense that they can and will adapt readily to the conditions of Structural Adjustment; our impressions are that they are not very adaptable. Rather we emphasize the difference in presumption, for it is also our impression that private bodies are not adaptable. Moreover, there seemed to us to be valid reasons why private firms should not adapt readily. Take, for example, the reducing of employment in a manufacturing firm facing foreign competition, as a result of the liberalization of imports. The local firm might decide not to reduce employment, even if it could produce at the lower *direct* cost as a consequence. First of all, those employees who lost their jobs with the firm would claim (a claim enforceable under legislation) substantial redundancy pay (in the case of Ghana, to a few *years'* salary or wages), amounting to a sum that the firm could not easily afford. To the firm, the alternative of continuing to produce for months, or even years, at higher direct costs, might be preferable. Even if the firm eventually went bankrupt (as many private firms in our four countries have) at least it would have avoided the redundancy payments, and the immediate offence it would have given to a government confronted with widespread unemployment. For the private firm, it may well be better to carry on, unadapted.

What we would urge is that the adaptability of private firms, particularly private manufacturing firms, be investigated too, for the presumption that the opening up of formerly protected markets to foreign competition will force local enterprises to lower their costs needs to be examined. Will on-the-job training, an important element of advance of science and technology, increase if private firms are subject to increased competition? Will private firms devote *more* resources to R&D, to product and process improvement, etc? More information is needed, and, in its train, more attention from abroad, to the private as to the public sector.

Elevation of intent: proper structure as a cure

The final implication of the shift in decision-making from local to foreign bodies attendant upon the adoption of Structural Adjustment Programmes is an elevation of intent. By elevation of intent we mean a shift from minutiae of development to the eternals. It also involves a shift of outlook, from process to structure, and from the dynamic to the static.

An illustration will make the distinction clearer. Let us seize again upon the thesis of comparative advantage, not as a principle derived from economic theory, but as a rule governing the allocation of foreign donations; and let us see the implication of following this general rule. We will take the case of bananas in Uganda, as illustrating what we called the 'Banana Syndrome' when we encountered it in Chapter 6. Bananas are not exported from Uganda, nor are they likely to be, given the country's distance from the sea coast. Yet bananas, along with their sister crop plantains, form probably the most important local food crop. The diseases afflicting bananas are many and presumably capable of eradication. The Ugandans would like to conduct more R&D into improving banana production, but have been unsuccessful in evoking foreign support, without which the intensity of R&D cannot be increased beyond a mere trifle. But the allocation of scarce scientific and technological resources to improving banana cultivation does not meet the criterion of increased export earnings. Coffee does, so it is coffee that receives support. As a consequence, the shift from a concern on minutiae – in this case the minutiae of food production by individual farmers, each operation being on a small scale for the local market – to the application of a general principle – in this, as in most other cases, that of comparative advantage – has the consequence that what in all probability has taken place is a misallocation of resources. As a result of the elevation of intent, accompanying an increasing dependence upon foreign contributions for advancing science and technology, Uganda's prospects for the future have been reduced.

One objective of the foreigners is to alter the structure of the Ugandan economy so that it better reflects the inducements and deterrents arising under a regime of world market prices. If world markets were open (rather than restricted), and if world market prices were perfect, we suspect that there would be an inducement in Uganda to produce more bananas and less coffee, for the reasons given in this and the previous sections. Yet science and technology, whose advances so influence the attractiveness of future production, are being directed in the opposite direction. There are, of course, other plausible explanations for foreign preferences, as far as the sponsoring of R&D is concerned, but we believe that the misallocation is best explained by the combination of change in the aim of development (from domestic expansion to export promotion) and elevation of intent (from pragmatic detail to guiding principle) that has occurred with the shift in the locus of decision-making.

Whether or not foreigners to Sub-Saharan Africa are capable of making decisions on anything other than guiding principles is a matter for the next chapter, on policy, so we shall not raise it here. Nor shall we expand here our temporal horizon to consider the long term, within which the fruits of scientific and technological advance mature. Nor shall we suggest remedies. These comprise our tasks for the final chapter.

11 Policy recommendations

INTRODUCTION

In this, our final chapter, we shall try to derive a set of micro-economic policies, as alternatives to these currently imposed on the countries in Sub-Saharan Africa, in the hope that our set will yield a better future for their economies. We shall offer the alternative set after having projected into the future the likely structure and performance of the economies under the current set of policies strongly urged by foreign assistance bodies, particularly the IMF and the World Bank.

Our first task, therefore, is to imagine what the Sub-Saharan economies will look like, say, a generation from now, if present policies are fully implemented. We choose a generation as our time horizon, because it is only over this long an interval that the structures of the Sub-Saharan economies will have altered and that current advances in science and technology will have been exploited. In our projection, we shall focus on four items in sequence: first, the likely effects, over the relatively short term, of the adoption of Structural Adjustment programmes; secondly, the consequences of such adjustment on the Sub-Saharan economies; thirdly, the exogenous changes that will arise over the next generation, particularly the growth of the countries' populations; and fourthly, the likely changes in the outside world, in which Sub-Saharan Africa is increasingly embedded.

Subsequently, we will postulate a better picture of the Sub-Saharan economies a generation from now. We shall then ask what alternative set of policies, that is alternative to those imposed at present, might be more likely to create this better picture. We shall next guess at what changes in current policy would be required, to shift to the better alternative, on the parts of the Sub-Saharan countries themselves, the international financial agencies, and assistance groups in the developed countries. Finally, we shall ask if these changes are feasible in the present economic and political environment, and, if not, what actions are possible. But first to the picture of the Sub-Saharan economies a generation from now.

THE SUB-SAHARAN ECONOMIES IN 2023

How can the economies of Ghana, of Kenya, of Tanzania, of Uganda, of all the other Sub-Saharan African countries, be portrayed in the year 2023? In proceeding to make our portrayal under the current set of policies we shall make two assumptions: first that the current set of policies persist, and secondly, that progress towards their attainment continues.

As to the second of these two assumptions, the progress we should expect the economies to have made by 2023, we shall guess at this by extrapolating the progress made so far. Thus, in those areas in which progress has been rapid, we shall assume that the conditions underlying the Structural Adjustment loans have been fulfilled; and in those in which progress has been slow, we shall assume that the conditions have been only partially fulfilled. The difficult areas are those in which no substantial progress has yet been made; what assumption would be most appropriate for them? To assume that no progress will be made in the future is plausible, for any of three reasons: the conditions may be too stringent, or too difficult to bring about, given the resources available for their fulfilment; the conditions may be politically unpalatable, and the developing countries willing to jeopardize relations with the IMF and World Bank in resisting them; or finally, the conditions may be abandoned by the international financial agencies as infeasible, or no longer necessary, or undesirable. At the other extreme, to assume that the conditions, unfulfilled till now, will be fulfilled between now and 2023 is not plausible. The intermediate assumption – that the conditions will begin to be fulfilled – is plausible, for these conditions currently rank large in the eyes of the development agencies and do, so they presumably feel, warrant continued attention. Since, to take one example of a condition that ranks large in the Fund's and Bank's eyes, government expenditures so need to be curbed that pressure to reduce them will be unrelenting, ultimately with effect. It would be quite unrealistic, therefore, to assume that there will not have been some curtailment of government expenditures by 2023.

It is this last, modest, assumption – of partial fulfilment of currently frustrated conditions – that we shall adopt. So far as the economies of 2023 are concerned, therefore, our assumptions of progress towards fulfilment of conditions are summarized as complete for those towards which major progress has already been made and partial for all the remainder. How then will the economies shape up?

It would be well to recognize how numerous and radical are the changes sought for the Sub-Saharan African countries. The average number of conditions imposed upon them in the course of borrowing from the IMF/ World Bank is 28 (World Bank, 1990), with such multiple objectives as 'fiscal austerity, monetary tightness, currency devaluation, liberalization in various forms, and wage restraint.' (Taylor, 1988: 9) Achieving, even partially, these objectives will, as it is supposed to do, alter substantially the Sub-Saharan African economies.

Alter towards what? In brief, the economies of the Sub-Saharan African countries will approach more closely the canons of *laissez faire*. Their economies will be more nearly 'liberalized' than those of the developed countries. This may seem an extraordinary statement, but the developed countries are under no compulsion to 'adjust' their economies: there is no body equivalent to the IMF/World Bank forcing the European Community to eliminate income supports to its farmers, and tariffs and quotas on imports of temperate foodstuffs; there is no equivalent body forcing Japan to open its domestic distribution system to imported goods; there is no equivalent body standing guard over the USA preventing it from subsidizing its exporters. *Laissez faire* is presumed to be good for all, but only the developing countries are to be obliged to follow its dictates.

The Sub-Saharan populations in 2023

Between 1962 and 1992, the population of Ghana doubled; the population of Kenya increased to nearly two-and-a-half times its early figure; the population of Tanzania more than doubled; and that of Uganda nearly doubled. It would be folly to assume anything other than a continued growth of the countries' populations at approximately the same rate. Efforts to raise public health, aided by foreign donations, will persist; the scourge of AIDs will have been contained; while efforts to reduce birth rates, both locally and foreign inspired, are unlikely to increase. By 2023, we would expect the population of Ghana to double again; similarly those of Kenya, Tanzania and Uganda. In 2023 the population of the Ghanaian economy would approach 30 million, of the Kenyan 50 million, of the Tanzanian 55 million, and of the Ugandan 30 million. Together these four countries would contain 165 million people, as against a little less than 40 million at independence.

Of the other resources with which these people will be combined in producing goods and services no such increase can be expected. The state of the arts – the consequence of advances in science and technology – will be discussed later, but the other resources at the economies' command will either have remained static – land, rainfall, etc. – or have declined – forests, fertility of the soil. Debatable are the direction of change of capital and skills, including entrepreneurship and technological capability. Capital may well increase in volume, as foreign firms invest in the natural resources the countries contain, but skills could fail to keep pace. The last item, technical skills, is also a part of the topic of science and technology, and so will be considered separately later.

On a per capita basis, the economies of 2023 can therefore be assumed to have less land but possibly more capital, all applied with an efficiency which may be greater or lesser on the average than that currently observed. What would be most likely would be substantial variations in the efficiency with which resources were combined: enclaves of high efficiency in large tracts of low efficiency, rather like Latin America today.

In what sorts of activities will the extra people be engaged? It would seem unlikely that agriculture could employ more people than it does today, at the level of productivity that must be attained for successful production of exportable crops. The existing work may, of course, be spread over more people, all residing in the countryside; but more likely, in countries in which government is less involved than today in regulating the lives of its people, is a migration of population to the towns and cities. The phenomenon which has been observed in other developing countries but has been largely absent in Sub-Saharan Africa to the present – a burgeoning of the population of the cities – is almost sure to appear. Given current rates of immigration and internal population growth the capital city of Nairobi could have a population in excess of four million people, Dar es Salaam in excess of three million, Accra in excess of two million and Kampala/Entebbe in excess of one-and-a-half million.

Given the prominence of such huge urban clusters, the question reduces to what sorts of activities will their residents engage in? History provides probably the best answer to this question: it is that some will be engaged in highly productive jobs, yielding relatively high incomes, but that the vast majority will be in marginal activities, earning relatively low incomes. Bombay, Calcutta, Rio de Janeiro, Lima and Mexico City are the models; 'informal' is the term used to describe the economic activities of the bulk of their residents, and pitiful the word to describe their prospects.

The rest of the world in 2023

Structural changes, population growth: what else will most affect the state of the economies of Sub-Saharan Africa in 2023? The final factor will be the state of the economies of the rest of the world, within which the Sub-Saharan economies, via their increased trade, will be more embedded.

So far as the demands which the rest of the world places on the commodity exports of Sub-Saharan Africa are concerned, we have argued throughout this study that they will not have increased proportionately to the increases in the economies' exportable output. Relative prices, that is prices of Sub-Saharan African commodity exports relative to prices of the goods and services they import, will almost certainly fall. With worsening terms of trade, the contribution of commodity exports to the national incomes of the Sub-Saharan African countries will also fall. What of other export earning activities? Revenues from tourism, even now so important to the balance of payments of Kenya and Tanzania, can be expected to increase, although under a regime of *laissez faire* much of these revenues will accrue to foreign investors in the necessary facilities – hotels, travel agencies, transport, banking. Other export categories seem absent, at least in the magnitude needed to generate the additional earnings for the increased population.

What will be needed to fill the gaps, both in urban employment for the expanded population of the cities, and output available for consumption by the population, can only be obtained through a greatly increased domestic production of domestically consumed goods and services. It is towards attaining this increase that a major portion of the advances in science and technology must be directed.

THE AIMS OF POLICY

The preceding sections have provided an indication of the direction in which science and technology should advance in the countries of our sample, and in Sub-Saharan Africa in general. Some advance is desirable in improving the production and distribution of exportable commodities, although less than is currently being sought. Greater advance should be sought in those activities which provide employment for a rapidly expanding population and which generate the production of goods and services for domestic consumption. In the countryside, generous advances will be needed to enable more food and fibre to be grown for countries as a whole; in the cities great advances will be required to make possible huge increases in employment and production of goods produced in competition with imports. It will not be enough that employment alone increase, if domestic markets have been seized by foreign producers able to undercut domestic firms; it will not be enough if a few domestic firms are able to reduce their costs sufficiently to survive foreign competition: what must happen is that a very large number of domestic firms, employing a very large number of people, must be able to produce at world market prices. *Laissez faire* will demand that domestic firms produce at low cost; the welfare of the populations of the countries will require that there be enough firms, all producing at low costs, to provide incomes for all.

So, the aims of advancing science and technology are modest gains in the area of export commodities, and immodest gains in the areas of non-traded goods and of activities, like tourism, which use relatively abundant resources to earn foreign exchange. Let us call the last area 'stable-terms-of-trade goods', in order to distinguish them from exportable commodities like coffee, whose terms of trade will continue to deteriorate in the future. Summarizing, the aims of policy in science and technology in the countries of Sub-Saharan Africa are to make reasonable advances in the area of exportable commodities and extraordinary advances in the areas of goods for domestic consumption and 'stable-terms-of-trade' goods.

THE REDIRECTION OF EDUCATION AND R&D

At present, the pursuit of science and technology in Ghana, Kenya, Tanzania and Uganda can hardly be said to be in the directions indicated by the above aims, nor can foreign donors be said to be assisting in the necessary redirection. In fact, as we have argued, foreign advisors and donors seem to be moving the pursuit away from, rather than in, the proper direction. Hence, our policy prescriptions will impinge as much upon the foreign as they will upon the domestic community; they will devote as much attention to how foreign agencies should change their ways as to how domestic agencies should change theirs.

Prescribing policy is no simple task. There is no theory of policy prescription to guide us, nor are there a common set of procedures or rules of thumb. What is often done by policy-makers is to establish a list of priorities, commencing with that policy towards which most attention should be directed and terminating with that towards which least need be directed. A list of priorities has the advantage that it is clear and precise for those who are responsible for the execution of policy; they know that their performance will be judged on their enforcement of the first policy on the list, then on the second, and so forth. A list of priorities has the disadvantage that it provides little guidance when trade-offs are involved between different items. If, for example, the first item in the list, assigned the highest priority, is to reduce government expenditures, and the second, assigned the next-to-highest priority, is to increase government expenditures on the pursuit of science and technology, the first cannot be achieved in practice without sacrifice of the second, nor the second without sacrifice of the first. Some compromise, some judicious mixture of the two, is needed; and a mere list does not indicate where the balance lies.

Nonetheless, we shall attempt to construct such a list of priorities; but we shall also attempt to give some indication of where trade-offs exist, and where the balance between conflicting policies might best be set. Our list of priorities will be relatively short, in part because it will be enough at odds with the list underlying the Structural Adjustment programmes of the IMF/World Bank and in part because no long list of priorities could possibly be carried out within the context of countries, like Ghana, Kenya, Tanzania and Uganda, so poor and so improvident.

The pursuit of science and technology will not be at the top of our list of priorities, although it will, naturally enough, receive the most attention, that being the *raison d'être* of this study. To place the pursuit of science and technology first would be to put undue emphasis on it, and to risk rejection of the whole list: important as we believe the pursuit of science and technology to be, even we will admit that it could not possibly carry the weight, and command the support, that several other items do.

Above the pursuit of science and technology as an objective of policy we place domestic expansion – the expansion of employment and of the output of goods and services that satisfy local demands or add to export revenues. Within the latter category we include both commodity exports, chiefly primary commodities whose terms of trade can be expected further to deteriorate, and stable-terms-of-trade goods, chiefly tourism. Also above the pursuit of science and technology we place the dissemination of methods of birth control, so as to encourage a reduction in family size. If domestic expansion is sufficient to reduce the deficit in the balance of payments this need not be a separate objective, but it is conceivable that additional measures may be necessary, such as seeking additional loans or grants from the developed countries.

The last of these priorities – reducing the rate of growth of the population – is a complement to the swifter pursuit of science and technology. The faster the rate of growth of the population, the larger the share of total public expenditures that must be devoted to providing social overhead capital – primary schools, health care, urban facilities (land, housing, roads, water, sanitation, etc.). If spent on social overhead capital, the funds are not available to advancing science and technology, since both sorts of expenditure come almost entirely from public funds.

DEVOTING MORE RESOURCES TO ADVANCING SCIENCE AND TECHNOLOGY

The next in our list of priorities for policy is expanding the volume of resources devoted to the pursuit of science and technology. We have placed it high on our list for two chief reasons, having to do with future benefits and current costs. Neither reason is obscure: the returns to advances in science and technology, provided that the advances are in areas appropriate to the countries involved, are great and long-lasting; and the costs of pursuing science and technology in Sub-Saharan countries, given current wage and salary scales for their nationals and the generosity of foreign donors, are low. The benefit/cost ratio appears to be high.

The conclusion that we come to is that the quantity of resources devoted to the pursuit of science and technology in Sub-Saharan African countries should be increased substantially. In previous chapters we estimated the present proportion of GDP allocated to R&D, and found the figures to vary over the four countries in our sample from a high of about 1 per cent to a low of about 0.5 per cent. We estimated the expenditures per capita and found them to be no more than a few US dollars per year. If these figures were to double they would still not exceed the proportions in the rapidly growing Asian countries, countries which starting from similar levels of GDP per capita, have reached levels of output and consumption far in advance of those in the countries in our sample. If the Sub-Saharan African countries are to grow at equal rates, let alone begin to catch up with their Asian counterparts, they may well have to exceed the Asian countries' expenditures on R&D, as well as those on technical education and training.

We shall attempt an estimate of the additional resources needed in the countries in our sample, if science and technology are to be sufficiently stimulated, but we prefer to postpone this task until after we have discussed the direction which should be pursued, the next topic in this chapter.

THE DIRECTION IN WHICH R&D SHOULD MOVE

No one will deny that science and technology should be pursued more actively in Sub-Saharan Africa, and few will deny the need to allocate more resources to the pursuit: the arguments will arise over the direction in which science and technology should move. We are therefore approaching the most controversial part of our policy statement.

Our thesis has been that the Sub-Saharan African countries should not count on the export of those primary commodities on whose production they are currently concentrating for their economic salvation. These primary commodities in which they currently have a comparative advantage, primarily non-alcoholic beverages, face deteriorating terms of trade. Increasing still further their production will only serve to worsen the Sub-Saharan African countries' economic position *vis-à-vis* the developed world; and allocating scarce R&D to their improvement will merely accelerate the deterioration. R&D, and the activities which back them up, should be directed elsewhere.

The questions then arises: 'Where else?' and 'Should R&D currently allocated to export commodities such as, say, coffee, be redirected?' Let us try to answer these questions in reverse order. First what should be the policy towards those activities, currently commanding the bulk of the resources, which attempt to advance science and technology in the production and export of primary commodities with deteriorating terms-of-trade? Our recommendation is that they continue to be allocated to their current activities, in their current amounts. We would be content to see advances continue at their present pace for two reasons, one negative and the other positive. The negative reason is that we do not believe, from what we have observed, that *re*allocation of resources devoted to the pursuit of science and technology in developing countries at the low level of expertise of Sub-Saharan Africa can be carried out with much chance of success. It may be possible to shift slightly the direction of R&D within a single institution; for example some scientists working in a R&D institution whose primary focus is coffee might be reassigned to improving the production of crops grown in conjunction with coffee; but their institution as a whole could not be expected to survive with any effectiveness if its entire focus were to shift to, say, maize. The mobility of resources, particularly resources long organized and directed towards the carrying out of one activity, is very low.

The positive reason for not attempting to reallocate scientific and technological resources currently assigned to improving the production of export crops is their demonstration effect upon the pursuit of science and technology in general. The R&D institutes assigned to improving the production of export crops with deteriorating terms-of-trade are those of greatest longevity and greatest prestige in the Sub-Saharan African countries. The Tropical Pesticides Research Institute in Tanzania, the Coffee Research Foundation in Kenya, the Coffee Research Group of the Agriculture Ministry in Uganda, and the Cocoa Research Foundation in Ghana are the pre-eminent R&D institutes in their countries, not only accomplishing admirable things, but also serving as a model for newer bodies. To try to convert them to other activities, under different authorities and with, undeniably, different personnel, would be to remove the most effective institutions advancing science and technology in these countries. Competence takes many years, even decades, to create; but it can be destroyed in a flash.

Leaving in place those resources already devoted to the improvement of export crops with deteriorating-terms-of-trade does not mean that R&D should not be concentrated in other directions. If the *total* volume of resources to be allocated to R&D were to increase substantially, and if the entire increment were to be devoted to activities other than stimulating the production of deteriorating-terms-of-trade goods, there would be a relative reallocation. Instead of nearly all the country's scientists and technicians being assigned to R&D in coffee and tea and cocoa only a decreasing portion would be; the growing remainder would be assigned to R&D in new stable-terms-of-trade earners of foreign exchange and in improving the performance of producers for the domestic market.

We have illustrated, at the close of Chapter 9, the effect of the growth of resources devoted to advancing science and technology in the latter directions by extending the international trade model laid out in Chapter 2. In Chapter 9 we merely reproduced the model, showing the likely consequence, over the long run, of undertaking R&D in the proper direction, 'proper' signifying the direction in which the terms of trade are expected to improve. We also compared the outcomes, for production, international trade and domestic consumption, with the likely consequences of increasing, alternatively, R&D in the improper direction, namely toward increasing the productivity of resources devoted to the production of deteriorating-terms-of-trade goods.

In Figures 9.1 – 9.4 we displayed both alternatives. The growth paths, or trajectories, were shown as heavy, solid lines, capped with arrow heads. The dashed lines of increasingly steep slope, from the origin, represented the changing terms-of-trade between the goods labelled Y (primary commodities whose terms-of-trade were deteriorating) and goods labelled X (the combination of new, 'stable-terms-of-trade' exports and goods for domestic expansion). Comparison of the two cases (Case I, in which R&D was concentrated in good X, the good with favourable prospects in its terms of trade; and Case III, in which R&D was concentrated in good Y, the good with deteriorating terms of trade) revealed that at some arbitrary date in the future the economy following Case I would have a production regime devoted more heavily to good X; a similar, balanced pattern of trade (continuing to export good Y and import good X) but in lower volume; and a substantially higher standard of living for its population. Case I embodies our policy recommendations.

ADDITIONAL RESOURCES NEEDED TO INCREASE THE ADVANCE OF SCIENCE AND TECHNOLOGY

We shall now make a quick estimate of the additional resources needed in each Sub-Saharan African country, if it is to propel science and technology in the proper direction and at a rapid rate. Let us start by assuming that between now and 2023 their economies grow at a rate sufficient to maintain

GDP per capita constant, i.e. at a rate of somewhat over 3 per cent per annum. For 2023, total GDPs, in real terms, should be roughly twice what they are today.

Let us continue by assuming that resources allocated to advancing science and technology need to be provided in the same proportion to GDP as they are currently in those East Asian countries that are developing so swiftly (South Korea, Taiwan and Singapore) say 2 per cent of GDP. Currently the Sub-Saharan countries invest roughly 0.5–1 per cent of GDP on R&D, and an equivalent percentage on technical education and training. Two per cent of a GDP roughly twice the current value, would entail at least a four-fold increase (from 1 per cent of today's GDP to 2 per cent of the next generation's GDP).

Let us carry on by adopting our recommendation that R&D in those activities producing deteriorating-terms-of-trade goods should remain constant in real terms. Currently this R&D consumes, on average over the four countries in our sample, about one-half of each country's total. If this part of all R&D remains constant in amount, and if the total increases four-fold, the amount directed towards R&D in stable-terms-of-trade goods and goods for domestic consumption would have to increase eight-fold over the next 20 years. In addition, the amounts invested in technical education and training would also have to increase by an equal multiple. To achieve these expansions, the country would have to increase its allocation of resources devoted to advancing science and technology by at least 10 per cent per year (compounded). This we believe to be the size of the task facing the Sub-Saharan African countries, if they are to achieve substantial advances of science and technology in the proper directions.

POLICY IMPLICATIONS OF PROVIDING ADDITIONAL RESOURCES

Implications for the developing countries

An eight-fold expansion of R&D in those fields with favourable prospects, and an equivalent expansion of technical education and training, are daunting tasks. Where could the necessary resources come from? Briefly, the resources that must be provided more abundantly are institutions, personnel, administration and finance. Elsewhere we have covered the first three of these matters (see Enos, 1991), so we shall not go into any detail here, other than to state that the implications of such an expansion and redirection of R&D, and such an increase in education are formidable undertakings for any Sub-Saharan African country, involving as they will a substantial increase in technical and managerial education at the tertiary level, an even more substantial increase in vocational education, and an equally substantial increase in entrepreneurial and administrative capability in central government.

These – greatly expanding the human resources needed for R&D – are the immediate implications for the developing countries, but they are not the only ones. Many foreign observers of Sub-Saharan African countries have noted common failings in their governments (a lack of formalization of the country's goals, insufficient power to be able to influence the behaviour of individual economic agents and to implement changes, etc.). These deficiencies have been most frequently aired where the choice of technique has been at stake (e.g. James 1989), but we believe that they are appropriate to the choice of direction and subsequent administration of R&D. What the objectives of economic development are, and how and in what direction advancing science and technology can best contribute to achieving these objectives, are worthy of much more attention than they are currently given. Even when so much of the nation's scarce political and administrative talent has to be devoted to carrying out the ordinary activities of government, and to conforming to the rigours of Structural Adjustment, time and energy should still be invested in planning for the future, and in advancing the future's instrument, science and technology.

In particular, the Sub-Saharan African countries should put more effort into choosing, in detail and for the future, the direction of R&D – on what products, what processes, into what markets. There are two reasons for putting more effort into specifying what are likely to be and what are not, fruitful ventures. The negative reason is that if the Sub-Saharan African country does not specify, foreign donors will; the positive reason is that the knowledge and experience acquired in choosing the right direction for R&D can be valuable in carrying out the subsequent stages of product/process/market design, production and distribution. R&D is only the first link in a long chain of activities that connects the present with a prosperous future.

If we are brief in the implications we draw for the developing countries from a long-term programme of greatly expanded R&D, it is because we believe that the developing countries will see that it is in their interest to devote attention to choosing the proper direction of, and resources to the conduct of, future R&D. Difficulties will arise, of course, in committing their country to a sustained programme of R&D, in the face of competing claims for scarce resources, and in branching out in new, unproven areas of research. Yet we do have faith in their abilities to recognize what is in their best interest and to persevere in seizing the opportunities that arise.

Implications for foreign donors

Our faith does not extend to the actions of foreign donors, however, to whom we devote the next section. What are the implications to foreign donors, actual or potential, of a greatly expanded programme for advancing science and technology, often in novel directions, in Sub-Saharan Africa? Why do we believe that the implications are more contentious for foreign donors than they are for the developing countries themselves, or even for the IMF/World Bank? In summary, we believe that both the expansion of assistance, and its redirection, will encounter more opposition among the foreign countries currently granting assistance than it will in either of the two other groups.

There are three areas in which opposition will arise, the first bureaucratic, in the administration of foreign assistance; the second political, in the purposes to which it is put; and the third financial, in the size and duration of the developing countries' needs. Let us consider these in turn. Previously, we argued that a misallocation of R&D occurs when efforts are directed towards raising the productivity of resources engaged in producing a commodity specialized by other developing countries and facing inelastic demand in a slowly growing world market. We called this collective belief the 'Kaffee Klatsch', after that predominant commodity. Chapter 9, Case III illustrated the future course for a developing country which persists in concentrating its R&D in such deteriorating-terms-of-trade commodities; it is our task now to explain how it comes about that those developed countries which contribute aid to Sub-Saharan Africa reinforce the misallocation of R&D, and how this behaviour might be altered, in the interests of the recipients.

The explanation involves examining the organization and staffing of the foreign assistance agencies where the decisions as to the size and direction of R&D are made, and the background of the advisors on whom the agencies rely. Foreign donors are faced with more appeals for aid than they can possibly satisfy; in such a circumstance they tend to screen out appeals that are novel (because evaluation is outside their experience), of long duration (because their resources are usually dependent on authorizations year-by-year), and of uncertain outcome (because they wish to avoid outright and conspicuous failures). Yet a reallocation of R&D in the developing countries *away from* those activities that are familiar, that do not involve long commitments, and that have had, in the past, successful outcomes and so have less uncertainty attached to future outcomes, is difficult for the foreign donors to contemplate.

To this typically bureaucratic conservatism should be added the vested interests of those who provide technical advice on the choice of projects. The advisors may be individuals, they may be organizations, but their own backgrounds have considerable influence on the advice they give. Experience dictates choice, as can be seen if we look at those organizations found among the former colonial powers. Their original purpose was to supervise the research initiated in their colonies on those primary products cultivated for the home country's behalf – coffee, tea, cocoa, rubber, copra, palm oil, etc. When, one after another, their colonies gained independence, the expatriate scientists and administrators returned home. They brought back with them their experience in R&D covering the same primary products. Many were employed in what became research groups attached to their home countries' aid agencies. In these positions, and with these backgrounds, what would be more natural than to recommend that R&D be continued to be carried out on the traditional crops, whether at home, or, via foreign aid, in the former colonies?

Political opposition is likely to arise among foreign donors if the developing countries attempt to shift the direction of R&D into novel areas, areas that is that are novel to the developing countries. Many of the novel areas will already be occupied by firms domiciled in the donor countries, which will not appreciate foreign aid being used to engender competition. The growing of crops competing with temperate foodstuffs; the processing of primary commodities; the manufacture of relatively simple consumer non-durables (often distributed in the developing countries by the affiliates of multi-national firms); the perfecting of 'appropriate' machines that substitute for sophisticated capital goods; brokerage, insurance and other financial services; armaments; these and other areas will be considered to be the preserve of the developed countries. In each donor country there will be lobbies, well-staffed and with excellent contacts, whose objective will be to make certain that funds are not allocated to the area they represent. To them, a little competitive R&D, in the developing country, is a dangerous thing.

The third objective that will be raised in the donor countries is the magnitude and duration of the developing countries' needs for funds for R&D (Helleiner, 1992). In Sub-Saharan Africa, assistance will be needed for a very, very long time. The developing countries themselves cannot afford sums such as we estimated will be required (rapidly to advance science and technology in the proper directions) and the World Bank and other international financial agencies, and private firms in the developed countries, are not currently prepared to lend money for such speculative, unappropriable R&D, so donations from the developed countries are the only possible source. Yet substantial, long-term commitments of untied aid for uncertain purposes are not popular either in the countries themselves or in their aid agencies. Harmless these donations, whose purpose is to advance science and technology in the developing countries, may seem to the populace at large; but harmful each single donation is sure to seem to at least one vested interest.

Implications for the World Bank and other international financial institutions

The IMF, the World Bank and the regional development banks are first and foremost banks, institutions lending money against securities or sureties for undertakings that generate the income from which repayment can be made. Unlike foreign aid agencies, they are not in the business of extending loans unsecured in the borrowing countries or of making gifts. A bank (we shall use this as short-hand for all the international financial institutions) develops a set of rules which apply to all loans, and a set of administrative procedures and standards which apply to all borrowers. Borrowers may differ in their size, in their political system, in their culture and in their financial prospects, but they tend to be treated by a bank as identical (see, in the context of education, Jones, 1992). General rules, procedures and standards are easier to formulate, agree upon, implement and evaluate than particular ones unique to each borrower for each loan.

The existence of general rules, procedures and standards may facilitate lending, but it does not necessarily assure that loans are well designed and that the funds are productively used. To do so would require that each loan take notice of the specific needs of the borrower, in the light of his unique characteristics. This in turn would require a flexibility on the part of the bank that it lacks. There needs to be a flexibility of mind, an admission that developing countries *are* different; there needs to be a flexibility in the design of loans, a willingness to consider the particular nature of the borrower's requirements and capabilities; there needs to be a flexibility in the administration of loans, an adaptability to changing circumstances, so likely to occur in such long-lived projects as education or R&D; and there needs to be a flexibility in the evaluation of the success of loans, a cost-benefit analysis, not just an audit.

These are recommendations that one encounters frequently in volumes addressed to the policy issues confronting the international financial institutions (*ibid.*), and so we shall say no more about them. What we should like to terminate with is a specific recommendation directed both at banks and at foreign donors, namely that they, too, devote some attention to discovering the 'proper' direction for R&D. Recall that 'proper' signifies in the best interests of the developing countries, and that, so far as advancing science and technology is concerned, it signifies focusing on those products/processes/markets that have favourable prospects for producers in the developing countries.

Generally these are products/processes/markets with stable or improving terms-of-trade and/or satisfying domestic consumption; but we have not attempted to identify them in more than a general sense. To do so, we would need to conduct product/process/market research. To do so, the banks and the foreign donors would also have to conduct product/process/ market research. Product/process/market research is not our province, nor has it ever been the province of banks and foreign donors. Choice of product, design of project, has generally been done without systematic enquiry as to what is best for the developing country, what is feasible in that country, and what that country can or cannot contribute to the task. To the extent that product/process/market research is undertaken by the banks or the foreign donors it is usually with their own interests in mind; more frequently none is undertaken at all. Choice is based upon past decisions, which in turn were greatly influenced by the interests of the former colonial powers and their accumulated scientific and technical expertise.

If banks and foreign donors are to base their loans and grants on evidence systematically obtained from product/process/market research, how can they go about doing so? The difficult answer – all answers are difficult – is to invest in these facilities themselves. Let them establish product/process/market research departments within their institutions. Private companies of equivalent size have such departments; they would never consider engaging in a new activity without thoroughly investigating the products that would be produced, the processes that would be utilized, the markets that would be served. In today's world of ideas, private profit-seeking enterprises are our models of economic rectitude: here is one area in which they should be imitated. The huge multinational firms producing and distributing branded consumer goods – the tobacco and soap and cosmetics and soft-drink firms – should be the models. They are profitable at least in part because they 'know' their products and their processes and their markets; and they 'know' their products and processes and markets because they have studied them systematically. Even commercial and merchant banks, and private philanthropists – the nearest equivalents in the private sector banks and foreign donors – study their 'markets' carefully before committing funds: it should not be too much to recommend that public institutions do the same.

To recommend that banks and foreign donors conduct product/process/

market research, before lending or giving, is straightforward, based as it is on the need to identify the proper direction for advancing science and technology; but to expect banks and foreign assistance agencies to establish, operate, and take the advice emerging from product/process/market research departments would be overly optimistic. Think of the administrative changes necessary: allocating part of the institution's budget to a new department; absorbing members of a vulgar profession (market researchers) within an austere community of bankers, economists and auditors; breaking links with previous advisors and contending with vested interests; recognizing the great diversity among products, processes and markets; and, finally and most difficult, admitting that a particular product/process/market necessitates a loan or gift, and a set of rules procedures and standards, that is just as particular as the product itself.

In other words, what is needed from banks and foreign assistance agencies are 'bespoke' programmes, tailored for each country at each instant. According to the dictionary, the word 'bespoke' means to speak about; to discuss, advise upon, determine; to stipulate; to auger for the future. Thus what are needed are programmes that are carefully determined, that stipulate where science and technology are to be advanced; and that are devised with the long-term always in mind.

SUMMARY OF POLICY RECOMMENDATIONS

We will commence our summary with what we believe to be our most important recommendation, the one from which all the others stem. It is that the main task in advancing science and technology in the developing countries, and specifically in Sub-Saharan Africa, is to identify the most attractive direction in which to proceed. We have argued that this proper direction is that which best represents the interests of the developing countries, and that this interest is not congruent with the interests of banks or foreign donors.

Identifying the best interests of the developing countries will be no easy task, for there is much current advice and some assistance directed towards advancing science and technology in the opposite direction. To specify the proper direction will involve discovering favourable products/processes/ markets, which in turn will require establishing product/process/market research organizations both in the developing countries and, more importantly, in the developing countries' servants – the banks and the foreign assistance agencies. Only with advice emerging from systematic studies of the potential, well into the future, of generally new products, processes and markets, and with that advice being taken, can science and technology be harnessed to pull the developing countries along the road to development. Only then can 'bespoke' programmes be designed and carried out.

These may be the major policy implications of providing additional resources for, and altering the direction of, future R&D, but they are not the only ones. Where the conditions applying to Structural Adjustment loans are concerned, we have cautioned against the severe application of the conditions of reducing government expenditures, because of their depressing affect on R&D, almost all of which is financed by government; and of privatizing the commodity marketing boards, which out of their own revenues support the most effective R&D institutes formed in Sub-Saharan Africa. Moreover, an overall shift of activities from the public to the private sector, a course of action so enamoured by the banks, will reduce the intensity with which science and technology are pursued; even in the rich countries the external economies so abundant in the output of R&D are secured chiefly through public sponsorship.

There are implications for the developing countries as well as banks and foreign donors. Implications primarily for policy in the developing countries alone are that any *additional* resources available for R&D should be channelled into the (new) areas indicated by product/process/market research as having favourable prospects (while maintaining steady R&D in traditional areas), and that all R&D institutes should attempt to devote a larger fraction of their expenditures to those items complementary to personnel – supplies, books and journals, equipment, extension services etc. (i.e. devote a smaller fraction of their expenditures to wages and salaries of core staff). Finally we recommend that the developing countries resist the usurping of choice of direction of R&D by banks and foreign donors. Resistance will come partly instrumentally, through the creation of their own, local product/process/market research organizations, partly intellectually through awareness that foreign bodies are currently not likely, and may continue to be unlikely, to propel advances in science and technology in the directions beneficial to the developing countries.

Bibliography

Andrea, G. (1981) *Industry in Ghana*, Uppsala: Scandanavian Institute of African Studies.

Apter, D. (1955), (1973) *Ghana in Transition*, Princeton: Princeton University Press.

Bacha, E.L. (1990) 'A Three-gap Model of Foreign Transfers and the GDP Growth Rate in Developing Countries', *Journal of Development Economics*, 32: 279–96.

Berg-Schlosser, D. and Siegler, R. (1990) *Political Stability and Development: A Comparative Analysis of Kenya, Tanzania, and Uganda*, Boulder, Colorado: Lynne Rienner Publishers.

Birmingham, W., Neustadt, I. and Omaboe, E.N., eds (1966/7) *A Study of Contemporary Ghana*, 2 vols, Evanston, Illinois: Northwestern University Press.

Buatsi, S. (1991) 'Interaction by Institutions of Higher Education in Sub-Sahara Africa with Industry: The Model Developed at the University of Science and Technology, Kumasi: Ghana', Kumasi, Technology Consultancy Centre (30 July).

Campbell, B.K. and Loxley, eds (1989) *Structural Adjustment in Africa*, New York: St. Martin's Press.

Coffee Research Foundation, 1989. *Annual Report and Accounts*, Ruiru, Coffee Board of Kenya.

Colclough, C. and Manor, J., eds (1991) *States or Markets: Neo-liberalism and the Development Policy Debate*, Oxford: Clarendon Press.

Commander, S., ed. (1989) *Structural Adjustment and Agriculture*, London: James Currey for the ODI.

Commins, S.K. (1988) *Africa's Development Challenges and the World Bank: Hard Questions, Costly Choices*, Boulder, Colorado: Rienner Publishers.

Coughlin, P. and Ikiara, G., eds (1988) *Industrialization on Kenya: In Search of a Strategy*, Nairobi: Heinemann Kenya.

Coulson, A. (1982) *Tanzania: A Political Economy*, Oxford: Clarendon Press.

Denison, E.F. (1967) *Why Growth Rates Differ: Post-War Experience in Nine Western Countries*, Washington, DC: The Brookings Institution.

Donovan, D.J. (1982) 'Macro-economic Performance and Adjustments under Fund-Supported Programs', *IMF Staff Papers*, 29 June: 171–203.

Duncan, A. and Howell, J. eds (1992) *Structural Adjustment and the African Farmer*, London: Overseas Development Institute.

Duncan, R.C. (1993) 'Agricultural Exports Prospects for Sub-Saharan Africa', *Development Policy Review* 11/1 (March): 31–45.

Economic Development Institute of The World Bank (1989) *Successful Development in Africa: Case Studies of Projects, Programs, and Policies*, EDI Development Policy Case Studies, Analytical Case Studies No. 1, Washington, DC: The World Bank.

Enos, J.L. (1991) *The Creation of Technological Capability in Developing Countries*, London: Frances Pinter, Mathematical Appendix.

Elgström, O. (1992) *Foreign Aid Negotiations: The Swedish-Tanzanian Aid Dialogue*, London: Avebury.

Ewusi, K. (1986) *Industrialization, Employment Generation and Income Distribution in Ghana*, Accra: Adwensa.

Faini, R., de Melo, J., Senhadji, A. and Stanton, J. (1991) 'Growth-Oriented Adjustment Programs: A Statistical Analysis', *World Development*, 19/8 (August): 957–68.

Fitzgerald, E.V.K. and Vos, R. (1989) *Financing Economic Development: A Structural Approach to Monetary Policy*, Aldershot: Gower.

Fitzgerald, M.A. (1993) 'Western Aid Donors Endorse the Tough Economic Options', *International Herald Tribune*, Paris, 21 September: 9.

Forje, J.W. (1989) *Science and Technology in Africa*, Harlow, Essex: Longman.

Foster, P. and Zolberg, A.R., eds (1971) *Ghana and the Ivory Coast: Perspectives on Modernization*, Chicago: Chicago University Press.

Fosu, A.K. (1991) 'Capital Instability and Economic Growth in Sub-Saharan Africa', *Journal of Development Studies*, 28/1 (October): 74–85.

Fung, K-y.M. and Ishikawa, J. (1992) 'Dynamic Increasing Returns, Technology and Economic Growth in a Small Open Economy', *Journal of Development Economics*, 37: 63–87.

Gaillard, J. (1991) *Scientists in the Third World*, Lexington: University of Kentucky Press.

Ghana, Republic of (1990) *Provisional Estimates*, Accra: Ministry of Finance and Economic Planning.

Ghana, Republic of (1991) 'Enhancing the Human Impact of the Adjustment Programme', Report prepared for the South Meeting of the Consultative Group for Ghana, Paris (May 14–15).

Goka, A.M., Mihyo, P.B. and Osunbor, O.A. (1990) *Performance Review of Institutions for Technology Policy in Ghana, Nigeria and Tanzania*, Nairobi: IDRC Manuscript Report 241e (January).

Green, R.H. (1987) 'Ghana: Country Study', Vol. 1 of *Stabilization and Adjustment Policies and Programmes*, Helsinki: World Institute for Development Economics Research (WIDER).

Grossman, G.M. and Helpman, E. (1989) 'Growth and Welfare in a Small Open Economy', Working Paper 2970, Cambridge, MA: National Bureau of Economic Research.

Gulhati, R. (1988) 'The Political Economy of Reform in Sub-Saharan Africa', Washington: DC: World Bank EDI Policy Seminar Report No. 8.

Hackl, P. and Westlund, A.H. eds (1991) *Economic Structural Change: Analysis and Forecasting*, Berlin: Springer-Verlag.

Harrigan, J. and Mosley, P. (1991) 'Evaluating the Impact of World Bank

Structural Adjustment Lending: 1980–87', *Journal of Development Studies*, 27/3 (April): 63–94.

Helleiner, G.K. (1992) 'The IMF, The World Bank and Africa's Adjustment and External

Debt Problems: An Unofficial View', *World Development*, 20/6 (June): 779–92.

Heller, P.S. *et al.* (1990) 'The Implications of Fund-Supported Programs for Poverty', Washington, DC: *IMF Occasional Paper 58*.

Hodd, M. (1991) *The Economies of Africa Trends and Forecasts*, Hanover, NH: Dartmouth University Press.

Hutchful, E. (1987) *The IMF and Ghana: The Confidential Record*, London: Zed Books Ltd.

ILO (1992) *Yearbook of Labour Statistics 1992*, Geneva.

Hyman, E.L. (1993) 'Production of Edible Oils for the Masses and by the Masses: The Impact of the Ram Press in Tanzania', *World Development*, 21/3: 429–43.

IMF (1987) 'Theoretical Aspects of the Design of Fund-Supported Adjustment Programs', Occasional Paper No 55.

James, J. (1989) 'Bureaucratic, Engineering and Economic Men: Decision-making for Technology in the United Republic of Tanzania's State-Owned Enterprises', J. James, ed., *The Technological Behavior of Public Enterprises in Developing Countries*, London: Routledge.

Jones, P.W. (1992) *World Bank Financing of Education: Lending, Learning and Development*, London: Routledge.

Jolly, R. (1991) 'Adjustment with a Human Face: A UNICEF Record and Perspective on the 1980's ', *World Development*, 19/12 (December): 1807–22.

Judd, A., Boyce, J. and Evenson, R. (1983) 'Investing in Agricultural Supply', New Haven: Yale University Economic Growth Centre Discussion Paper 442.

Khan, M.S. (1990) 'The Macro-economic Effects of Fund-Sponsored Adjustment Programs', *IMF Staff Papers*, Vol. 37.

Khan, M.S. and Montiel, P.J. (1989) 'Growth-oriented adjustment programs: a conceptual framework', *IMF Staff Papers*, 36/2 (June): 279–306.

Killick, T. (1978) *Development Economics in Action: A Study of Economic Policies in Ghana*, New York: St Martin's Press.

Killick, T. (1983) 'The Role of the Public Sector in the Industrialization of African Developing Countries', *Industry and Development*, 7 (April): 47–88.

Komba, A.Y. (1990) 'Technological Innovation and Public Policy in Tanzania: A Study of Innovation in Industry, R&D Institutions and TASTA Awards', Research Report within the East Africa Technology Study (EATPS), submitted to the International Development Research Centre (IDRC) of Canada, Dar es Salaam, (June).

Krueger, A. (1978) *Foreign Trade Regimes and Economic Development*, Cambridge, MA: Ballinger.

Lall, S., Navaretti, G.B., Teitel, S. and Wignaraja, G. (1994) *Technology and Enterprise Development: Ghana under Structural Adjustment*, London: Macmillan.

Lancaster, C. (1991) *African Economic Reform: The External Dimension*, London: Institute of International Economics.

Lewis, A.W. (1953) 'Reports in Industrialization in The Gold Coast,' Accra: Government Printing Office.

Leys, C. (1975) *Under-Development in Kenya*, London: Heineman Educational Books.

Loxley, J. (1989) *Structural Adjustment in Africa*, London: Macmillan.

Lucas, R.E. (1988) 'On the Mechanics of Economic Development', *Journal of Monetary Economics*, 22/1 (January): 3–42.

Makau, B.F. (1988) 'Survey on Private Sector R&D (R&D) Resources and Activities in Kenya', Nairobi: National Council for Science and Technology (NCST Bulletin No. 26, May).

Martin, M. (1991) 'Negotiating Adjustment and External Finance: Ghana and the International Community 1982–1989', in D. Rothchild, ed., *Ghana: The Political Economy of Recovery*, Boulder, Colorado: Lynne Rienner Publishers.

Meier, G.M. and Steel, W.F. eds (1989) *Industrial Adjustment in Sub-Saharan Africa*, New York: Oxford University Press for the World Bank.

Mjema, E.A.M. and Kundi, B.A.T. (1993) 'A Study of Maintenance Problems in Tanzania', *The Tanzania Engineer* 4/5 (April): 13–20, Dar es Salaam: The Institution of Engineers, Tanzania, PO Box 2938, Dar es Salaam.

Mlawa, H.M. and Sheya, M.S. (1990) 'Profiles of R&D Institutions in Tanzania', prepared for the Secretariat of the Future Actions Committee of Management of Science and Technology for Development (MANSCI), Dar es Salaam (December), mimeo.

Mlawa, H.M. and Sheya, M.S. (1990) 'Science and Technology Situation in Tanzania', prepared for the Secretariat of the Future Actions Committee of Management of Science and Technology for Development (MANSCI), Dar es Salaam (November), mimeo.

Mosley, P., Toye, J. and Harrigan, J., eds (1991a) *Aid and Power: The World Bank and Policy-Based Lending*, Vol. 2, London: Routledge.

Mosley, P, Harrigan, J. and Toye, J., eds (1991b) *Aid and Power: The World Bank and Policy-Based Lending*, Vol. 2, *Case Studies*, London: Routledge.

Mosley, P. (1991) 'Kenya', in Mosley, P., Harrigan, J. and Toye, J. eds (1991) Chapter 16: 270–310.

Mwamadzingo, M. (1991) '*The Interface of Science and Technology with Industry and Government in Kenya*', Nairobi: African Centre for Technology Studies (ACTS), [May].

Ndulu, B. (1988) 'Structural Adjustment in Tanzania', Helsinki: WIDER.

Nelson, J. (1990) *Political Choice and Adjustment*, London: Macmillan.

Nelson, R.R., Peck, M.J. and Kalachek, E.D. (1967) *Technology, Economic Growth and Public Policy*, Washington DC: The Brookings Institution.

OECD (1992) *Flows of Financial Resources of Developing Countries*, Paris.

Olsen, M. (1982) *The Rise and Decline of Nations*, New Haven: Yale University Press.

Opio-Odongo, J.M.A. (1992) *Designs in the Land: Agricultural Research in Uganda, 1980–1990*, Nairobi: African Centre for Technology Studies.

Overseas Development Institute (ODI), (Foreign and Commonwealth Office, London, UK) (1991a) 'What Can We Know about the Effects of the IMF Programmes', *ODI Working Paper 47* (by T. Killick *et al.*).

ODI (1991) 'Country Experiences with IMF Programmes in the 1980s', *ODI Working Paper 48* (by T. Killick *et al.*).

Page, J.M. Jr. (1980) 'Technical Efficiency and Economic Performance: Some Evidence from Ghana', *Oxford Economic Papers*, 23/2 (July): 319–39.

Papageorgiou, D., Michaely, M. and Choksi, A.M., eds (1991) *Liberalizing Foreign Trade*, Vol. 7, 'Lessons of Experience in the Developing World', Cambridge, MA: Basil Blackwell.

Phelps, E.S. (1966) 'Models of Technical Progress and the Golden Rule of Research', *Review of Economic Studies XXXIII*: 133–45.

Polak, J.J. (1957) 'Monetary Analysis of Income Formation and Payments Problems', *International Monetary Fund Staff Papers*, 6: 1–50.

Psacharopoulos, G., ed. (1987) *Economics of Education: Research and Studies*, Oxford: Pergamon Press.

Psacharopoulos, G. and Woodhall, M. (1985) *Education for Development: An Analysis of Investment Choices*, Oxford: Oxford University Press.

Roemer, M. (1984) 'Ghana, 1950–1980: Missed Opportunities', in Harberger, A.C., ed., *World Economic Growth*, San Francisco: ICS Press.

Romer, P. (1989) 'Increasing Returns and New Developments in the Theory of Growth', *Working Paper 3098*, National Bureau of Economic Research.

Romer, P. (1990) 'Endogenous Technical Change', *Journal of Political Economy*, 98: S71–S102.

Rothchild, Donald, ed. (1991) *Ghana: The Political Economy of Recovery*, Boulder, Colorado: Lynne Rienner Publishers.

Saha, S.K. (1991) 'Role of Industrialization in Development of Sub-Saharan Africa: A Critique of World Banks' Approach', *Economic and Political Weekly*, 30 November.

Schleuter, L. (1993) 'Quarterly Progress Report: April–May–June 1993', Arusha: Village Oil Press Project, mimeo.

Simons, S. (1989a) 'Raising Agricultural Productivity: the Role of Research and Extension', Nairobi: Ministry of Planning and National Development, Long Range Planning Unit, Technical Paper 89–8 (January).

Simons, S. (1989) 'Kenya's Research Institutions: Problems and Solutions', Nairobi: Ministry of Planning and National Development, Long Range Planning Unit, Technical Paper 89–11 (July).

Simons, S. and Gitu, K.W. (1989) 'Funding Agricultural Research and Extension: the Implications for Growth', Nairobi: Ministry of Planning and National Development, Long Range Planning Unit, Technical Paper 89–10 (February).

Smillie, I. (1986) *No Condition Permanent: Pump-Priming Ghana's Industrial Revolution*, London: Intermediate Technology Publications.

Solow, R.M. (1957) 'Technical Change and The Aggregate Production Function', *Review of Economics and Statistics XXXIX*, (August): 312–20.

Sowa, N.K., Baah-Nuakoh, A., Tutu, K.A. and Osei, B. (1991) 'The Impact of the ERP on Small-Scale Enterprises', Legon: University of Ghana, Department of Economics, October.

Steel, W.F. (1972) 'Import Substitution and Excess Capacity in Ghana', *Oxford Economic Papers*, 24/2 (July): 212–40.

Steel, W.F. (1977) Small-Scale Employment and Production in Developing Countries: Evidence from Ghana, New York: Praeger.

Steel, W.F. (1988) 'Recent Policy Reform and Industrial Adjustment in Zambia and Ghana', *Journal of Modern African Studies*, 26: 157–64.

Steel, W.F. and Webster, L.W. (1990) 'Small Enterprises in Ghana: Responses to Adjustment', Industry and Energy Department Working Paper, Industry Series Paper No. 33, [September], Washington, DC: The World Bank.

Stewart, F. (1991) 'The Many Faces of Adjustment', *World Development*, 19/12 (December): 1847–64.

Strack, D. and Schönherr, S. (1989) *Debt Survey of Developing Countries*, Munich: IFO Institute for Development Research.

Tanzania, Planning Commission/Ministry of Finance (1986) *Economic Recovery Programme* (ERPI), Dar es Salaam: The Government Printer.

Tanzania, Planning Commission/Ministry of Finance (1989) *Economic and Social Action Programme* (ERPII), Dar es Salaam: The Government Printer.

Tanzania, Commission for Science and Technology (COSTECH) (1990) 'Human and Financial Resource Flows to Science and Technology in Tanzania (1978/79–1988/89),' Report submitted to the United Nations Centre for Science and Technology for Development (UNCSTD), Dar es Salaam, July.

Tanzania, Ministry of Agriculture, Livestock and Cooperatives (1991) *National Agricultural and Livestock Masterplan*, The Hague: International Service for National Agricultural Research (ISNAR).

Tanzania, Planning Commission (1990) *The Economic Survey 1989*, Dar es Salaam: The Government Printer.

Tanzania, Planning Commission/Ministry of Finance (1993) *Rolling Plan and Forward Budget for Tanzania 1993/94–1995/96*, Dar es Salaam: Government Printer.

Taylor, L. (1988) *Varities of Stabilization Experience*, Oxford: Clarendon Press.

Toye, J. (1991) 'Ghana', in Mosley, P., Harrigan, J. and Toye, J. (1991) Chapter 14: 151–200.

UNCTAD (1987) 'Impact of Technology Transfer by Foreign Small- and Medium-sized Enterprises on Technological Development in Kenya', New York: UNCTAD/TT/85.

UNDP (1989), (1991), (1992) *Development Cooperation: Tanzania 1988 Report, 1989 Report, 1990 Report*, Dar es Salaam, July 1989, May 1991, August 1992.

UNDP (1993) *Development Co-operation: Kenya, 1991 Report*, Nairobi (August).

UNDP/World Bank (1992) *African Development Indicators*, New York and Washington, DC.

UNESCO (1990) *Statistical Yearbook 1990*, Paris: United Nations Economic, Scientific and Cultural Organization.

UNESCO (1990) *World Tables*, Washington DC: World Bank.

Uzawa, H. (1965) 'Optimal Technical Change in an Aggregated Model of Eonomic Growth', *International Economic Review*, 6/1 (January): 18–31.

van der Hoeven, R. and Vandermoortele, J. (1987) 'Kenya', WIDER Stablilization and Adjustment Policies and programmes Country Study 4, World Institute for Development Economies Research.

van der Hoeven, R. (1991) 'Adjustment with a Human Face: Still Relevant or Overtaken by Events?', *World Development*, 19/12 (December): 1985–1986.

Westphal, L.E. (1986) (Book review of Kim, K-S. and Park, J-K. (1985) *Sources of Economic Growth in Korea: 1963–1982*, Seoul: Korea Development Institute) in *Journal of Economic Literature*, 24 September: 1245–7.

Wildavsky, A. (1979) *The Politics of the Budgetary Process*, Boston: Little Brown.

World Bank (various years) *World Debt Tables*, Washington DC.

World Bank (1981) *Accelerated Development in Sub-Saharan Africa: An Agenda for Action*, Washington DC.

World Bank (1983) World Development Report, Washington DC.

World Bank (1984) 'Economic and Industrial Profiles for Sub-Saharan Countries',

Economic Development Institute, *EDI Training Materials, Document 400/033*, Washington, DC: (September).

World Bank (1988a) 'Adjustment lending: an evaluation of ten years of experience', Country Economics Department, *Policy Research Series No. 7*, Washington DC.

World Bank (1988b) *Education in Sub-Saharan Africa: Policies of Adjustment, Revitalization and Expansion*, Washington, DC.

World Bank (1990) 'Conditionality in Adjustment Lending FY 80–89: the ALCID Database', Industry Series Paper No 28 (May), Washington DC: Industry and Energy Department of The World Bank.

World Bank (1991) *World Tables 1991*, Washington, DC: World Bank.

World Bank (1991) 'Ghana: Progress on Adjustment', Washington, DC: Report no. 9475-G.H. (April).

World Bank (1992) *Kenya: Re-investing in Stabilization and Growth through Public Sector Adjustment*, Washington DC.

World Bank (1993) *World Tables 1993*, Washington DC: World Bank.

Younger, S.D. (1989) 'Ghana: Economic Recovery Program – A Case Study of Stabilization and Structural Adjustment in Sub-Saharan Africa', in Bheenick, R. ed. *Successful Development in Africa*, Washington DC: The World Bank, EDI Analytical Case Studies 1: 128–73.

Zymelman, M. (1990) *Science, Education and Development in Sub-Saharan Africa*, Washington DC: World Bank

Index